Recycling the Family

Recycling the Family

Remarriage after Divorce

Frank F. Furstenberg, Jr.
Graham B. Spanier

 SAGE PUBLICATIONS Beverly Hills London New Delhi

For information address:

SAGE Publications, Inc.
275 South Beverly Drive
Beverly Hills, California 90212

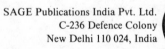 

SAGE Publications India Pvt. Ltd.
C-236 Defence Colony
New Delhi 110 024, India

SAGE Publications Ltd
28 Banner Street
London EC1Y 8QE, England

Printed in the United States of America

Library of Congress Cataloging in Publication Data

Furstenberg, Frank F.
    Recycling the family: remarriage after divorce.

    Includes index.
    1. Remarriage--United States--Longitudinal Studies.
I. Spanier, Graham B.   II. Title.
HQ536.F95   1984   306.8′4   83-24699
ISBN 0-8039-2260-4

FIRST PRINTING

Contents

Preface

Divorce, once discussed in hushed tones, is now an integral part of the life course of millions of Americans. As divorce has become commonplace in our society, so has remarriage; but social scientists have been slow to turn their attention to remarriage, perhaps because it is such a complicated process. This volume reports the results of a longitudinal study of the social, psychological, and economic adjustment of the transition from marriage to divorce to remarriage. Although the principal data collection took place during a three-year period, the project encompasses an eight-year span beginning in 1975. Our data include findings from two surveys which together asked more than 1,000 questions, as well as from several dozen in-depth case studies amounting to hundreds of hours of interviews.

This volume is the product of a happy collaboration between the authors, and demonstrates the feasibility as well as the complexity of research across universities (University of Pennsylvania and Pennsylvania State University). Our collaboration was made possible, in no small measure, by the efforts of the field staff of the Institute for Survey Research at Temple University and by a very great number of our students and colleagues.

We gratefully acknowledge the contribution of those who worked with us at various stages of the study: Elaine Anderson, Robert Casto, Rodney Cate, Albert G. Crawford, Patricia Dalto, Deborah Gabriel, Sandra Hanson, Mary Hart, Rebecca Hicks, Cliff Hirschhorn, Carolyn Jenne, Margie Lachman, Lauren Levine, Randie Margolis, Anthony Mixon, Carol Pfeiffenberger, Julia Robinson, Nancy Rothschild, Gisela Schonrock, Judy Shea, James Shockey, Ellin Spector, Catherine Surra, Linda Thompson, and Debra Ward.

This research would not have been possible without the generous support provided by the National Institute for Mental Health, the American Council of Life Insurance, and the Administration for Children, Youth, and Families (grant 90–C–1767). A grant from the Guggenheim Foundation freed Frank Furstenberg's time to prepare the introductory chapter.

As we describe in greater detail in the introductory chapter, nearly all of the chapters in this volume have previously appeared in professional journals or as chapters in edited collections. Because the demand for these materials has been enormous, we decided to make them available in a single volume. We have revised them only slightly, deleting redundant passages, updating references, and making minor improvements in style. Although some attempt has been made in the introduction to integrate the chapters, the work published here is admittedly selective and somewhat arbitrary, expressing our special interest in the topic. Much is left out, but we hope this volume will provide a partial agenda of issues that require further investigation.

Chapters 1 and 2 were written for this volume, while the remaining chapters are adapted from previous publications and presentations, as described below: Chapter 3 from, "Conjugal Succession: Reentering Marriage after Divorce," pp. 107-146 in Paul B. Baltes and Orville G. Brim, Jr. (eds.) *Life-Span Development and Behavior*, Volume IV, New York: Academic Press, 1982; Chapter 4 from, "Patterns of Parenting in the Transition from Divorce to Remarriage," pp. 325-343 in Phyllis W. Berman and Estelle R. Ramey (eds.) *Women: A Developmental Perspective*, National Institutes of Health, Washington, D.C., 1982 (with Nancy Rothschild); Chapter 5 from, "Renegotiating Parenthood after Divorce and Remarriage," presented at the biennial meeting of the Society for Research in Child Development, 1981; Chapter 6 from, "Remarriage and Intergenerational Relations," pp. 115–142 in Robert Fogel et al. (eds.) *Aging: Stability and Change in the Family*, New York: Academic Press, 1981; Chapter 7 from, "Marital Dissolution and Generational Ties" (with the assistance of Albert G. Crawford) presented at the annual meeting of the Gerontological Society, 1980; Chapter 8 from, "Remarriage after Divorce: A Longitudinal Analysis of Well-Being," *Journal of Marriage and the Family*, 43 (August): 709–720, 1982; and Chapter 9 from, "The Risk of Dissolution in Remarriage: An Examination of Cherlin's Hypothesis of Incomplete Institutionalization," *Family Relations*, forthcoming.

The appendix is the interview schedule developed by the authors, in consultation with the Institute for Survey Research at Temple University. This interview schedule was used in the Time-2 follow-up survey of respondents and their new married or unmarried partners. The interview schedule used in the Time-1 survey is presented in the appendix to a companion volume, *Parting: The Aftermath of Separation and Divorce,* by Graham B. Spanier and Linda Thompson.

—Frank F. Furstenberg, Jr.
University of Pennsylvania

—Graham B. Spanier
*State University of New York
at Stony Brook*

CHAPTER 1

Recycling the Family
Introduction

Divorce and remarriage trends have taken American society by surprise. Few, if any, experts foresaw the rapid rise in marital dissolution. Who would have predicted a generation ago that more than half of all marriages contracted in the latter part of the twentieth century would end in divorce? It is far easier to chart the change than to say what its implications are for our family system. Already, however, it is clear that changing marriage practices have vastly complicated both our images of family life and the structure of family relations.

The chapters in this volume assess how family images and family relations have been altered by both the expectation and the occurrence of marital instability. Most of the essays report on empirical findings from a longitudinal study of the transition from divorce to remarriage carried out from 1977 to 1979 in Centre County, Pennsylvania. This study is one of the most ambitious attempts to date to trace the impact of divorce and remarriage on American perceptions of marriage, parenthood, and intergenerational relations. However, as we shall describe in greater detail, the data must be considered preliminary. We envisioned the study, even at its inception, as a point of departure for raising significant issues that may warrant closer investigation.

This introduction, which might also be read as a postscript to the papers, summarizes some of the central themes that run through the discrete analyses. Some of these themes were recognized before the project was launched; some developed in the course of carrying out the research; still others surfaced when we began to analyze and interpret the data. As we chronicle the history of the project and summarize some of the major results, our aim is to recapture for the reader the elusive but exhilarating process of discovery through research.

The Origins of the Central Pennsylvania Study

It is difficult to trace the beginnings of any research undertaking, for they are usually an amalgam of both intention and accident. The Central Pennsylvania study is certainly no exception. In the most literal sense, the research came about as a result of a series of conversations between the two of us about our mutual interests in the sociology of the life course and the sociology of the family. The discussion began at a colloquium visit by Furstenberg to Pennsylvania State University in 1977, during which the two of us discussed the desirability of longitudinal research; Spanier mentioned that he had contemplated the possibility of following up his recent study of adjustment to marital separation to examine the longer-term accommodations to separation and divorce.

Spanier had begun his research in 1976 when, aided by two small grants, he conducted 50 open-ended case-study interviews with recently divorced men and women. This was the first step in what would become a more systematic investigation the following year into the social, psychological, and economic adjustment to marital separation. The in-depth case-study interviews resulted in more than 1,000 pages of field notes. This method seemed appropriate because in the 20 years since Goode's (1956) pioneering study of divorce, virtually nothing new on the subject had been published, and it wasn't clear what questions should be asked in a survey. In 1977, following two rounds of pretesting, Spanier collected a considerable body of cross-sectional data, allowing for the possibility of a future longitudinal study, but with no specific plans at the time for such a follow-up.

Furstenberg, meanwhile, had just completed a series of historical investigations concerning the changing social organization of the life course, focusing especially on the timing of marriage. One of the principle findings of this research was that the process of family formation had become more uniform. The timing of marriage, childbearing, and the establishment of a separate household became far less variable in the twentieth century. In describing the results, Furstenberg and his colleagues observed that the finding might not have held up had they examined final rather than first marriages (Modell et al., 1978). Furstenberg and his colleague, Modell, had a cursory exchange about the desirability of looking at changing patterns of remarriage. The idea had intrigued Furstenberg because of a long-standing interest in unscheduled life events. A couple of years earlier, he had concluded a study of teenage childbearing that had focused on early motherhood as "a departure from the normative schedule" (Furstenberg, 1976). He had been considering the possibility of looking at a similar departure in a later part of the life course.

The specific idea for a study of the transition from divorce to remarriage came to Furstenberg at the Philadelphia airport in the summer of 1977 as he stepped off a plane and was greeted by a shower of rice and confetti. Ahead of him was a middle-aged couple being welcomed home from a honeymoon by a crowd of friends. One of them waved a sign with the words, "Recycled Lovers." At that moment, Furstenberg decided to begin work on a proposal which ultimately was entitled, "Recycling the Family: Experiences in Remarriage."

On a sabbatical in the fall of 1977, Furstenberg began to review the literature on remarriage. Expecting to be overwhelmed by a vast number of studies, he was both dismayed and delighted to discover a paucity of social science research on the topic. With the exception of a core of demographic reports on the tempo of divorce and remarriage and a scattering of clinical reports, all the citations were to a literature that was nearly a generation old. Having explored the conventional bibliographic routes, he began to read family textbooks in the hope of accumulating more recent references. Virtually nothing new turned up, but the exercise proved to be interesting nonetheless. As recently as five years ago, remarriage was virtually ignored by family sociologists even though divorce received extensive treatment. Reentering marriage was an invisible transition so far as scholarship was concerned.

Social scientists seemed to be ignoring the possibility, suggested by the rapid rise in marital dissolution, that the institution of marriage was undergoing a fundamental transformation. Family sociologists continued to regard divorce as a deviation from accepted marriage practices, and remarriage as a mechanism for restoring the integrity of the family, much as if the broken fragment of an object might be mended in order to return it to its ideal form. The point was not to reveal the cracks.

The sparse literature on the experiences of remarried persons indicated that this conventional model of divorce and remarriage might be inadequate for understanding the experiences of individuals who moved from one marriage to the next. In the process of recycling the family, it appeared that those entering remarriage might experience marriage, parenthood, and kinship differently from persons marrying for the first time. Such processes as courtship, mate selection, marital socialization, childbearing and child rearing, and intergenerational relations are recast against the backdrop of previous marital history. And the structure of the new marriage and set of family relations has to be built upon the remnants of an existing system. In attempting to conceal the cracks, family sociologists had overlooked the strong possibility that the form and functioning of first and second marriages might not be the same.

Early in 1977, Spanier was in the midst of writing up what he and his colleagues had learned from the case-study data, while at the same time beginning to construct a comprehensive interview schedule to study approximately 200 recently separated men and women. The case-study research produced many insights, but one particular finding was to guide the subsequent study: Separation—not divorce—was discovered to be the critical event in the disruption of the marriage. For various reasons, including the vagaries of the adversarial legal framework governing divorce in Pennsylvania during the 1970s, divorce could occur soon after the separation, several years later, or never. Clearly, separation, its timing, and its circumstances were the keys to under-standing the breakup of marriage and its aftermath.

Studies of divorce were also being launched in the mid-1970s by other investigators (among them Weitzman, Chiriboga, Kitson, and Sussman) but there was still so little known that each investigator proceeded in his or her own way with only a modest degree of shared interests. In the Spanier investigation, a decision was made to focus on the adults involved and leave the study of the children to others. There was special interest in social, psychological, sexual, legal, and economic variables, and the interview schedule reflected these emphases. Finally, Spanier's growing interest in demography, which was to lead to a visiting research appointment at the Census Bureau during the summer of 1978, led to the inclusion of a substantial amount of demographic material in the survey.

Later in 1977, after several more discussions between the two of us, Furstenberg set to work on a research proposal that elaborated the theoretical rationale for examining the transition from divorce to remarriage and devised a research design for exploring the area. He elaborated a lengthy agenda of topics for investigation, revolving around the ways that individuals renegotiated the passage from divorce to remarriage. The theoretical section of the proposal assembled ideas from several pioneering studies of divorce and remarriage carried out by Waller, Bernard, and Goode, as well as from the more recent research of Bohannon, Walker, Rogers, Messinger, and Cherlin. The issues raised in the proposal were diverse but shared in common the life-course perspective which Furstenberg had applied in his previous research and which Spanier had come to appreciate during five years of discussion and collaboration with Penn State colleagues Baltes, Huston, Lewis, and Lerner.

THE RESEARCH DESIGN

Having discovered a rich and virtually unexplored problem area, Furstenberg began to ponder a research design for a study of remarriage. Torn between a desire to launch a large-scale longitudinal survey and the recognition that the costs of initiating a long-term project would be immense, he contemplated ways of acquiring data that could be used longitudinally without undertaking a longitudinal study. The strategy of coupling a follow-up to an existing study seemed especially appealing. The attractiveness of this option increased after an abortive attempt was made to use Philadelphia marriage records as a potential sampling frame. While he was drafting the proposal, Fursten-berg had carried out a pilot study that involved contacting individuals who had recently remarried. The investigator hoped to obtain some baseline information for inclusion into the proposal. This approach proved to be unworkable because of the difficulty of finding individuals who had recently remarried. The great majority had moved from the address listed in the records and could not be easily located. It was clear that finding a representative sample would involve considerable time and expense. A decision was made to defer a large-scale study and concentrate on more intensive methods of data collection in the first stage of the project. It seemed to Furstenberg that funding sources would be skeptical about supporting a large, expensive survey unless the way was paved by a good deal of preparatory research.

It was at this point that Furstenberg proposed to Spanier that they collaborate in following up Spanier's sample of separated and divorced persons. Although relatively small and not selected in such a way as to ensure representativeness, Spanier's sample offered a number of distinct advantages over initiating a new study. The first and most important was the data collected in the initial wave of the Spanier study. When first contacted, all the participants were recently separated, and 75 percent had already been divorced. Few had reentered marriage, although a number were in the midst of forming new relationships. Spanier had collected a vast amount of information on their experiences in the latter stages of their marriages and more recently in the transitional period after their marriages were dissolved.

A follow-up approximately two and a half years after the initial interview would reach many of the respondents in the early stages of a second marriage or during a period of cohabitation. Extrapolating from national statistics, we estimated that close to half would have reentered marriage or would be cohabiting. The remainder would have lived through the early trauma of separation or divorce without having yet taken the next step of forming new relationships. Thus, it would be possible to compare the experiences of individuals who remarried again with counterparts who remained, at least for the time, outside of marriage. Although there would no doubt be some selection in the sorting process, the contrast nonetheless would be informative of the kinds of adjustments required in self and family under quite different life circumstances.

Spanier's sample included individuals who had separated in the 26 months preceding the interview. Assisted by a research team of graduate and undergraduate students, Spanier undertook to interview recently separated persons in Centre County, Pennsylvania, in the spring of 1976. The search began in the county courthouse, where clerks who had never seen a sociologist before had to be convinced that divorce files were public. The community had to be convinced too, Spanier suspected, and he made sure that all court employees, attorneys, and journalists were briefed on the study. Feature articles about the study in the local newspaper were more successful in generating cooperation from reluctant participants than any other "tactic" used to encourage responses.

Eligible respondents included persons known to be living within a 50-mile distance of the county who were either separated, had filed for child support or custody, were in the process of divorcing, or had recently obtained a divorce. This underrepresents individuals who had recently separated but had not taken any legal action. Efforts were made through snowball sampling techniques and newspaper articles to locate such individuals. A few were found.

Of the more than 900 potential respondents who were identified as eligible, Spanier had been able to locate only 344 (37 percent) and interviewed just 210—slightly less than a quarter of the designated population. This low response rate is consistent with the results of other studies of marital dissolution. High rates of mobility make it difficult to find recently separated and divorced individuals when court records have been used as the sampling frame; when located, individuals in a marital transition frequently are reluctant to participate in research. The high rate of unlisted numbers for recently divorced individuals was also no small problem. Given the necessary but unorthodox sampling procedure and the relatively low rate of response, it is important to keep in mind that the results from Central Pennsylvania cannot be generalized.

Nonetheless, there are certain strengths to the sample. Unlike most previous investigations, it is not clinically based or known to consist of a special subgroup of the formerly married such as a self-help group or a college-based sample. Indeed, the sample is extremely diverse in social class, religion, age, gender, and parental status.

Just over three-fourths (76 percent) were divorced at the time of the first interview, and the remainder were separated. About 9 percent of the divorced persons had remarried at the time of the interview. Of the sample, 56 percent was female. The ages of the respondents ranged from 20 to 67 with a mean of 33. For both the respondent and his or her former spouse, the mean level of education was 14 years.

The sample was 12 percent Roman Catholic and 60 percent Protestant. Other religious preferences were stated by 9 percent, and 19 percent were atheist, agnostic, or had no religious preference. The total yearly income was less than $5,000 for 28 percent of the sample. Of the respondents 31 percent had a total yearly income in 1976 between $5,000 and $9,999 while 23 percent had an income range of $10,000 to $14,999. The remaining 18 percent had income greater than $15,000. The income distribution of the sample reflects the marital status of the population—a high proportion were living as singles or as single parents in 1976. Also, the cost of living in Central Pennsylvania was quite low.

The mean length of marriage was 9 years, with a range of four months to 45 years. Eight percent of the respondents had been divorced more than once. Of the respondents, 128 (just over 60 percent) had children—a total of 279. (Some of the children, of the older respondents, were adults.)

The sample was not selected to ensure that it would be representative. However, it is heterogeneous enough in most respects to permit subgroup comparisons of important demographic attributes. The diversity of the sample suggests that many of the results may, indeed, not be limited to the study population. The Central Pennsylvania sample was just large enough to permit statistical examination but not so large as to limit the possibility of more extensive qualitative treatment.

Following a decision by the two researchers to join forces, Furstenberg completed a proposal seeking funds to reinterview the 210 participants in the Central Pennsylvania study and to collect data from their spouses or unmarried partners in the event that they had entered a new relationship. Data from the spouses and partners would be used to augment information collected from the primary respondents, corroborate their reports, and provide contrasting information on the experiences of persons who had never been married before, as we suspected that a substantial proportion of the spouses would have been entering marriage for the first time. As it turned out, the spouse and partner interviews proved difficult to obtain, and we were able to make only limited systematic use of the dyadic data in our analyses.

The proposal also called for a set of qualitative interviews to precede the survey. We planned to use this information to formulate hypotheses, identify important topics for exploration, and refine specific questions. In fact, the qualitative interviews became a far more prominent feature of the study than we had envisioned and provided a great deal of source material for the analysis.

In the final section of the proposal, a number of limitations of the study were acknowledged: the small sample size and its geographic restrictions; the absence of data from some of the relevant parties (such as the former spouse and children); and the fact that most respondents were in an early stage of remarriage, which might distort the picture we would get were the study extended in time. A rather ambitious plan was outlined for a subsequent stage of research that would test the preliminary findings obtained from this small-scale, local study on a national level. At the time, the plan appeared grandiose, even to the author of the proposal; but, in fact, a second study was carried out and is currently showing that many of the results from the Central Pennsylvania study are quite robust (Furstenberg and Nord, 1982; Furstenberg, 1982a; Furstenberg, 1983).

PREPARING FOR THE FIELDWORK

Late in 1978, the proposal was funded by the Administration for Children, Youth, and Families, which was particularly interested in the implications of divorce and remarriage for family services. As so often happens, the start-up period for a new study was slow. It was not until the spring of 1979 that Furstenberg began to conduct a series of qualitative case studies of remarried couples in the Philadelphia metropolitan area. Respondents were drawn largely from among those who had been located the preceding year from marriage records, and Furstenberg and his associate, Gisela Schonrock, taped lengthy interviews with about 25 recently remarried couples.

The couples, primarily middle class and exclusively white, presented an extensive range of issues for exploration. Some stemmed from the previous marriage and included how to deal with the previous spouse, coparenting practices, relations with former in-laws, and the courtship process. Others were concerned with the transition to the new marriage, strategies of stepparenting, and the process of acquiring new kin.

Although we came to the interviews prepared with a shopping list of questions, it was hardly necessary to ask them. Generally, the couples had a story to tell. We listened, probed, and as we began to organize the information into more general interpretations, we would check them out with the couple. We attempted to make the interviews as conversational as possible, sharing information that we had obtained from other couples and occasionally mentioning our own personal experiences in order to minimize the inevitable sense of distance and formality that can permeate a research interview. We explained to the participants that they should think of themselves more as informants than respondents and, when that distinction was made clear, they generally assumed a more active role in the interview process.

After about 10 or 15 case studies, a curious pattern developed in the interviews. It was almost as if the couples were speaking from scripts. Certain themes recurred with such regularity that we sometimes had a sense of déjà vu although the details of the stories were quite varied. Our informants did not hold an identical view of the remarriage experience, but the set of issues that they faced were similar. Individuals encountering common concerns often adopted quite different strategies to resolve them—a fact that became even more evident from the survey data. What we learned from the case studies was which questions to ask and how they must be formulated in order to capture the important realities of remarriage. The case studies transformed us from naive academics to informed observers.

Meanwhile, Spanier and his Penn State colleagues had analyzed much of the data from the first wave of what was to become the longitudinal study. These data were satisfactory for answering some of the questions we had, but not others. A growing list of questions for the follow-up was emerging at the same time questions were being generated from the qualitative data.

By the late spring, we began to prepare for the fieldwork, which was to begin at the end of the summer. Although the fieldwork was to be conducted by the Institute for Survey Research at Temple University, we were responsible for the tracing of the sample and the development of the interview schedule. Both of these tasks proved to be far more complex than had been anticipated.

Tracing information had been collected during the initial wave of the study, and almost all of the respondents had consented to participate in a possible follow-up. However, there was considerable, unexpected mobility in the two-year period. Names changed following remarriage, and individuals fleeing from the aftermath of a first marriage sometimes became socially invisible. Starting over for some participants obviously meant severing previous ties. When the fieldwork began, a substantial number of respondents still had not been located. Eventually, however, we located 95 percent of the respondents who had been interviewed in 1977.

The interview schedule began to take shape early in the summer of 1979 when Furstenberg moved up to State College and, with Spanier, put together a lengthy instrument. About half of the questions (300 in number) were repeated from the first interview schedule, and 300 new questions were added. After a series of drafts, a team of graduate students conducted a dozen or so interviews. The result was disastrous. The interview was too long, the question sequencing was poor and, worst of all, respondents were confused and frustrated by a number of questions. The most vexing area by far were the sections of the interview that concerned the children. We had asked the respondents to report on contact with children, the quality of relationships, and child-rearing strategies. Invariably they asked the interviewer, "Which children do you mean? My children from my first marriage, my stepchildren, or the children from this marriage?" Naturally, their responses often differed for different categories of children.

Following the initial pretest, the interview schedule was completely redrafted. We pruned the first draft, removing nonessential and redundant items. Respondents were asked parallel questions about four sets of children (biological and stepchildren living in the household, and biological and stepchildren living outside the household). Despite misgivings about boring the respondents with a repetitive series of questions, the new structure of the interview so simplified the questions that respondents experienced little difficulty in negotiating them even when they were asked about two, three, and sometimes even four sets of children.

A second pretest was conducted in July, and the results were reassuring. The interview was considerably shorter. Respondents were more likely to make appreciative rather than negative comments at its conclusion. Best of all, the interviewers no longer felt uncomfortable about the process of data collection. After further refinements and following a third pretest, we were ready to launch the fieldwork.

CONDUCTING THE FIELDWORK

All of the interviewers, hired by the Institute of Survey Research (ISR), were women residents of Centre County where the study was located. Nearly all had extensive interview experience although some were unfamiliar with the process of conducting an academic project. Most of the trainees were housewives looking for part-time employment although there were a sprinkling of graduate students and full-time workers. The fieldworkers generally had some college experience, and most were in their middle years.

There was a three-day period of training before the fieldwork convened, during which each interviewer was thoroughly briefed on the questionnaire, was tested on its contents, and conducted a practice interview. Inevitably, some of the fieldworkers were eliminated or dropped out along the way. Of the 15 who began, 13 eventually worked on the study and 10 interviewers completed 8 or more interviews. Typically these interviewers completed about 10 to 20 interviews; the field coordinator carried a larger share as she completed a large number of the cases that were difficult to obtain and picked up the residual cases that were sent back by other interviewers when they no longer worked on the study.

The site of the interview varied according to the respondent's preference. All were given the option of being interviewed on the campus of Penn State, at home, or at another location. One-half elected to be interviewed at home while two-fifths of the sample opted to be interviewed at the campus, in a public place, or in the home of the interviewer. The remainder (11 percent) had moved from Central Pennsylvania and were interviewed by phone. Even though the phone interviews usually lasted for more than an hour, cooperation was generally excellent.

The fieldwork began in late August and was concluded in November. During this three-month period, 181 of the 210 participants in the initial survey were reinterviewed. (Nearly 70 percent of the eligible spouses and partners were interviewed as well—a number which, however, only totaled 60 persons.) Just 11 respondents (5 percent of the sample) could not be located. There were 18 persons (9 percent) who refused to participate in the follow-up. Originally the number of refusals was more than twice that number, but we found that a call from Spanier, who was well known in the area, convinced many of the participants to cooperate. In addition to converting about half of the refusals, Spanier was able to obtain partial interviews from 9 of the 18 persons who refused to participate in the study.

All of the interviews were verified through a mailed questionnaire that provided some indication of the validity of the information obtained. The reports from the mailed questionnaires revealed that respondents were generally very satisfied with the quality of the interview, and the information they provided by mail validated their responses in the face-to-face interview. Further corroboration of the veracity of the responses was provided by data collected in the follow-up case studies conducted after the structured interviews were completed. These follow-up visits, as we shall report below, increased our confidence in the quality of the information obtained by the fieldworkers.

Evaluations by the interviewer at the conclusion of each interview uncovered few significant problems with the fieldwork. Nearly all (95 percent) described the respondent as cooperative, very communicative (81 percent), honest (96 percent), and friendly (97 percent). The vast majority experienced no problems during the interview; most of the problems that did arise were occasioned by the presence of another person within hearing range, usually a child or relative. But this situation occurred rarely.

A final indication that the interviews had gone well came from the respondent's expression of willingness to participate in further follow-up. When asked whether we could contact them again in the future should we need additional information or want to update the study, almost all granted permission; most consented to be contacted again in the next month or two to provide more extensive information in the form of case studies.

THE DELAYED PROBE INTERVIEW

Following the conclusion of the structured interviews, we recontacted a subsample of 25 of the remarried respondents and their new spouses carrying out what could be called a delayed probe interview. All had one or more children living at home. Our principal aim was to collect additional qualitative information that would extend beyond the responses provided in the structured interview.

As indicated earlier these call-backs also provided some confirmation of the quality of the interviewing, the validity and reliability of the information collected, and offered the respondents a chance to reflect in an unrestricted way on what they had learned from recounting their personal histories of the past several years. Their appraisals broadened our perspective on the meaning of the data we had collected. What had the respondents thought of the study? Did they have any second thoughts about their responses to questions posed in the interview? Had they discussed the research with their partners, children, or friends?

In order to promote a free-flowing discussion, our postinterview case studies were always with the couple. Even though we promised to preserve the anonymity of their responses in the individual interviews, such assurances generally turned out to be unnecessary. The participants, with a few conspicuous exceptions, freely shared many of the opinions that they had expressed in the structured interviews. One of the reasons we felt confident about the quality of the survey data was the high degree of consistency in the responses to questions posed in the two interview situations. We were impressed that often the respondents would repeat phrases in the delayed probe interview that had been recorded in the prior structured interview. In general, the accounts did not change even though the context of the interview was quite different.

Almost invariably, we began the case studies by asking the participants to describe their responses to the interview in which they had participated a month or so earlier. There were several advantages to beginning this way. It was an easy and straightforward question to answer. It also provided some feedback about the interview process itself and the meaning of the interview to each of the respondents. But as can be seen below, it revealed a great deal about how couples manage the information about their previous life and how they communicate with one another on sensitive subjects.

Reactions to the survey interview varied widely, ranging from respondents who found it tedious, routine, and uninteresting, to those who were tremendously involved and stimulated by the experience. Among the former, one man replied with mock enthusiasm, "It was a great experience! No, it was all right. It took longer than I thought it was going to take, but it was nice because I was sitting outside in the sun." His wife went on to add that she reacted pretty much the same way, summing up by saying "it was okay." For individuals like this pair, the interview was neither memorable nor meaningful.

A larger number of respondents reported that they found the interview enjoyable, although typically they wanted to express their feelings about some of the subjects at greater length than they were permitted in the structured interview.

> WIFE: I just thought it was very interesting . . . it makes you realize the source of problems that you have had or just what sort of interesting encounters or situations can arise and do arise. . . . Some of them are thought provoking; some of them are amusing.
>
> HUSBAND: Many times there were not enough alternatives to give an answer.
>
> WIFE: Or it's something you wanted to qualify or else [your answer] didn't make sense.

Apart from the form of the questions, which some respondents found too restrictive, a few participants complained that they did not like covering old territory. Clearly some couples avoid what they regard as prehistory, the time before their current relationship began. Males particularly were disinclined to dwell on their previous relationship.

> HUSBAND: Well, I found some of [the questions] hard to relate to. . . . They're asking questions about my former wife and I tried not to think about any of those things.
>
> WIFE: Right. Sometimes you don't want to remember a lot of happenings in that time period.

It might be suspected that individuals who felt most strongly that way might not have participated in the study at all. No doubt these individuals are underrepresented in the sample, but a number of the participants commented that although it was painful to review the past, they were prepared to do so because they thought it might be beneficial to others.

> HUSBAND: You know, every now and then, it opens an old
> wound or something when you get to thinking . . . if it's
> something that will help somebody else get through a period like
> that, well, it's worthwhile.

Female respondents generally had fewer qualms about discussing some
of the sensitive topics, especially their former relationships. Accordingly, they were usually more willing than their husbands to acknowledge
that they derived some direct benefit from the interview.

> WIFE: I think it helped me to evaluate myself a little bit more
> about how I was doing and how I had grown from the divorce
> and how I had grown as a person. Maybe that is selfish but I
> think it did help me realize that I did grow and could get over
> something that was very unhappy in my life.

The evaluations of the interview experience exposed a certain amount of
information about the relationship between the couple; in particular,
their style of communication. Some couples reported that they had had
almost no discussion after the interviews were completed. In a few
instances, couples expressed some curiosity about one another's answers
to specific questions. Others felt that it was intrusive to probe each
other's opinions. "It's his business," one woman told us, indicating that
a discussion about intimate feelings would be off limits.

Several couples who had discussed the interview with each other
sheepishly admitted that they had inquired about their partner's
responses to the questions concerning sexual activity. The interview
apparently provided an occasion to seek reassurance or perhaps broach
a topic that was generally taboo. Approximately half of the couples had
extensive conversations about the interview, comparing notes on each of
their responses. For some, this process reaffirmed their common
perspective on marriage.

> WIFE: Well, when we were talking about the different questions, it
> usually turned out that what we said was pretty much the same
> thing . . . we're very close and we talk a lot. We don't hold
> anything back from each other so I think that's probably a lot to
> do with it.

As couples began to talk about their responses to the interview, they
comfortably moved into other areas of their marriage. If they began by

discussing their styles of communication, we generally preceeded to talk about their marriage, eventually working back to their former relationship. If they focused on their review of past relationships, we usually focused the early part of the interview on their former marriage and worked our way to their present relationship. With relatively little prompting, participants generally covered most of the topics on our agenda. We made no effort to give equal emphasis to the areas we covered, electing instead to let couples point the way to the important issues in their relationship. Sometimes the interviews dwelled on their former marriages, sometimes on relations with children and stepchildren, sometimes on the problems of managing the competing claims of work and family. Little effort on our part was required to manage the content of the interview.

As we had done in preparing for the structured interviews, we let the participants know that they were regarded as informants, not respondents. We sat back and listened, occasionally prompting a new question or probing an incomplete or incomprehensible response. As we formed impressions of their views on particular subjects, we would try to sum them up for their comment. Sometimes we put forth hypotheses for their opinion as we tried to make sense of their accounts. By stating or sometimes deliberately misstating their reports of the remarrige experience, we were permitted to enter into—at least to some degree—their private marital world.

More than anything else, the delayed probe interviews guided our subsequent analysis of the data. Many of the themes of the chapters in this volume emerged in the course of the discussions, for we were continually attempting to understand the information collected in the structured interviews. We were compelled by the process of making sense of the data to examine the structured responses in light of what we learned from the unstructured interviews. And, we were often forced to temper or reinterpret the qualitative data by the distribution of answers from the structured interviews. The interplay between the two types of data provided many of the ideas explored in the analysis.

The chapters in this volume summarize the results of that analysis. They have not been cosmetically treated to conceal the rather unorthodox manner in which the analysis was carried out. As the final results of the survey were not available to us until the spring of 1980, we plunged into the data using the transcripts from the two sets of qualitative interviews. Indeed, the earliest paper, "Remarriage and Intergenerational Relations," was prepared even before the survey was launched. The survey itself provided systematic information that permitted us to test some of the ideas developed from scrutinizing the case-study materials. Our approach throughout was to generate as many ideas as we could from the qualitative interviews, attempting to ground our observations in the responses to the survey whenever possible. The survey was never regarded as the primary or ultimate source. Even when the survey material became available, we attempted to move beyond the limitations of the data set by introducing demographic and public opinion data. The conclusions we reached are based, then, on a patchwork of data derived from a variety of sources. The reader searching for conclusive findings will no doubt find the results unsatisfying. Those interested in locating useful points of departure for further study will, we hope, be more tolerant of the form of the analysis.

ISSUES FOR FURTHER INVESTIGATION

What is common to most of the chapters is the way that divorce and remarriage is revising commonly accepted notions of marriage, parenthood, and kinship. As mentioned at the outset, we are persuaded that the process of conjugal succession has helped to bring about a change in family imagery and family relations. In the chapters on conjugal succession, parenting, and intergenerational relations, we identify a number of conventional conceptions that have been eroded as divorce and remarriage have become more common. Several incipient trends seem to us to warrant further attention by students of family change.

In the chapter on conjugal succession, we pose the question of whether the meaning of marriage has changed in response to the growing prevalence of divorce and remarriage. We examine changes in the meaning of marriage at two levels which are discrete but at the same time interlinked. At a cultural level, marriage expectations have been altered as a result of changing patterns of family formation and changes in the economy—most centrally, the entrance of married women into the labor force. At the individual level, the passage from marriage to divorce inevitably shapes the nature of the remarriage experience. Specifically, this means that individuals must develop strategies to explain their biography of failure and to ensure that the second marriage is not merely a reiteration of the first. The result is a subtle change in marital expectations, which reinforces the general trend toward viewing marriage as a conditional commitment.

This hypothesis—and it cannot be argued that our tentative interpretation is anything more than that—deserves a more searching empirical examination. We know relatively little about the socialization process in first marriages, and even less about how it works in second marriages. Elsewhere, Andrew Cherlin (1978) has argued that individuals entering remarriage face special problems of accommodating to family life because the guidelines for how to behave are less clearcut than they are for individuals in first marriages. The incomplete institutionalization of remarriage, Cherlin tells us, leads to a greater amount of marital strain. We have questioned Cherlin's conclusion although not his contention that remarriage is currently an anomolous arrangement. In both the chapter on conjugal succession and the one dealing directly with Cherlin's argument we have advanced an alternative interpretation of how individuals adapt to remarriage. That process of adaptation is further examined in the analysis of the adjustment to remarriage. Taken together, these indicate that most individuals cope rather well with the strains of divorce and remarriage. Our results parallel the findings on the effects of divorce on children that have shown that the short-term trauma is often quite considerable but that the long-term effects—if they exist at all—are much less severe (Hetherington et al., 1978, 1982; Wallerstein and Kelly, 1980; Furstenberg and Seltzer, 1983). Given sufficient time, most individuals— whether children or adults—are able to adapt to unexpected life changes. This conclusion, if it is true, should be regarded as an opportunity for future exploration of the mechanisms by which individuals mobilize personal and social resources in the process of negotiating unscheduled transitions.

As divorce has become more commonplace, the custody issue has resurfaced as both a practical matter for families who have experienced marital disruption and a policy dilemma for the courts, the welfare system, and service providers who must deal with problems of child care. Marital dissolution forces parents to reallocate time and resources for child rearing. The results are rarely satisfactory to either the parents or children involved. The chapters that describe parenting after divorce reveal that most nonresidential parents opt out altogether. Typically, child support is nonexistent or meager at most, and the level of contact between the parent and child usually dwindles to an occasional visit. Our aim in the analysis was to understand the rapid disintegration of ties between the nonresidential parents and their offspring.

The conflict that leads to divorce obviously makes collaboration between the parents difficult, if not impossible. Lingering resentments between the formerly married partners are often played out in parental roles. But even with the best of intentions it is difficult to manage child rearing when parents live apart. Residential parents claim that outside parents are abandoning their responsibilities while outside parents, in turn, feel excluded and unappreciated. The very different situations of the two parents lead to divergent perspectives—what we referred to as the "his and her" views of divorce, borrowing Jessie Bernard's phrase for describing contrasting perspectives of husbands and wives.

Remarriage, as we show in the two chapters on parenting, further complicates the situation both by introducing additional actors and by expanding the demands on the parents. There is, of course, no uniform response to remarriage. The data from Central Pennsylvania show that remarriage sometimes relieves the strain between the formerly married partners; but sometimes it has just the opposite effect. In either case, it often results in a realignment of family priorities. Nonresidential parents who are only marginally involved in child rearing frequently withdraw altogether, turning their attention to their second family. It would seem that sociological parenthood takes precedence over biological parenthood.

In a recent paper describing the results of a national survey of children from maritally disrupted families, the pattern of child care after divorce and remarriage was characterized as "a system of child swapping" whereby fathers exchange one set of children for another (Furstenberg and Nord, 1982). This description of current arrangements may be something of an overstatement, but it rings true for most families that have experienced divorce and remarriage. Successful coparenting is extremely rare, far less common than we are led to believe from accounts in the mass media or from personal observations. Whether, and how much, coparenting has been increasing in recent years is not known. It is a question that certainly merits attention. It is even more important to discover how and why certain formerly married couples can manage the difficult task of parenting despite living apart.

An elaboration of the nuclear family occurs after divorce and remarriage. Divorce, as David Schneider observes, creates two "incomplete families" if one adopts the position that the nuclear family remains the cultural ideal. The family is no longer contained within a single household, which violates commonly accepted notions of the integrity of the family. Remarriage reestablishes a nuclear family, but not in replica. The pieces do not join together neatly. Most people, as the data from Central Pennsylvania show, discriminate between steprelations, kin acquired through marriage, and blood relations (or what are colloquially referred to as "real relatives"). The two chapters on the impact of divorce and remarriage on the kinship system explore how individuals manage new relations and the circumstances in which they retain ties to former in-laws. We discovered that the kinship system established by divorce and remarriage functions somewhat differently for adults and children.

Adults generally trade one set of relatives for another when they move from one marriage to the next. Although they have the option of maintaining ties with in-laws from their previous marriage and even of continuing to regard them as relatives, they do so infrequently and selectively. Intimate relationships sometimes survive; distant ones almost never do. By contrast, the new marriage automatically creates a new family network. On my wedding day, the brother of my wife becomes my relative. It is far less clear whether my former wife's brother remains my relative. The chapter titled "Intergenerational Relations" reveals that families ratify the marriage by extending temporary kinship to in-laws. Not to do so might be divisive. Not to acknowledge an in-law as a kinsperson could jeopardize relations with blood kin. Loyalty to in-laws may not be very deep and is certainly not lasting, but it has the consequence of strengthening bonds to kin related by blood.

The situation for children is almost reversed. They cannot so easily exchange kin for their ties to the relatives of their noncustodial parent are by blood. Presumably, blood ties take precedence over the ties that are established by marriage to the relations of their stepparent. Nonetheless, relationships with kin still require contact and material support to become effective. The withdrawal of the noncustodial parent often disrupts intergenerational relations by breaking the link between the child and his or her noncustodial parents' extended family. Conversely, frequent contact with the extended kin of his stepparent forges close bonds with stepgrandparents, uncles, and aunts. Typically, children add on rather than forfeit relations. As a result, they acquire an expanded kinship network after a divorce and remarriage.

We know relatively little about the operation of this new family extended not only by generation but by marriage as well. As we point out in this book, a relatively small number of children are being shared by a large pool of adults. Children easily can have a half-dozen grandparents and maybe more. How this complicates or enriches the child's life has not yet been explored. The reciprocal question, equally intriguing, is how adults—grandparents in particular—manage the competing claims of biological and steprelations. Preliminary indications from the Central Pennsylvania study suggest that distinctions are sometimes concealed, sometimes blurred, and sometimes ignored in order to avoid conflict. But it would be revealing to examine inheritance patterns for traces of distinction.

Conclusion

The fact that the Central Pennsylvania study leaves so many loose ends is not a source of embarrassment to us. We expected no less. As stated earlier, we regarded the research as a point of departure for a more ambitious study of some of the unresolved issues. In the midst of analyzing the data, plans were made for reinterviewing a national survey of children and their parents who had participated in a 1976 study sponsored by the Foundation for Child Development. The study, directed by Nicholas Zill and James Peterson, had investigated the determinants of well-being in a representative sample of children between 7 and 11 years old. In 1981, 1,423 children from 1,071 households were reinterviewed. The results of the study, which directly replicated portions of the Central Pennsylvania interview, seem to indicate that the findings from Central Pennsylvania are likely to hold up for a representative population (Furstenberg and Nord, 1982; Furstenberg et al., 1983a, 1983b).

As the national survey was being launched, Andrew Cherlin and Furstenberg began to interview a sample of the children's grandparents to explore further the question of how intergenerational relations are reshaped by divorce and remarriage. The objective of the current studies is to pick up where the Central Pennsylvania analysis leaves off, exploring more intensively how conjugal succession alters the lives of children by changing the nature of the socialization process, restructuring the family, and reshaping the network of kin surrounding the child.

Our task is to discover how families respond to situations that are culturally uncharted. The solutions that families invent, we believe, provide a clue to emerging rules of behavior. These rules inform us both about what the family is today and what it is likely to become in the future.

CHAPTER 2

Demography of Remarriage

Our perspective on the contemporary family has been radically altered by a recent infusion of material on family life in previous centuries. Previously, a common misconception was that family variation, conflict, and instability were by-products of industrialization and urbanization. We now know better. The available statistical records and archival material provide ample evidence that family life was always fraught with tensions, subject to dramatic fluctuations, and full of diversity. The closer we get to the family of the past, the more it seems like the family of the present—buffeted by external forces and divided by internal strains (Hareven, 1978; Demos and Boocock, 1978; Tufte and Myerhoff, 1979).

Relinquishing our romantic illusions about the past does not lead to a sanguine view of the contemporary family. Nor do we embrace the comforting, but fatuous adage, "The more things change, the more they stay the same." To the contrary, we believe that fundamental and far-reaching changes are taking place in the nature of marriage and parenthood. We are uncertain whether the changes that we shall describe in this chapter completely justify the climate of crisis that currently prevails in American society over the state of the family. Whatever one's position on the strengths or weaknesses of the contemporary family, we do not think that glib comparisons of the crisis-ridden family of today with the putative stable family of the past serve the debate about policy.

No informed observer can question that the family, at least in the United States, is experiencing profound alteration. The magnitude of the perceived change depends in part on what is taken to be the baseline: Beginning at the end of the nineteenth century, the first period for which we have a large amount of reliable quantitative data, yields a vastly different picture than beginning in the middle of the twentieth century, when we have a much richer variety of demographic and social information.

It is striking that short-term family changes—those over the last few decades—are much more dramatic than the long-term changes—those over the last century. This is because in the period immediately following World War II, certain long-standing cyclical trends were temporarily reversed. Age at marriage, which had been relatively stable, plummeted. Fertility (which had been declining rather steadily) increased dramatically, creating the unprecedented baby boom. Divorce rose precipitously at the end of the war, but then declined to prewar levels. In short, for reasons not yet well understood, in the middle of the twentieth century Americans entered an era of mass production of families (Cherlin, 1981; Masnick and Bane, 1980).

It is against this backdrop that the changes in family formation of the past two decades appear to be revolutionary. Marriage age has risen close to historical highs for women, and fertility has declined to historical lows. Women have increasingly moved out of the home and into the workplace, or have combined homemaking with employment. However, our perceptions of these changes are exaggerated because the point of comparison is the baby-boom period. In reality, these changes are less discrepant with long-term trends in family formation. Nevertheless, the end of the baby boom has signaled some monumental changes that have no historical precedent.

This chapter examines some of the demographic trends that have occurred in divorce and remarriage during this century, contrasting patterns of family formation in American society with other developed nations. Our aim is to provide an historical and cross-cultural perspective for viewing the results of our study in Central Pennsylvania. In subsequent chapters it will become clearer that the participants in our study are displaying patterns that have their roots in a major transformation that has been taking place in the American family.

TRENDS IN DIVORCE AND REMARRIAGE

Remarriage was common in the early history of the United States, as it was in much of Western Europe, because of high mortality rates which ended many marriages prematurely (Griffith, 1980). On the other hand, divorce was extremely rare until the end of the nineteenth century and did not increase significantly even during the first part of this century (Plateris, 1979). Thus, until relatively recently, remarriage and family reconstitution implied something quite different from what they do today. The high rates of mortality meant that marriages were replaced rather than rearranged: Parents were removed rather than appended. While it is useful to recognize that high rates of family dissolution and reconstitution are not unprecedented, the parallels with the past can be misleading. Patterns of remarriage after divorce represent recent institutional innovations rather than historical continuities (Cherlin, 1981; Furstenberg, 1979).

Although the divorce rate began to rise after the Civil War, it hovered around the same level from the turn of the century until World War I when it nearly doubled in a matter of a few years. But while divorce became more visible around the time of World War I, it was still decidedly a deviant pattern in society. Indeed, as is shown in Figure 2.1, the rate of divorce dropped off during the interval between the two wars. During the Depression, the absolute number of divorces even declined and the ratio of divorces to marriages also fell off slightly.

Figure 2.1 reveals the sudden and spectacular rise in divorces that occurred during and just after World War II. The divorce rate doubled during the early 1940s and then declined just as suddenly toward the end of the decade. While the upsurge in divorce during World War II prompted a national discussion on the need to strengthen the family, experts observed that marriages were also on the rise and that the peak of marital instability was probably related to the disorganizing effects of the wartime mobilization (Modell et al., 1978). When the number of divorces waned and marriage rates remained high, public concern dissipated. Throughout the 1950s and into the early 1960s the divorce rate remained relatively stable. Actually, however, during this period more individuals were divorcing but more were also marrying—concealing the growth of divorce. In fact, an increasing proportion of all marriages were second unions, and the ratio of divorces to marriages continued to climb during this apparently quiescent period (Preston and McDonald, 1979).

During the 1950s, normative resistance to divorce was breaking down. Public opinion surveys from that period show that a substantial proportion of the population favored liberalization of divorce laws, and many states were beginning to reconsider their restrictive practices (Cherlin, 1981). The impetus to a quickening pace of change occurred in the 1960s when many societal values were subjected to searching examination.

Beginning in the mid-1960s, the divorce rate began to rise and continued to climb virtually unabated throughout the early 1970s. The steep upward trend appears unrelated to any specific external event,

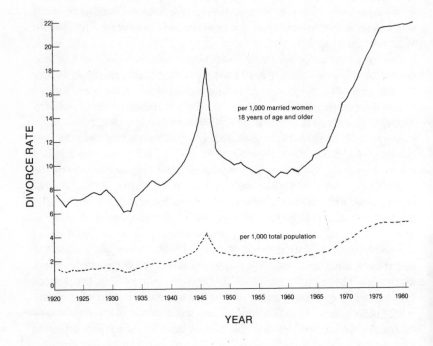

Figure 2.1   Divorce Rates: United States, 1920–1980

unlike the increases around the time of the two World Wars. The trend began during the Vietnam conflict, but it continued for nearly a decade. The annual rate of divorce more than doubled—from 2.2 in 1960 to 5.2 in 1980. Since then it has remained relatively stable.

These changing rates can be translated into more meaningful figures when we consider the estimated probability that any given couple will terminate their marriage by divorce before one or the other spouse dies. Weed (1980) has calculated that approximately half of all marriages recently contracted will end in divorce.

Not only is divorce occurring more frequently, but it seems to be taking place at an earlier point in the life course. The interval between first marriage and divorce has dropped sharply, bringing down the modal age of divorce. Whereas the typical divorced woman in the 1950s was in her early thirties, today she is in her late twenties (U. S. Bureau of the Census, 1976).

In many popular and scholarly accounts of divorce, the impression is given that it represents a withdrawal from marriage. On the contrary, divorce is generally a transitional rather than a terminal event. About half of all women and a somewhat greater percentage of men remarry within three years of the date of their divorce decree; eventually three out of four divorced females and four out of five divorced males reenter wedlock (U. S. Bureau of the Census, 1977). The pace and level of remarriage may be slowing somewhat, but if this is the case it is probably in part attributable to the increasing numbers of divorced persons who are cohabiting before they remarry—a trend that does not seem to reflect a diminished enthusiasm for the conjugal state (Glick, 1980).

Divorce is now commonplace in all Western societies, but no country approaches the United States with its sustained high divorce rate. There are now approximately 1.2 million divorces each year in the United States, involving 2.4 million adults and more than 1 million children. Altogether, about 3.5 million persons are directly affected by divorce each year (Vital and Health Statistics, 1982).

MARRIAGE RATES AND EXPERIENCE

As with divorce, remarriage has become a widespread phenomenon. Remarriage, viewed as a variation from traditional lifelong marriage to one person, is certainly the most prevalent alternative life-style. Close to 4 in 10 marriages in the United States involve at least one spouse who has previously been married (Vital and Health Statistics, 1980b). The incidence of remarriage in this country is among the highest in the world's developed nations. Sweden, Denmark, England, Wales, Egypt, and the German Democratic Republic follow. Countries in which remarriage is low relative to first marriage include primarily Catholic countries such as Peru, the Philippines, Portugal, Dominican Republic,

Ecuador, Italy, Chile, and Northern Ireland (Chamie and Nsuly, 1981) where divorce is still relatively rare.

Using combined information from vital registration data and census data, Chamie and Nsuly (1981) estimated remarriage rates for a substantial number of countries in the world. They point out that, except for a number of Catholic countries, the overwhelming majority of remarriages consist of divorced persons. Among countries with a high proportion of remarriages, about 80 percent of all remarriages involve at least one divorced person. This is in contrast with some Catholic countries where the proportion of remarriages involving at least one divorced person is less than 30 percent.

In all but one country (Austria) the ratio of remarriages to all marriages is greater for males than females. Remarriage rates for divorced males and females are higher than remarriage rates for widowed males and females in virtually all countries. In fact, across countries, divorced men and women are about 7 and 18 times as likely, respectively, to remarry as are widowed men and women (Chamie and Nsuly, 1981).

In the United States, remarriage rates are three times as high for men as for women. In 1978, the rate was 121.8 for men and 40.0 for women. (The rate refers to the number of previously married individuals who marry in a given year per 1,000 divorced and widowed individuals eligible for remarriage.) In other words, about 1 in 8 American men eligible to remarry does so each year, compared to 1 in 25 women. However, the differentials in remarriage rates are most striking when the behaviors of divorced people and that of widowed people are looked at separately. Widowed men remarry at a rate five times greater than widowed women, but divorced men remarry at a rate only 60 percent greater than divorced women (Vital and Health Statistics, 1980b).

Several demographic considerations undoubtedly account for these differentials. First, mortality rates are higher for men than for women. There is a substantial excess of women over men who are widowed. Thus, there are fewer men available for marriage, especially to women in their later years. Second, men tend to marry women who are younger than they, and this tendency increases with increasing age (Glick and Norton, 1977; Spanier and Glick, 1980a). Third, a divorced man is more likely to wed a woman who has never before been married than is a divorced woman to wed a never-married man (U. S. Bureau of the Census, 1978). These facts combine to result in a narrower field of eligible marriage partners for women than for men.

While both the American divorce rate and the remarriage rate were rising during the 1960s, during the 1970s the remarriage rate declined slightly. This decline may be accounted for in part by a trend to postpone remarriage after divorce. One related trend supports this interpretation: A substantial proportion (approximately half) of unmarried individuals who are living together have previously been married (Glick and Spanier, 1980). Thus, cohabitation with a new partner after divorce may be extending the period between divorce and remarriage (Glick and Spanier, 1980).

Cherlin and McCarthy (1983) report that of 45 million married-couple households in the United States in 1980, 9 million were remarried-couple households in which one or both spouses were remarried following a divorce. Thus, one in five households maintained by a married couple involves a remarriage. The proportion is slightly higher (one in four) among blacks, slightly less among households with a man of Hispanic ethnicity (one in six). Cherlin and McCarthy estimate that there were about 2.3 million households in 1980 with stepparents of either sex who were raising stepchildren. There were 4.8 million children living in a household with stepparents and another 4.8 million children under 18 who lived in a remarried-couple household in which neither spouse was a stepparent. A total of 9.6 million American children are in remarried-couple households—one-sixth of the children in the nation.

ANTECEDENTS OF REMARRIAGE

The increasing propensity to divorce in the United States has forced social scientists to reconsider their ideas about the permanence of individual marriages. As mentioned previously, the majority of marriages are now terminated by divorce rather than by the death of a spouse. This situation has existed since 1974, when the number of divorces in a given year exceeded the number of deaths of married persons for the first time (Glick, 1980). It has been true every year since, and is likely to be true for the foreseeable future. Two decades will pass before the large postwar baby cohort reaches the point in the life span when mortality rates begin a significant rise. Yet this cohort is experiencing continued exposure to divorce. As noted, it is projected that approximately half of the marriages formed in the 1970s will be terminated by divorce (Vital and Health Statistics, 1980a). This projection will continue to apply to individuals marrying for the first time in the early 1980s since divorce rates have remained slightly above the level used for projecting the survivability of those married in the 1970s.

Divorce more often affects young marrieds, and widowhood more often affects older marrieds. Moreover, each divorce introduces two additional persons to the field of persons eligible for remarriage, whereas widowhood adds only one person to the field of eligibles. Consequently, remarriage is much more likely to involve divorced rather than widowed individuals.

TIMING OF REMARRIAGE

The median interval from marriage to divorce fluctuates around seven years; the modal length of time between marriage and divorce for first marriage is two to four years (U. S. Bureau of the Census, 1976). The median length of time between divorce and remarriage is about three years, although there are indications that this period will increase in the next few years (Vital and Health Statistics, 1980b). Widowed men and women who do remarry tend to take longer to remarry than do divorced individuals, even when age is considered. Rates of remarriage after divorce are higher than rates of first marriage (Vital and Health Statistics, 1973), indicating that a divorced person at any given age has a greater likelihood of marrying a second time than a never-married person has of marrying a first time. Thus, the idea that divorce involves a rejection of the institution of marriage is not well founded.

FACTORS ASSOCIATED WITH REMARRIAGE

The pathways to remarriage are varied. White women are more likely than black women to remarry, and they remarry more quickly (Glick, 1980; Vital and Health Statistics, 1973; Spanier and Glick, 1980b). Younger women are far more likely to remarry quickly following a divorce, especially when their first marriages were relatively brief. Rapid remarriage is also more likely among women who were married at a relatively young age and who had less than a college education (Glick, 1980; Spanier and Glick, 1980b).

In the study we shall report on in this volume, we discovered every imaginable variation in the circumstances and sequences leading to remarriage. Although it is useful to know what the norms are, one must not lose sight of the great diversity in remarriage experience; such diversity appears to be considerably greater than that found in first marriages.

AGE DIFFERENCES IN REMARRIAGE

Men and women in remarriages tend to differ in age by a greater margin than do men and women in first marriages. In both first marriages and remarriages, the man is the same age or older than the woman in about four in five marriages (Glick, 1980; Vital and Health Statistics, 1973; Spanier and Glick, 1980a). However, the magnitude of the difference is significantly greater in remarriages than in first marriages. Glick (1980) speculates that persons who are marrying for the first time, because of their relative youth, may be more sensitive about the difference between their age and that of their marriage partner than are older persons who are entering marriage for the second time. Another explanation might be that the marriage pool provides less selection at younger ages.

CHILDREN AND REMARRIAGE

Slightly more than half of all couples have children at the time of divorce, and the number of children involved in divorces in a given year more than doubled from 1960 to 1980—rising from 500,000 to 1,200,000 (Spanier and Glick, 1981). Extrapolating from these annual figures, it is possible to estimate the likelihood of the child experiencing family dissolution before reaching age 18. Glick figures that by 1990 approximately one-third of all children will encounter a divorce before reaching 18 years of age (excluding those cases where parents separate but never divorce). Two recent studies that include separations indicate the proportion of children who will experience disruption will be at least two in five (Furstenberg et al., 1983a; Bumpass, 1983). Over half of these children will see the parent with whom they reside marry. Thus, about one child in four will grow up having more than two parents.

Approximately 9 in 10 children live with the mother following the divorce. Fathers are unlikely to obtain sole custody of children regardless of the socioeconomic characteristics or marital history of the wife. There is reason to believe that public attitudes concerning custody awards may be changing, but there is as yet little evidence to indicate that fathers are obtaining physical custody much more often than they did a decade ago. However, there is some evidence that when fathers challenge a custody determination or when they go to court to seek custody, judges have been increasingly willing to grant custody to them (Orthner and Lewis, 1979).

Fathers are somewhat less likely to have custody of all children if their former wives are still divorced rather than remarried (Spanier and Glick, 1981). The likelihood of fathers winning custody is increased when the mothers of their children remarry while the children are very young. They appear to be more likely to obtain custody if the children are all boys and are least likely to obtain custody if the children are all girls.

Spanier and Glick (1981) were able to estimate the extent of split custody in the United States by comparing data on household composition with data on child-custody arrangements. Split custody is defined as a situation in which the father has custody of one or more of the children *and* the mother has custody of one or more of the children. In other words, brothers and sisters may find themselves living in different households. This is in contrast to joint custody, in which both parents are designated as custodians of one or more children. Although about 9 percent of all children under 18 live with their father following divorce, only 4 percent of children live with fathers who have custody of *all* the children from the previous marriage. Split custody, then, involves about 1 in 20 divorced mothers and fathers. But a man who receives custody of any of the children is much more likely than a woman to be a part of a split custody arrangement.

Studies of child-care patterns following divorce suggest that split custody arrangements may assign parents and children of the same sex together, and that older children may be somewhat more likely to be in the father's care while younger siblings remain with the mother (Spanier and Glick, 1981; also see Chapter 4, this volume). Our Central Pennsylvania data, as we shall see, reveal that it is often difficult in practice to think in terms such as joint and split custody or even to be able to state with certainty what the history of custody has been for a particular child. Part of the adjustment for adults and children involved in a divorce and remarriage is reaching an acceptable understanding of these arrangements.

How do children affect the parents' chances of entry into remarriage? Spanier and Glick (1980b) found that overall, children seem to be a slight deterrent to remarriage. However, the effect of having children on the timing and the likelihood of remarriage is probably less than one would expect. Indeed, Koo and Suchindran (1980) found that the *age* of the parents at the time of divorce may be especially important in understanding the impact of children. Among women divorcing before age 25, having children decreased the likelihood of remarriage. Among women divorcing at 35 or older, however, having children increased the chances of remarriage. For women divorcing at ages 25 to 34, there was no effect. More than one-third of white divorced women and about one-half of black divorced women with three or more children never remarry (Spanier and Glick, 1980b).

PARENTING AND STEPPARENTING

As mentioned previously, nearly 10 million children under 18 were living with a biological parent and a stepparent or with two parents who were remarried, representing about one-sixth of all children under 18 years of age (Cherlin and McCarthy, 1983). The number is expected to grow (Glick, 1980). Among the families of remarried mothers, an estimated 70 percent of the children are living with their biological mother and a stepfather. The other 30 percent are living with both natural parents—in other words, these children were born after their mother had remarried (Glick and Norton, 1977).

Bumpass (1982) reports that about one-third of the children in recent remarriages were under five at the time of remarriage; one-sixth were teenagers, 14–17. Few of the children were without siblings, and half had two or more siblings at the remarriage. In making projections about future changes in the configuration of the newly expanded family, Bumpass estimates that about one-third of the children entering second families will have a half-sibling within four years and about two-thirds of the children entering remarriage are eventually likely to have either a step- or a half-sibling; about one-sixth will have both.

Women who remarry after divorce have lower fertility than do women in first marriages but higher fertility than women who divorce and do not remarry. Thus, a woman whose first marriage is interrupted by divorce can expect ultimately to have slightly lower fertility than other women in her marriage cohort, even if she remarries (Glick, 1980).

Until recently, only speculations and anecdotes were available to address the question of what degree of contact and material support exist between divorced or remarried men and women and their children from a previous marriage. We present some illustrative data on this question from our Central Pennsylvania study later, but it is instructive here to highlight some recent data from a national study that will help put the Central Pennsylvania data in perspective (Furstenberg et al., 1983a).

Perhaps most striking is the finding that nearly one-half of all children from maritally disrupted families have not seen one of their biological parents, usually the father, in the previous five years. Almost as remarkable as the proportion who have no contact with the nonresidential parent is the low frequency of visitation among those who have had some contact in the preceding five years. Of those parents who had been in some contact with the child in the past five years, one in five had not seen the child at all in the past 12 months. Furthermore, among those in contact during the last year, one-third saw their outside parent fewer than 14 days; a third between 14 and 51 days; and only a third saw them on more than 52 days during the preceding year. In other words, only one child in six whose parents were separated or divorced managed to see their outside biological parent on the average of once a week.

We shall later confirm from the Central Pennsylvania data some findings in the national study, namely that mothers living outside the home tend to maintain a much more active role in child rearing. Although few in number, nonresidential mothers are distinctly more likely to visit with their child on a regular basis, have overnight visits, and have more indirect contact by phone and letter (Furstenberg and Nord, 1982). The data also appear to suggest that the significance of biological parenthood may be waning in response to emerging patterns of conjugal succession. Put another way, sociological ties account for more, biological ties for less. This is illustrated by the finding that contact with the parent living outside the household normally takes the form of a social rather than an instrumental exchange. Common activities are going out to dinner, taking trips, or playing but rarely are helping with schoolwork or working on a project together. There is little enforcement of rules by the outside parent, and the socialization that exists seems to be done from a distance and with a great deal of laxity. Correspondingly, perhaps, residential parents commonly complain about low levels of involvement of outside parents in child-rearing tasks.

Finally, we should note that national data do not support speculations that stepfamily life is afflicted by problems created by the presence of too many parents. Typically, no more than two adults remain actively involved with the children following divorce. Furthermore, when the residential parent remarries and the outside parent remains nearby geographically, difficulties are typically not directly related to multiple parents. There is some preliminary evidence that when tensions emerge over stepparenting issues, they are more common for children with stepmothers than for children with stepfathers.

STABILITY OF REMARRIAGES

Are the quality and stability of marriage the second time around greater than the first marriage? The data suggest not. Divorce rates are actually higher among the remarried than among the first married. For example, whereas about half of all first marriages formed in recent years are projected to end in divorce, about 55 percent of remarriages can be expected to terminate. While the difference is not substantial, it is real (Vital and Health Statistics, 1980a).

There are different explanations for this phenomenon. Cherlin (1978) explains the higher divorce rate of remarriages by suggesting that remarriage poses special challenges. He theorizes that remarriage is an incomplete institution with no clearly defined norms to help guide the new relationship. The presence of stepchildren, for example, may pose unusually difficult adjustments not normally found in first marriages. We challenge Cherlin's reasoning, however. Our data suggest that an analysis of the difference should focus primarily on the one unique attribute that all remarried people share—namely, that they have been married and, typically, divorced before. The previous experience of divorce suggests the possibility that remarried couples are more willing to terminate a marriage that fails than are individuals in first marriages. This greater willingness, however tempered, will mean that previously divorced persons are more likely to divorce a second time than are never-divorced persons, many of whom are unlikely to divorce no matter what the quality of their marriage. Moreover, even if a previously divorced person is in principle opposed to divorce and is reluctant to do it, he or she nevertheless has survived the experience once; and the knowledge that it can be survived may make it more likely that the individual will allow it to happen again. (We will discuss this issue in some detail later in this book.)

In this chapter, we have attempted to set forth the demography of remarriage. There is no common profile of who divorces and remarries, nor is there a common set of experiences or social characteristics that apply in matters of child custody and parenting. Nevertheless, there are some generalizations that can be made which will set the stage for discussions that follow.

The propensity to remarry is one such generalization; Americans usually remarry after a divorce (despite some inclinations to the contrary) soon after the final separation from their spouse. Furthermore, they tend to remarry quickly. Finally, it is noteworthy that in a period when there have been some profound changes in family life, little has changed in how children are assigned following divorce. Children continue to be in the custody of their mothers, with less contact with fathers than one might imagine. With this general overview of the remarriage experience, we now examine data from our Central Pennsylvania study.

CHAPTER 3

Conjugal Succession

Divorce has become so commonplace that it represents, for much of the population, an optional stage in an increasingly variable conjugal career. Yet most students of the family continue to think of divorce as an anomolous departure from normal marriage practices rather than as an intrinsic, if not completely institutionalized, part of our kinship system. By treating divorce as a manifestation of family pathology and focusing almost exclusively on the potentially detrimental impact of divorce on adults and their children, social scientists have diverted attention away from the deeper implications of divorce for family functioning.

In the previous chapter, we observed a profound transformation in our kinship system in this century, moving from a time when divorce was a relatively rare event to the present arrangement in which close to one-half of those entering marriage will eventually divorce and the great majority of these individuals will remarry. Indeed, in a matter of a few decades we have replaced a set of rules requiring that people remain married even when they retained little or no emotional attachment to one another with one that virtually requires them to relinquish their relationship if they are not deeply emotionally involved.

Our initial objective in this chapter is to try to show how the pattern of conjugal succession is becoming articulated into a more general configuration of family formation. In particular, we shall try to show that changing patterns of divorce and remarriage are related to the emergence of more flexible life-course sequences. These structural changes in turn may be revising contemporary notions of marriage, parenthood, and extended kinship.

Our concern in this chapter, however, is less with the causes than with certain consequences of conjugal succession. Little is known about the process of nuptial transitions or the functioning of second marriages. We shall examine how ideas of matrimony change during the transition from the first to the second marriage. Our aim is to explore how and why marital beliefs and practices are altered in the remarriage process. We shall try to show that the movement from one marriage to the next takes a characteristic form that differs in important respects from that of the initial entry into marriage.

Sources of Change in Conjugal Stability

There are, of course, many possible explanations for the growing acceptability of divorce and remarriage (Ross and Sawhill, 1975; Masnick and Bane, 1980; Cherlin, 1981; Lasch, 1977). Prominently mentioned as reasons for the change are (1) the movement of women into the labor force combined with the declining significance of childbearing and child rearing as an exclusive role for married women; (2) the growth of the welfare state and the provision of economic alternatives to marital dependency; (3) the lowering of legal and social barriers that previously had served to constrain couples from ending an unrewarding marriage; and (4) the increasing emphasis in American culture on personal fulfillment which may have elevated our expectations of marriage.

While acknowledging the strong likelihood that each of these conditions may have contributed to the transformation in marriage practices, we would like to draw attention to a series of demographic changes that may also have promoted the pattern of conjugal succession by altering the meaning of marriage for large segments of the population. Briefly, we shall try to show that marriage was previously embedded in a tightly sequenced series of status transitions. As long as this configuration existed, matrimony implied a lifetime commitment because it was the keystone to a general life-course plan. Marriage was, in short, an essential part of a socially prescribed status sequence (Modell, 1980). Today, marriage is frequently a discrete transition removed from other events that make up the process of family formation. Because marriage has relatively fewer implications for the course of early adulthood, it is now far easier to contemplate its dissolution than it was a generation ago.

In the traditional sequence of family formation, marriage was tightly bound to a series of other events—the departure from the family of origin, the initiation of sexual activity, entrance into the labor force for men and withdrawal from the labor force for women, the inception of parenthood, and the establishment of independent residence. Although a familiar arrangement, in point of fact the traditional pattern of family formation is of relatively recent vintage. The nineteenth-century pattern of family formation depicted in Figure 3.1 permitted a good deal more discretion in the timing of life events than did the pattern that became common in the middle of the twentieth century. Historical data on the social organization of the life course in the nineteenth century indicate that the passage to adulthood—and specifically the transitions to marriage and parenthood—followed a looser schedule than it did in the more recent past. The timing of marriage was dictated by collective considerations (i.e., conditions set by the family of origin), and individuals were frequently unable to coordinate marriage to suit personal preference (Kett, 1977; Modell et al., 1976; Elder, 1978).

By the middle of the twentieth century, the pattern of family formation became much more uniform for both men and women (Modell et al., 1978; Modell, 1980). Marriage typically occurred shortly after schooling ended, particularly when both phenomena were precipitated by a premarital pregnancy. As marriage almost invariably implied imminent parenthood (and often was actually occasioned by impending parenthood), the male was required to make a full-time commitment to work while the female typically withdrew from the labor force and assumed full-time homemaker responsibilities. In a very real sense, the postwar period was the culmination of an ideal course of family formation which up until then had never been fully realized. When this ideal finally became operational, it proved to be enormously problematic culturally, economically, and psychologically. Beginning in the mid-1960s, there was a strong reaction against this domestic scenario as young people in general, and women in particular, began to depart from this tightly prescribed sequence of life events (Hirschhorn, 1977).

As is shown in Figure 3.1, the uniform design so evident at mid-century has vanished for large segments of the population, giving way once again to a motif of diversity. In the contemporary sequence of family formation, the marital transition has receded in importance and no longer serves as a central organizing event in the passage to adulthood. Whereas two decades ago marriage was part of a package of transitions that occurred more or less simultaneously, recently it has become less integrated with each of the other events that make up the process of family formation.

Most individuals have sexual relations well before they marry, and the decision to have sex no longer necessarily implies an intention to marry (Zelnik and Kantner, 1980). The double standard is on the decline, and women—as was once the case only for men—are

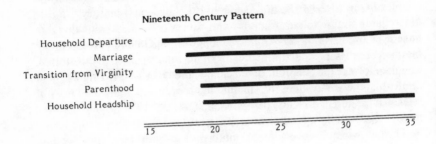

Nineteenth Century Pattern

Household Departure
Marriage
Transition from Virginity
Parenthood
Household Headship

15   20   25   30   35

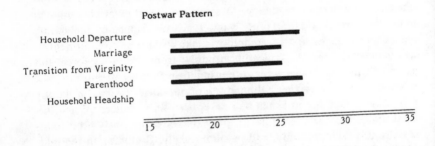

Postwar Pattern

Household Departure
Marriage
Transition from Virginity
Parenthood
Household Headship

15   20   25   30   35

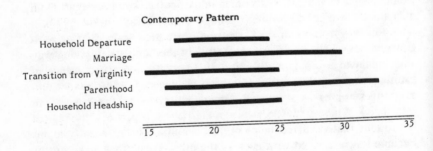

Contemporary Pattern

Household Departure
Marriage
Transition from Virginity
Parenthood
Household Headship

15   20   25   30   35

Figure 3.1   Three Modal Patterns of Family Formation: Women, United States (estimated spread of middle 80 percent who ever achieved transition)

permitted and sometimes even encouraged to have varied sexual experience before they marry (Clayton and Bokemeier, 1980). Accompanying the changing sexual mores is the unprecedented growth of cohabitation. Between 1970 and 1978 alone, the number of unmarried couples living together more than doubled (Glick and Spanier, 1980). No reliable figures exist on either the proportion of individuals who have ever lived with a member of the opposite sex or the percentage of married couples who live together prior to marriage. It is still only a minority of the population. Even so, cohabitation both reflects and reinforces the separation of sex and marriage and contributes to a relaxation of the tight schedule of family formation that prevailed in the middle of the twentieth century (Cherlin, 1981).

The growth of cohabitation as an acceptable way of delaying marriage means that matrimony has ceased to mark the transition to household headship. In the 1950s, the gap between the conclusion of school and marriage was so brief that most young women remained at home until they were wed. Setting up house signaled a shift of dependence from parent to spouse. As the period of schooling lengthened in the 1960s, young people—men and women—began to establish their own households, either independently or with peers well in advance of marriage. No longer is marriage required to set up independent residence (Masnick and Bane, 1980).

In another important respect, the significance of marriage in the process of family formation has declined. The rapid and automatic progression from marriage to motherhood that characterized the postwar period cannot any longer be assumed. A growing proportion of women are beginning childbearing outside marriage, although most who follow this course drift into—rather than elect—this option (Furstenberg et al., 1981). More often, women enter marriage without any immediate intentions of becoming parents. A small minority profess the desire to remain childless, while a much more sizable proportion resolve to delay parenthood until career lines are clearly established. A considerable number of women now delay childbearing for five or more years after entering marriage. Thus, parenthood no longer dictates marriage as it once did, and increasingly marriage does not dictate parenthood (Bumpass, 1979).

In general, the pathways of family formation have become less normatively prescribed insofar as behavioral regularities reveal social rules. Individuals have greater leeway to tailor family arrangements to their personal needs and desires. Hence, the early part of the life course has become more discretionary in both the timing and the order of family-related transitions, at least compared to a generation ago.

It is not difficult to see how these changes may signify a corresponding shift in the general cultural meaning of marriage. It is no coincidence that as marriage has been stripped of some of its importance as a ceremonial marker of adulthood, the pattern of conjugal succession has also become more widespread. In the first place, many more individuals now enter marriage after living alone as singles. They have had some experience managing a household prior to marriage and are equipped to do so again in the event that their marriage fails (Stein, 1981). Even if few regard being single as a preferred way of life, most younger people can contemplate living outside of marriage if such a contingency becomes necessary. This represents a large change from the situation a generation ago when many individuals, especially women, had little or no experience living outside of family settings (Masnick and Bane, 1980).

Moreover, the presence of children no longer serves as a deterrant to divorce as it once did when mothers with young children were incapable of commanding a position in the labor market. Single parenthood was once a term reserved for illicit parenthood. Today it applies to an undifferentiated category of unmarried and formerly married parents who are living without partners. If it has not become a highly regarded status, neither is it any longer a deviant one.

Finally, the contemporary process of family formation not only provides training and experience for managing marital dissolution, but probably also contributes directly to higher rates of disruption by creating more exacting marital standards. For example, some authorities contend that varied prenuptial sexual experience increases sexual adjustment after marriage, but this type of training probably means that individuals demand more sexual gratification from their marriages if only because they have a wider basis for comparison (Reiss and Furstenberg, 1981).

Similarly, cohabitation may contribute to a more realistic assessment of marriage by giving individuals an opportunity to develop emotional capacities and interpersonal skills prior to settling into a permanent relationship. But cohabitation not only enhances one's ability to form new relationships, it also prepares an individual to sever intimate bonds when they prove to be ungratifying. Longitudinal research on cohabitation suggests that most people living together at any given point in time will dissolve their relationship before marriage (Macklin, 1978). It seems likely that a growing number of young people enter marriage after cohabiting with one or more individuals other than their marital partner. Thus, many persons marrying for the first time are not completely unfamiliar with the process of divorce.

To sum up, there is reason to suspect that the rise of conjugal succession is related to a general shift in the pattern of family formation that has unraveled marriage from what was once a common strand of status transitions. As marriage has become independent of other events in the life course, it is seen as a more voluntary and less permanent arrangement. This does not necessarily mean that individuals today expect less of marriage. Indeed, it is entirely possible that as marriage has become less binding and inviolable, standards of what constitutes a gratifying and satisfying marriage have risen. As marriages have become less constrained by a preconceived agreement to remain wed, individuals may, so to speak, refer more to current market standards and believe that they can do better by making a nuptial change. It seems unlikely that marriages are less happy today than they were 50 or 100 years ago. Probably the contrary is true because a greater premium is placed on marriages that are more emotionally rewarding today (Shorter, 1975; Degler, 1980). But as standards have risen and constraints declined, individuals are more prone to get divorced with less provocation.

When viewed in this light, divorce can be seen as an intrinsic part of a cultural system that values individual discretion and emotional gratification. Divorce is a social invention for promoting these cultural ideals. Ironically, the more divorce is used, the more exacting the standards become for those who marry. Thus, the high rates of divorce in our society are not an indication that marriage as an institution is being devalued; in fact, just the opposite. But as the cultural importance placed on the personal gratification of marriage grows, the commitment any given couple makes to a marriage becomes more conditional as either partner must be able to exit from the relationship in the event that it is not living up to his or her expectations.

Divorce, then, serves not so much as an escape hatch from married life but as a recycling mechanism permitting individuals a second (and sometimes third and fourth) chance to upgrade their marital situation. A conjugal career is an apt metaphor, for most remarried individuals see themselves as taking a progressive step when they divorce and reenter marriage.

UNEXPLORED ISSUES IN THE STUDY OF SECOND MARRIAGES

The sequences of conjugal careers have obvious parallels to the ordering of occupational careers and the pattern of job changes over the life span. Yet in contrast to the rich literature on occupational transitions, no similar line of research has developed on nuptial transitions. The reentrance to marriage has been largely neglected until quite recently (Price-Bonham and Balswick, 1980), and the few existing studies ignore altogether what is involved in moving from one marriage to the next.

Moreover, many researchers have overlooked the most interesting properties of second marriages which differentiate them from initial unions. All marriages, as Berger and Kellner (1964) remind us, involve a building of a common *nomos*, or world view, which sustains the couple's dealings with one another. In the process of remarriage, individuals must both revise and disassemble the micro-culture of their first marriage and create a new belief system. Sometimes this process involves a radical revision, and sometimes it merely involves minor alterations. There have been no studies of how individuals go about shedding old expectations and acquiring fresh ones, and how much the first marriage shapes practices and beliefs in the second is not known. It is this question that will concern us in the rest of this chapter.

There are several reasons to suspect that the process of remarriage is different from, and probably more complicated than, the initial entry into marriage.

(1)   While difficult to factor out, there are undoubtedly lingering effects of the first marriage on the second. Two separate sources of influence are readily discernible. First, we have already alluded to the person's psychological experience of the first marriage which creates a layer of expectations and habits that may or may not be imported into the second union. Later, we shall present evidence showing that the first marriage provides a baseline against which the second relationship is judged. Married couples take considerable pains to differentiate marital styles in their first and second relationships, suggesting an unavoidable tendency on the part of these couples to apply the experience of their first marriage to their second.

(2)   Apart from any lessons learned from the failure of their first marriage, second marriages bear the continuing imprint of the previous relationship. Remarried persons, particularly if they are parents, often cannot

avoid continued interaction with the first spouse, and their current and previous mates are unwittingly linked in what can be described as a "remarriage chain" (Bohannon, 1970).

(3)   First and second marriages take place at divergent points in the individual's life span. Personal maturity, life experience, and social status variations create a different set of constraints in the two marriages if they are contracted at disparate ages. Because of these life-span variations, people often remarry under circumstances dissimilar to those of their first marriage, leading them to perceive first and second marriages as distinctively different.

(4)   Finally, a remarried individual is a member of two different marriage cohorts and accordingly is exposed and then reexposed to current cultural standards of how a marriage should operate. Individuals who marry at two very different historical moments—for example, those who were first married in 1965 and then married a second time in 1975—may be subject to very different expectations of how to behave in marriage. The process of remarriage may compel marriage partners to rethink marriage according to contemporary standards.

We now turn to some preliminary findings from our longitudinal study of the transition from divorce to remarriage. The objective of this analysis is to expand and illuminate the influences mentioned above which differentiate between couples reentering marriage and those marrying for the first time.

The Entrance to Marriage: Differences Between the First Marriage and the Second

Our respondents share one significant status when they enter marriage: They have all been divorced, usually after several years of marital conflict. This long-term process of disenchantment and disengagement from a previous marriage is extremely important in organizing the experience of marriage the second time. Individuals begin second marriage without the idealized image of marriage that most couples have when they first marry (Berger and Kellner, 1964). This is one reason why some divorced persons prefer to wed someone with previous marriage experience.

Individuals reentering marriage face a special problem related to their biography of failure. Having extricated themselves from a painful marriage, they may see divorce as a positive experience and remarriage as a potentially hazardous undertaking. As we shall see, individuals frequently refer to the time of their divorce as a period of personal liberation and growth. Consequently, recommitment to marriage requires the need to develop a plausible account that persuades an individual that it will be different this time. In the following discussion, our aim is to show how remarried people neutralize their fears that they are about to make the same mistake again.

At the time of the initial interview, most participants in the Central Pennsylvania study expressed a certain wariness about reentering marriage. About two-thirds indicated either that they definitely would not remarry or expressed a reluctance to do so, while only one-third admitted that they were eager to remarry or had definite plans to wed. This sentiment in fact proved to be virtually useless as a predictor of the occurrence of remarriage. Of the individuals who were reluctant to reenter marriage, 28 percent changed their minds and remarried by the second interview—just two and one-half years later. Only a slightly higher proportion (36 percent) of those who were eager to remarry found a suitable partner by the follow-up.

All indications from demographic data show that the process of deciding to reenter marriage is as rapid as, if not more rapid than, the initial decision to wed. Several studies have also indicated that remarried persons are less inclined to observe rules of homogamy (marrying persons of similar status) than are those who wed the first time (Peters, 1976; Dean and Gurak, 1978). Most participants in the Central Pennsylvania study insisted that they approached the decision to remarry with much greater caution and circumspection than they had before their first marriage.

> WIFE: Before marrying, we sat down and discussed different things that happen in a marriage. We brought out our views and ideas, and decided that the only way a marriage can work would be to be honest, outspoken, and ready to accept each other's criticism. We have made it a habit to sit down every week and discuss any problems or disagreements that came into our minds that week before they get out of hand.

When asked to describe the differences between their decision to marry the first and second time, respondents almost invariably stated that their first marriage often resulted from social pressure generated by family or friends. One out of five respondents reported that the decision to marry resulted directly from a premarital pregnancy, and an almost equal number reported that they married simply because it was expected of them. Others saw their first marriage as a way of escaping from a dreary family situation.

> INTERVIEWER: Is that a different kind of feeling than you had the first time you went into marriage?
>
> WIFE: I can't really answer that. I was 18 when I got married and I was also three months pregnant. It was back in the sixties. You got married, [because of] pressure . . . there was no keeping the child and staying home with your parents. . . . I didn't know really what I wanted, what I expected, or even what marriage should be like. Well, I know what I expected, I expected it to be perfect but I didn't know what marriage was really all about.
>
> HUSBAND: I think it was a culmination of . . . I came from, you know, I don't want to sound like an old sad song you've probably heard before, you know, I came from a poor family. There was ten kids plus my mother and dad, so there's twelve of us and we never had two nickels to rub together so I think . . . then my Dad died when I was 15 and I've been taking care of myself ever since so it was more or less just a chance to get away, you know, from that atmosphere and I think that was my wife's too, 'cause she came, well, from a poor family but she came from down in the sticks, out in the middle of nowhere and we moved to State College when we got married. It was more or less like we were getting away from home, you know, starting all over.

The respondents' willingness to succumb to such pressure is partly explained by the fact that they were young and impressionable. Repeatedly, in both the structured interviews and the qualitative case studies, we were informed that in their first marriage they subscribed to an illusory belief that at a certain age "everyone falls in love and lives happily ever after." Immaturity, insecurity, and impetuosity were frequently mentioned as reasons for marrying the first time. These personal limitations lead the individual into a false love relationship based on a romantic illusion.

> WIFE: I mean, I was 21 when I got married. Right out of college. I mean, I had dreams of going to graduate school. You meet THE MAN and you get THE RING and that's it. That's what happened. I was really insecure then. I guess I didn't feel strong

enough in myself that I could go on to graduate school by myself, be alone.

This lack of judgment, it was reported to us, figured heavily in the failure of the first marriage and presumably explains why most divorced women are willing to entertain the idea of reentering marriage. Nearly two-thirds reported that their first marriage did not work out because "I just didn't marry the right person." There was a widespread belief among the remarried respondents that they had selected their spouse with greater care the second time.

Although we lack information that would enable us to compare the courtship process in first and second marriages, it seems likely that in certain respects divorced persons do exercise more caution than persons marrying for the first time. Most of the former reported that they consciously attempted to rectify the ill-advised way in which they entered their first marriage. Two-thirds, for example, stated that they had explicit discussions with their prospective spouse about the risks of another divorce.

> HUSBAND: We talked about it, what if, or are we making a mistake? . . . Are you now mistake prone? . . . Not necessarily in depth, planning for the eventual demise, but that we still felt the same [way].

Their approach to dating and courtship was typically guided more by pragmatic than by romantic considerations. Many couples either never adopted or very early in their relationship abandoned the traditional form of dating; instead they quickly settled into a pattern of informal association at any time of the day or night (see Schonrock, forthcoming). Living together before marriage is, of course, an extreme expression of that informality, and nearly two-thirds of our sample cohabited before they married.

In the in-depth interviews, informants pointed out that they deliberately tried to present themselves honestly rather than projecting an ideal image. Being seen in old clothes or with their hair in curlers was considered an important part of early courtship. Thus, couples often by-passed the romantic, idealistic stage of courtship, preferring instead to see each other's warts as quickly as possible. If they did not live together before marrying, couples with children spent a great deal of time promoting contact between their children and their prospective partner. A number of informants reported that even after they decided that they wanted to marry, they withheld making a fixed decision until they had their children's assent.

> HUSBAND: We talked about everything, any possible problems that could come up over the next so many years. What happens if . . . or when if . . .
>
> INTERVIEWER: Were there any discussions with Marge and you about the boys? Were the boys brought in from time to time?
>
> HUSBAND: Oh yes. This was something else too that the boys and I, like I said earlier, well, I don't know if I said it, I said I was very fond of the kids but I've always been very close to them and we had discussed a lot of times, should we get married again.
>
> WIFE: Well, they all asked me to marry them.

Although the remarried people in our study believe that they staunchly resisted the kinds of social pressures that led them into their first marriage, studies of the transition to divorce consistently revealed that the status of the divorced woman is an uncomfortable one and that previously married persons are importuned by both friends and family to reenter wedlock (Goode, 1956; Hunt, 1966). And, a prevailing myth is that many people remarry on the rebound to prove to others, as well as themselves, that they are capable of getting married. Very few of the respondents acknowledged that their decision to remarry was prompted by loneliness, economic need, or the difficulties of managing a household alone, although these reasons must have entered into their decision to remarry. Thus, while the motives for matrimony may change from first to second marriages, individuals do not seem any more aware of the external pressures to marry the second time than they did the first.

Nevertheless, there is some reason to suspect that remarried persons are less fettered by romantic illusions about the perfect union. When asked to compare the qualities in a spouse that were important the first time and this time, the respondents were somewhat less likely to emphasize appearance, ambition, and occupational status, and were more likely to place importance on stability, consideration, and shared interest. Remarried persons indicate that they are willing to make concessions regarding qualities that have social currency in enhancing status and instead opt for traits that may improve the viability of the union.

WIFE: I admired my first husband, I admired what I thought [were his] strengths—which were his determination, and his self-confidence and his abilities to set forth a difficult goal and meet it. . . . Now that I know more about him, I know how he does those things, and they are not as important to me. But at that time, that was sort of the basis for my love. . . . We did not have a lot of common goals. . . . I also bought into the stereotype version of what marriage was, what it would be—and it wasn't that way, and probably never is. I had a kind of romantic view of what man and woman should be together. . . .

I thought that if he got a Ph.D., that he had to be super-intelligent, and I admired that. . . . At the same time that I married him, he was very funny. And really he wasn't easygoing, but he was the life of the party. That kind of thing. And my family's values, my parent's values, were always very interested in education, a Ph.D. would be just like the top thing.

INTERVIEWER: What about your feelings for your second husband?

WIFE: Well, Roger is stable, he is very competent, and, confident in himself, but he has room for mistakes. Stan would never admit a single mistake he ever made. . . . Roger has such a character that you can depend on his doing the thing that would be the admirable thing. Now, I am saying that I admire him. And I do. But it's for a very different kind of reason.

As is illustrated in this quote, remarried couples commonly down play the importance of romantic love or, at least, redefine it. Nearly three out of four in the Central Pennsylvania sample agreed with the statement that "remarried persons have a different conception of love than couples in their first marriages." In the unstructured interviews, many couples expressed their mistrust of a marriage based on romantic attachment. Of course, there are exceptions, such as individuals who broke up their initial marriage because they fell in love with someone else; but these situations do not seem to be as frequent as popularly imagined.

While no one rejected the importance of strong emotional feelings as a sine qua non for marriage, they sometimes entertained suspicions about the necessity of falling in love. Frequently, respondents contrasted their more mature feelings of love with the irrational attachment they experienced the first time they wed. In part, this may reflect a change in the cultural meaning of love and marriage that occurred in the past decade or two.

Moreover, the implications of romantic love—uncontrollable emotional feelings, indulgence in fantasies, and unconditional commitment—do not suit the needs of many remarried persons. They experienced the souring of romantic sentiments in the first marriage and, consequently, are prepared to accept a more measured and qualified level of attachment in their second union, foregoing the ecstatic love. Even when they retain a commitment to romantic love, they are more inclined to discount its permanence, expecting their romantic feelings to diminish in time.

> WIFE: I think one reason why we have so many divorces is that marriage and all the stuff around it has been made into a myth and you expect perfection and fulfillment and all kinds of things from it and you just don't get it and when you find out, it takes about four years to find out you are not going to get it, with your relationship, some people get disillusioned and leave.
>
> INTERVIEWER: When you think of it, . . . would you describe yourself as being caught up with falling in love, with romantic love?
>
> WIFE: Well, I'm still caught up in that but I think I've made some perspective and I realize what it is.
>
> INTERVIEWER: What is it?
>
> WIFE: Well, romantic love is, I think, temporary. It comes and after awhile it will leave. You know, it always has. So, you know, I figured that this is just an emotion and it's transitory and it's not going to stay. But there are other things underneath that are more permanent, so that even though they aren't quite as intense as romantic love is, they are still necessary.

Remarried couples also establish marital relations with less grandiose expectations. They speak a language of domestic veterans. In the case studies, frequent reference was made to "the need to give and take," "the importance of compromise," and "the willingness to work things out." Partly because people begin their second marriages later in life and partly because they have gone through a disillusioning first marriage, second marriages from their inception typically take on the appearance of advanced relationships. Illusions are shed before the marriage begins as a protection against the fear of disappointment.

Remarried couples are extremely sensitive to the popular conception that in second marriages individuals merely recapitulate the problems encountered in the first marriage. Close to half of the remarried couples subscribed to the view that people often make the same mistake in getting married the second time as they did in their first relationship. The apprehension that they, too, may become recidivists partly explains the tendency of remarried persons to enter relationships with modest emotional expectations. It is as if they cannot afford to indulge in the lavish fantasies of the perfect marriage. Their view of love and marriage is more pragmatic and less hedonistic.

In summary, evidence from the Central Pennsylvania study points to the fact that those who marry a second time enter marriage with a different outlook from the one they held when they married the first time. How much their recollections of entering marriage the first time are distorted cannot be ascertained from these data. Whether the differences are imagined or real, they appear to reveal a perspective derived at least in part from the experience of going through an unsuccessful marriage. Respondents have altered their criteria for selecting a mate. Appearance and status count less in finding the right person, while judgment and maturity are accorded more weight in courtship. Romantic love is desired but at the same time distrusted. Remarried persons enter marriage with lower expectations or, as they put it, with a more realistic sense of what can be gained. For all of these reasons, a substantial majority (72 percent) thought that remarriages are generally more likely to work out than first marriages.

While generally subscribing to this view, two out of three of our respondents also expressed the opinion that remarried couples are less likely than those in first marriages to stay in an ungratifying marriage. In the case studies, couples frequently alluded to the fact that while they were totally committed to making their marriage a good one, they had agreed that they would not remain married if they were unsuccessful in creating a satisfying relationship. A number of informants told us that the experience of enduring an unhappy marriage convinced them that divorce was a better alternative to a marriage that is not working out.

> WIFE: He said, and I've said this many times, I'm willing to go through another divorce but I'm not willing to go through another bad marriage. The divorce isn't half as bad as a bad marriage.
> HUSBAND: That's right.

WIFE: So we're both committed to that and we're also committed to working at this one. I think the thing that I've learned is to be myself and not to be somebody different because somebody else expects that of me.

Because they are not innocent of the possibility of failure, couples who have been married before must hedge their commitment to marriage even more than those married the first time. Persons who remarry are increasingly likely to view marriage as a conditional contract. As we shall see later, remarried couples monitor the relationship very closely for they are all too familiar with the signs of deterioration. Their principal strategy for avoiding failure is to maintain a high level of vigilance about this ever-present danger. Second marriages appear to be designed to anticipate rather than deny problems. Remarried people, then, are inclined to embrace, if not exaggerate, the contemporary view of marriage as a difficult and even hazardous undertaking.

THE ROLE OF THE FORMER SPOUSE

Serving as a reminder of the possibility of failure, the former spouse looms large for many couples—especially in the early stages of the relationship. It is outside the scope of this chapter to discuss in detail the relations between the formerly married couple, but it is important to note the symbolic place of the former spouse in the second marriage. We refer to the symbolic role of the spouse because evidence from our study suggests that, with some exceptions, the former spouse has a very low level of involvement with either marital partner.

In many instances, particularly if the first marriage produced no children, relations between former spouses approximate a kind of ritual avoidance. In most such cases, the current partner either has never met his or her counterpart in the first marriage or has had only the briefest contact with the ex-spouse. However, when there are children from the first marriage, contact is almost inevitable if the couple is involved in an intricate system of common child care. At best, this relationship is cordial and businesslike; usually it is tense and carefully controlled; not infrequently, it is overtly hostile. Regardless of the quality of the relationship, contact between the former partners is, with few exceptions, deliberately restricted to the business of raising children. This is illustrated in the example below, where a couple contrasts their differing situations vis-à-vis their respective former spouses.

INTERVIEWER: Have you any contact with his wife?

WIFE: No, none. Never.

INTERVIEWER: Have you seen her at all since the two of you got married?

WIFE: We've seen her in public.

INTERVIEWER: Have you had any contact other than that?

HUSBAND: I haven't talked to her, hardly at all. . . .

INTERVIEWER: So, when that marriage ended, it really is something like a past history chapter in your life?

HUSBAND: Yes. It's very easy to just forget. I don't want to say it that bluntly, but. . . . There's no reason for it to keep coming back. [Other people have got to go back over] their marriage. They've got to talk about the kids. They're in constant rememberance that they were married, whereas I have no contact whatsoever.

INTERVIEWER: Is that more or less the way you would see it? In some sense your marriage is still existent, in at least, around the children?

WIFE: No. I don't feel the marriage is . . . I don't feel any existence of the marriage, but I feel like, somewhat like my privacy is invaded. Fred and I can't go on and live our own lives, that part of my life is there, you know, it's back and forth because of the kids but, I don't feel like I'm partially married to him or anything.

Even when involvement is manifestly confined to matters of mutual concern regarding the children, relations with a former spouse usually produce some emotional spill-over into the second marriage. And even when there is little or no actual involvement, the former spouse sometimes assumes a presence in the current marriage if only in the couple's imagination. Managing relations with the former spouse becomes a preeminent concern.

Many couples seem to put the former spouse to use as a contrast heightener, so to speak. As we have already seen, constructing a new relationship requires sustaining a belief that this time things are different. Casting the former spouse in a negative role—whether it be irresponsible provider, untrustworthy lover, or indifferent companion— distances the formerly married partner by subjecting him or her to invidious distinctions. By comparison, the negative image of the ex-spouse enhances the position of the current spouse.

WIFE: In being married and divorced the first time and knowing what went wrong and knowing where all the problems lie, you know what you really want and the things you want to avoid and you start to recognize what real love is in another person.

HUSBAND: You really look for somebody. I mean, when I started dating her, if anything, if she would have leaned in any way in any actions towards my previous wife, I would not be here.

INTERVIEWER: You mean, if she had been like your first wife, if she had reminded you of her . . . ?

HUSBAND: I'd have walked away from her.

WIFE: Well, see, our first spouses were very similar. They're very greedy. Very materialistic. The world owed them everything and they'd get it any way they could. They were very similar and I was, I always had the attitude that people are more important than things. As long as I've got a roof over my head and food on the table and clothes on my back, I'm fine. I don't need anything else and that's what he needed. He was so sick of grab, grab, grab, grab, me, me, me, me, I was like a breath of fresh air to him because, you know, I don't need those things.

A private language was sometimes developed to refer to the former spouse. Many couples we interviewed had invented some derogatory term for their ex-spouses, such as "the bitch," "Mr. Wrong," or "the clown." Most interviews yielded liberal expressions of hostility displayed toward the former partner, even when informants had professed to have neutral feelings toward their previous mate.

Repudiating the former spouse heightens solidarity in the new relationship. Expressions of hostility serve to demonstrate loyalty to the new spouse, thus reducing the potential for jealousy. The couple could unite in outrage over past injustices inflicted by a former spouse. In the in-depth interviews, a partner would sometimes tell stories that had become part of the lore of their marriage. In recounting such incidents, the current spouse can provide reassurance that things really are different now. The husband or wife hearing his or her biography replayed can affirm just how much change has occurred and usually responds by declaring that he or she is married to the right person this time. Through this dramatic interplay, assurance is provided that the second marriage is essentially different from the first.

It should come as no surprise that almost all of the remarried respondents in the Central Pennsylvania study reported that their current marriage was a vast improvement over their first relationship.

The initial interview included the Dyadic Adjustment Scale, developed by Spanier (1976), measuring the functioning of their marriage in the few months before separation occurred, and in the follow-up interview the respondents rated their current marriages on the same scale. As might be expected, the differences are enormous. There is virtually no overlap between the two sets of reports; that is, the best rating of a former marriage was hardly ever as high as even the worst rating of a current marriage.

No doubt, these differences are magnified by the fact that the report on the initial marriage was obtained retrospectively, after its dissolution, while the current marriages were still in the early stages. The qualitative case studies provided abundant evidence that at least some of these changes are real and are related to the remarriage process. As we shall see, informants perceive probably correctly that *their* second marriages are different. But it is not necessarily the case that remarriages *generally* have distinctive dynamics. Let us look at the evidence available to us on the functioning of second marriages, and then return to the question of whether first unions and remarriages are actually structured differently and operate according to a different set of rules.

Three major areas were mentioned repeatedly in discussions of why the current marriage was different. First, many respondents said that they had learned to communicate differently; the differences involved ways of discussing matters of mutual concern and handling conflict in the marriage. Second, remarried persons claimed that because they communicated differently, they had altered the way they made decisions. Finally, we learned that the division of labor in second marriages was frequently modified. As we examine these changes in more detail, we shall discover some of the reasons marriage is experienced differently the second time and how individuals go about developing a new *modus vivendi* in the second marriage.

PATTERNS OF COMMUNICATION AND DECISION MAKING

Both the case studies and the longitudinal survey revealed that almost all remarried persons believe that they communicate differently in their second marriages. Invariably, the case-study informants began with a litany of complaints about the problems that they encountered in discussing even routine matters in their first relationships. Sometimes, they attributed the difficulties to themselves; most often, however, they placed the blame on their former partner's failure to give them a chance to express themselves, refusal to take them seriously, or unwillingness to credit their point of view. In sharp contrast, the process of communication in the current marriage is portrayed as more open, shared, and mutually sympathetic. Respondents describe their partner as willing to listen, to solicit their opinions, and to understand their point of view.

> WIFE: We feel a lot more comfortable now. Before, if something bothered me or something . . . anything, I could not go to Frank and talk to him about it because he'd get very upset or he wouldn't talk or he'd stomp out the door or whatever. . . . Robert and I can talk about it. Sometimes we don't even need to talk to each other, you know. We know how each other feels and it's very comfortable. It's very easy.
>
> INTERVIEWER: He understands you.
>
> WIFE: He does. He really understands me and he doesn't make me feel funny, you know, if I say something. Even if I say something, I have silly little ways of saying something stupid every now and then that makes me look like a moron. But he doesn't laugh at me. He'll talk to me about it. And it's just another part of being able to talk to each other and to be able to get along.

Quantitative data from the structured interviews support the reports of a very different communication pattern in the first and second marriage (see Tables 3.1 and 3.2). Clearly, couples in current marriages are reported to be much more likely to exchange ideas, to laugh together, to discuss issues calmly, and to confide in each other. It is important to keep in mind that comparisons are exaggerated by contrasting the first marriage in its waning period with the current marriage in its early stages. Nonetheless, the differences are so considerable and so consistent with the qualitative data that it is difficult to dismiss them merely as an artifact of this comparison.

How and why do these developments come about and what do they tell us about the impact of remarriage in altering communication patterns within the marital dyad? There are several ways of accounting for these differences. Many respondents attribute them to the fact that they are married to the right person for them. The respondents believe that they have not changed significantly in their second marriage, but

TABLE 3.1
Respondents' Reports of Their Frequencies of Communication with Their Spouse, for Former and for Current Marriages (in percentages)

		Never	Less than Once a Month	Once or Twice a Month	Once or Twice a Week	More than Once a Day	Once a Day	(N)
How often would you say the following events occur(ed) between you and your (former/current) spouse? How often did/do you								
have a stimulating exchange of ideas?	former marriage	36	29	16	16	3	0	(62)
	current marriage	2	2	10	54	25	8	(62)
laugh together?	former marriage	13	8	24	32	18	5	(62)
	current marriage	2	0	2	3	52	42	(62)
calmly discuss something?	former marriage	21	16	16	26	16	5	(62)
	current marriage	2	0	2	13	47	37	(62)

have merely found someone who understands them, allows them to be themselves, or who sees them as they really are.

> WIFE: I think this relationship is more built on trust and being open with one another. I think that with Larry, I've been able to be much more myself, my real self than I was with Alvin.
>
> INTERVIEWER: Do you think that's because Larry is a different kind of person or you're older?
>
> WIFE: No. I think it's because he's a different kind of person and also because he's just willing to accept me how I am. . . . I didn't have to be somebody else or put on another mask just to make somebody else happy. . . . I think that we've been able to talk to each other about all sorts of things, which haven't been easy to talk about and haven't been easy, you know, for each other to handle at times. . . .

A variant interpretation, not necessarily mutually exclusive of the one described above, is that the respondents changed because they had married someone with communication skills very different from those of their first partner. In this version, the right person is one who manages to develop their previously unrealized capacities for communication and mutual understanding.

TABLE 3.2
Respondents' Reports of Their Frequency of Confiding in Their Spouse, for Former and for Current Marriages (in percentages)

	Never	Rarely	Occa-sion-ally	More Often than Not	Most of the Time	All of the Time	(N)
former marriage	19	21	11	13	19	16	(62)
current marriage	0	2	0	2	47	50	(62)

HUSBAND: Our first months together were not, you know, blissful, open communication. I was still learning.

WIFE: Yeah, he's right.

HUSBAND: I learned from her implicitly and explicitly, you know, just . . . tell me what you want and that's no guarantee you're going to get it, but tell me what you want and I can cope with it.

WIFE: I just saw this person trapped with all these feelings and just a wonderful person who hadn't been allowed to express a lot. And I knew that it would be fun to just let him know that it was okay to be who he was.

A third way of explaining the change in communication patterns derives more directly from the experience of the first marriage and its dissolution. Some individuals were determined not to repeat that experience and felt transformed by the negative experience of an unsuccessful marriage. Sometimes with professional help, sometimes on their own, they made a determined effort to correct what they viewed as a deficiency in their first relationship. The interim period between the two marriages was viewed by many as an opportunity to grow, experiment, and develop.

Along with an enhanced ability to communicate with their new partner came a different attitude toward conflict. It hardly needs to be stated that individuals in our sample report lower levels of conflict in their second than in their first marriages. Again, the differences are exaggerated by comparing the level of conflict at the end of the first marriage and the beginning of the second. However, the overall level of conflict is not necessarily the most sensitive or revealing indicator of the changes that occurred in the transition to a new marriage. When we

TABLE 3.3
Respondents' Attitudes Toward Conflict in Marriage, for Former and for Current Marriages, for Males and Females (in percentages)

		Readily Accept as Normal	Dislike but Live with	Try to Avoid at All Costs	(N)
Husband	former marriages	36	39	25	(28)
	current marriages	46	50	4	(28)
Wife	former marriages	38	50	12	(34)
	current marriages	53	35	12	(34)

inspected the data more closely, they appeared to show that even when conflict did not diminish, it was often experienced differently.

In the initial interview and the follow-up, respondents were asked to describe their views of conflict in their previous and in their current marriage. In each instance, they were asked if conflict in their marital relationship was something that they "accepted as normal," "disliked but lived with," or "avoided at all costs." A shift took place in their views about conflict during the transition between the two marriages. In their first marriage, 37 percent of the respondents thought that conflict was a normal part of a marriage while in the second marriage, precisely one-half of the remarried persons subscribed to this view (see Table 3.3).

Most remarried persons who changed their views usually did so consciously; about 60 percent of the sample said that they felt differently about conflict in their current marriage. Slightly more than half of those who felt differently explained that in the first marriage, they had attempted to avoid conflict at all costs by concealing their differences of opinion and going along with their former spouse. In their current marriage, they are much more open in expressing their point of view. Some of these respondents reported fighting more but fearing conflict less.

> HUSBAND: I don't think that she's willing to put up with the stuff in this marriage that she did in the first marriage. . . . There will be situations where I'll say that I don't think we ought to do that and then she'll sit there for the next ten minutes and tell me why we shouldn't do that. What she's doing is, she's getting her opinions out.

WIFE: Yeah, some of our arguments will be over [the fact] that we agree. . . .

HUSBAND: We get in arguments and we're both on the same side.

WIFE: Yeah, but it's just the fact that I got to get my two cents in or ten cents, whatever it is. . . . There's no way around it. I have strong opinions.

HUSBAND: It gives her the opportunity if she is emotional about something. She can express that emotion rather than holding it in.

About one-fifth of those who altered their views about conflict had a slightly different interpretation of how the change had come about. In their first marriage, they had fought about everything because arguing was the only mode of communication. In their present marriage, they were able to exchange views in a more reasonable way and therefore experienced a lower level of conflict.

HUSBAND: There's more treating of each other as equals and respecting each other's opinions. Things are discussed and not argued; it's a calmer atmosphere which I find I like in my tottering old age.

Small but interesting gender differences appear in the respondents' descriptions of styles of conflict in their first and second marriage (see Table 3.3). Both the men and women are more likely to see themselves as accepting conflict in their second marriage than in their first. The men were much less likely to report avoiding conflict in their second marriage than in their first; they report correspondingly more grudging or ready acceptance of conflict. While the women were less likely than the men to avoid conflict in their first marriage, they did not report less avoidance in their second marriage; however, many of the women have shifted their attitudes from grudging to ready acceptance. It would seem that the women have assumed a less submissive stance in their second marriage and hence have become more receptive to open controversy. The men, who may well have expected less acquiescence, have accommodated by discussing differences of opinion more openly (as illustrated by the quotation above).

From the structured interviews, there is a clear indication that the balance of power is indeed different in first and second marriages. When asked who is the boss in their current relationship, three out of four respondents replied "both of us." By contrast, fewer than half had

TABLE 3.4
Respondents' Reports of Who Is "the Boss in the Relationship,"
for Former and for Current Marriages, for Males and Females
(in percentages)

		Man	Both	Woman	(N)
Males	former marriages	31	46	23	(26)
	current marriages	19	73	8	(26)
Females	former marriages	28	47	25	(32)
	current marriages	19	75	6	(32)

given a similar response when asked the same question about their first marriage in the 1977 interview. There is some corroborative evidence indicating that these characterizations about the balance of power are valid. At the very least, they are consistent with the respondents' reports about decision making in their first and second marriages (see Table 3.4).

In the initial interview, the respondents were asked to report who made various decisions in their first marriage. The questions were repeated in the follow-up interview when a remarriage had taken place. An index was developed to summarize the number of decisions shared by the spouses (i.e., those in which according to the respondents each partner had equal weight). The index was based on six items: who decides whether the male should take a certain job; what car to buy; where to go on vacation; what house or apartment to live in; whether the female should work or not; and how much money they can afford to spend per week on food. As can be seen in Table 3.5 significant changes occurred in the respondent's perceived patterns of decision making, in the direction of greater sharing of decision-making authority.

We speak of *perceived* patterns of decision making because there is ample evidence from our study and from previous investigations that husbands and wives may not share a common view of how decisions are made. Comparing the views among the couples interviewed in the Central Pennsylvania study, women typically report a greater number of shared decisions than men while men generally indicate that they make more decisions than women say that they do.

TABLE 3.5
Respondents' Report of the Number of Shared Decisions,
for Former and for Current Marriages (in percentages)

	0	1	2	3	4	5	6	(N)
Former marriage	10	11	21	25	18	14	2	(63)
Current marriage	2	2	11	24	25	13	24	(63)

NOTE: See the text for a description of the items and the index.

As we observed in regard to communication and conflict, remarried persons were acutely conscious of these shifts. Nearly 80 percent said that decisions were made differently in the second marriage, the principal distinction being that in the current relationship decisions were arrived at jointly rather than being imposed by one or the other. In a small number of cases, respondents reported that they had previously been required to make all the decisions as their former spouses refused to take any responsibility for the maintenance of the household. Far more often—in about half the cases—we were told that in the first marriage, respondents either were given too little say in the important decisions or had to fight tooth and nail to make their own views known.

> WIFE: I avoided disagreements at all costs, they were always there. It seemed like I always gave in and did what he wanted. I felt like a doormat.
>
> HUSBAND: Whew! It was such a struggle . . . it was such a problem. Conflicts were there all the time. If I was in a bad mood, I'd just go back to work to get away. Such a damn change. In my previous marriage, if I wanted conflict, all I had to do was go home. I'd get it. Now I enjoy coming home. I'm a clock watcher, so I get the hell out and go home.

Do these changes in the structure of first and second marriages reflect a difference in the nature of second marriages in general or do they merely indicate that a change of partners initiated a different balance of power? As before, our informants provided support for each of these interpretations. In the case studies, most made some reference to finding the right partner as the reason they have been able to share decisions more in their second marriage.

> WIFE: We decide things together. He asks me a lot about what we should do, although . . . like he plays on the stock market, and I don't know, I think about that, and I just let him do it.

. . . And he comes into some areas, like decoration or something. If he doesn't particularly like something, he will say "I don't really like that very much, but if you want to get it, it is all right." And I know it is. We make decisions about the children together. If I am worried about the children, then I ask him his opinion, and he will tell me. But most of the time he pushes me. I guess the real reason I chose him is that I have to be on my own, that he would always ask me to make my decisions. I really felt that it was time that I became a real person, a person with her own values.

However, the sense of participation, of being taken seriously and of being respected, sometimes becomes a stimulus for personal change. Especially women describe a growing confidence in their ability to make important decisions after receiving a larger share of responsibility in their current marriage. After being frustrated and angry at having been excluded from important decisions in their former marriage, they are often lavish in their praise of their new partner. In this arena (as in others) there is a powerful shake-up effect created by a bad marriage which confers a sense of potential for change in a second relationship. Determined not to repeat the same mistakes ("keeping my mouth shut," "always taking responsibility") respondents enter a second marriage willing to experiment or to try a different approach to marriage.

WIFE: A standing joke between my remarried friends is that you have to get married the first time in order to get it right the second.

The shake-up effect seems especially pronounced when both partners have been married before. When both individuals have been marital refugees, they appear to find it easier to alter their definition of the marital situation. Having a different partner, particularly one who has also experienced an unsuccessful marriage, establishes a license to change the rules of marriage. Husband and wife adopt a similar account of how each was misunderstood or mistreated in their first relationship. They are able to behave differently in their new marriage because their current partner recognizes the "way they really are" or helps them to change to be the person "they really want to be." This personal reconstruction is viewed by many as the essential source of change in the marriage.

WIFE: The responsibility and trust is very mutual in our second marriage. The trust is a very necessary thing. If you're looking for a second marriage, first find a friend or compatible mate. To me, that is more important. All other things fall into place, naturally. You need flexibility to have your own thoughts. I didn't have this before.

In some instances, the emergence of a new self begins prior to the marriage and crystalizes after the new relationship commences. Frequently, informants in the case studies told us how the process of divorce itself made them aware of the need to make decisions for themselves. Women, in particular, described the terror of being on their own for the first time in their lives and being unable to act independently. More than a few recounted that the experience of living on their own transformed their perspective on how to behave in marriage.

WIFE: Now, this process started while I was alone and standing on my own two feet, so to speak, making my own decisions and all that kind of stuff, and I just continued to be that same kind of person.
INTERVIEWER: So you've got a marriage now that allows you to be the kind of person that you wanted to be in that first marriage?
WIFE: Yeah, that's right. And some of that was my fault. I grew up in the fifties when the ideal was to be a wife and mother and do what your husband wanted and clean the house and change the baby's diapers, all that stuff. I really, at 18, was committed to that, and I grew to the point where I just said, this is not what I [want].
INTERVIEWER: So you were just younger? But you don't think it has anything to do with the fact that . . . there may be different things expected of women today?
WIFE: Yeah, I think that was part of it.
INTERVIEWER: You are nodding your head a little bit on that Jimmy.
HUSBAND: I think the times helped.
WIFE: Back when I was growing up, the big goal for a woman was to get married, you know, and today the big goal is to have a career and I think that was a big change.

Second marriages are restructured in part because individuals enter them with different resources, gained either from the experience of an unsuccessful first marriage or from having to adapt to living on their own after divorce. Remarried couples generally believe that they are far more independent in their second marriages, and they often think of their marriages as being more in line with the contemporary standards of marriage discussed in the first part of this chapter. Our respondents do not eschew traditional gender roles altogether, but many for the first time have altered the role conceptions that they held when they entered marriage. These modifications often involve different shifts for men and women. Some males feel that they were not sufficiently willing to rely on their former partners; women are sometimes wary of being as dependent as they were in their previous relationships. The result is a different balance of power, evident in the style of decision making.

> HUSBAND: I think in my first marriage, I tried to control it or thought I was controlling or I was wanting to control it and being the macho man I guess. I'd always say, this is right but then everything would kind of be the opposite. . . . Now, I don't myself, I don't try to force myself on Susan. I mean, here I am. Take me or leave me, you know.
>
> WIFE: I think he's an easy person to get along with and he doesn't seem to be too forceful. He's very generous and loving.
>
> INTERVIEWER: Does this mean that the kind of day-to-day marriage is different, the way you do things around the house, the way you make decisions from your first?
>
> HUSBAND: Well, in a sense I'm more involved in the doings, the mechanical doings in the house and the property and so forth, like that, than I ever was before.
>
> INTERVIEWER: Do you have a fairly clear division about labor around the house? Did you take over the kitchen and he takes over the outside of the house or do you both do both?
>
> WIFE: Well, no. We just try to help each other because there's times where, you know, I can't handle the busy schedule of, you know, the harvest and canning and things like that and Jeb is a real help with that and there's times, you know, when I go out and help him outside and things like that.
>
> INTERVIEWER: Is that something that wasn't part of your Macho, as you put it, your Macho life before or did you do those kinds of things?
>
> HUSBAND: Well, only if I had to. . . . Doing it now with Susan is different than before because when I did it before it was always something wrong or this should have been done this way. Now

with her, it's not. Even if she does say, well, I do it this way, I don't take offense to it.

As can be seen in the interview quoted above, the renegotiation of marital roles is also evident in the changes which occur in the division of labor between the first and second marriages. Slightly more than half of the remarried persons in the sample expressed the view that couples in second marriages generally have an easier time dividing up household chores than couples in first marriages. However, there are substantial gender differences in these perceptions, males being far more likely than females to subscribe to the view that allocation of tasks is easier in a second marriage (29 percent of the males disagree occasionally or more often versus 41 percent of the females).

Table 3.6 presents the actual reports by the remarried persons in our sample about the allocation of six household decisions and six household tasks in the first marriage (reported at the time of the initial interview) and in the current marriage (reported at the follow-up). The six tasks are repairing things around the house, servicing the car, keeping track of the money and bills, doing the grocery shopping, cleaning the house, and doing the evening dishes. Two ratios summarize the degree to which these decisions and tasks are evenly borne by husband and wife. A ratio of one means that decisions and tasks are divided equally between the two partners, either because each performs the same number (as is more often the case) or because they are done jointly.

It is immediately apparent that males and females have very different perceptions of how decisions are made and tasks performed. The men report a much higher level of male involvement in household tasks than the women do; the gender differences in the decision-making ratio are much smaller. Bernard (1973) has referred to these variations as "his and her" views of marriage and has suggested that it is less relevant to determine which view is objectively correct than to explore the consequences of these differing conceptions of reality.

While the accounts of the two sexes diverge sharply, both shift markedly toward viewing their second marriages as more egalitarian than their first marriages. Females are less likely than males to see their partners as sharing decisions and tasks more or less equally in their second marriages. However, the females even more than the males experience a sharp movement away from a marriage based on strictly defined gender roles. How does this process of change come about

TABLE 3.6

Distribution of Ratios, Means, and Standard Deviations of Male to Female Involvement in Task Performance and Decision Making, for Former and for Current Marriages
(in percentages)

	(N)	0–.17	.18–.33	.34–.50	.51–.67	.68–.83	.84–.99	1.00	1.01–1.20	1.21–1.33	1.34–1.50	1.51–2.00	2.01–3.00	3.01+	Mean	Standard Deviation
Task performance: males																
former marriages	(28)	0	7	7	4	7	0	21	0	18	4	18	14	0	1.37	.76
current marriages	(28)	3.5	0	3.5	7	3.5	0	25	3.5	15	10	22	3.5	3.5	1.44	1.05
Task performance: females																
former marriages	(34)	11	12	31	17	15	0	9	0	3	0	3	0	0	.58	.32
current marriages	(34)	6	3	23	6	21	0	15	8	9	3	6	0	0	.84	.44
Decision making: males																
former marriages	(28)	4	4	14	8	10	0	21	10	7	0	17	4	0	1.07	.61
current marriages	(28)	0	0	4	7	14	0	46	4	18	7	0	0	0	1.01	.24
Decision making: females																
former marriages	(34)	0	0	3	6	26	0	24	6	9	5	6	12	3	1.39	1.04
current marriages	(34)	0	3	0	9	20	0	47	3	12	0	3	3	0	1.03	.44

NOTE: See the text for a description of the items and the indices.

during the transition from one marriage to the next? For some couples, merely being released from the former marriage engenders a change of attitude about gender roles. They confessed that, having struck a certain bargain in their first marriage, they found it extremely difficult to revise their ways of doing things until the marriage dissolved. When that occurred, they felt free to reconsider what had seemed an unbreachable contract. What was referred to earlier as the shake-up effect of divorce provides part of the impetus for restructuring gender roles. Many females felt exploited in their first marriage, and some males recognized that the rules set in the first marriage no longer applied. In the case studies, frequent reference was made to the fact that times have changed since the informant first married. Couples today are more often expected to share household duties. To some extent, current cultural expectations provide a new set of guidelines for determining a fair division of labor within a marriage.

> INTERVIEWER: Let me ask you about other kinds of things, about how you divide up the tasks in the house or don't divide? You're laughing now. Can you explain?
>
> WIFE: I went out shopping with a friend on Monday and I got home and he'd done the dishes, vacuumed the house, burned the garbage, cleaned the basement. He does all my work on his days off and I don't have anything to do now for the rest of the week [laughing]. He does all the laundry too, five loads. He sits down there and he watches the agitator and he hums . . . he's singing into the washing machine.
>
> INTERVIEWER: Is this different from your first marriage, the kind of arrangement that you have now?
>
> WIFE: Oh jeez, I'd work all day and come home and do all the housework, and be told that I had to do all the housework because that's what women were for, you know. I mean, "don't ask me to do anything, any of that stuff," he'd say, you know, "what do you think I am." So this is a real switch for me.

The rationale for the change is not always put in such global terms. Many couples arrive at a different division of labor out of necessity. The merging of households and families creates such a complicated structure that the marriage is placed on a different footing, as is also true in dual-career families (Rapoport and Rapoport, 1976). Women frequently referred to the fact that if their husband did not help out, they simply could not manage the household.

Males, especially those who brought children into the marriage, felt an obligation to provide household assistance. The difficulties of scheduling visits by the nonresidential parent and of importing noncustodial children into the household meant that tasks often became less routine and predictable. Marital partners frequently cited the ever-present danger of being overwhelmed by child care and household management. Moreover, in most marriages both partners worked, adding further complexity to daily routines. Consequently, many men in second marriages were propelled into a different domestic role than the one they performed in their previous marriage.

> WIFE: [laughs] I don't know if we'll ever get it all organized. It's a very busy house. It's a small house. There's somebody coming and going constantly. . . . And both of us hold down a full time job and so there's usually one of us at home and about two days a week both of us are at home.
>
> INTERVIEWER: That requires a lot of planning doesn't it?
>
> HUSBAND: No [both laugh], actually it didn't. I don't think it took any planning at all. Things were just there and they just fell right into place. If we would have tried to plan everything, I don't think we could have done it really.
>
> INTERVIEWER: It sounds like because of the ways that your work fits together . . . each of you takes a fairly equal share of caring for the children or how does that work?
>
> WIFE: Oh, yes.
>
> INTERVIEWER: . . . That was almost a smile. What does that mean?
>
> HUSBAND: Oh, we were talking the other day. You know, Ann has this thing about saying that she doesn't think there's any other husband that would do things that I do.
>
> INTERVIEWER: You think he does more than most men that you . . . ?
>
> WIFE: Yes. . . . Dave never says anything. I work 3–11 and he doesn't complain about getting dinner for the children. Once in a while, but not very often, I will plan something in advance for dinner and he does not complain about having to fix dinner.

It is impossible to say whether, had they remained married to their first partner, some of the individuals in our study might have shifted their marital roles in the same direction taken in their second marriages. After all, many couples revise their marriages over the life course as childbearing and work careers impose new constraints on relationships, as individuals acquire experience living with one another, and as they respond to changing cultural expectations. We have relatively little firm knowledge about the alterations that take place in intact marriages over time, although it is safe to assume that successfully married couples often negotiate fresh understandings and arrive at different ways of doing things over the course of a marriage (Schonrock, forthcoming).

The Remarriage Process: Summing Up

The evidence we have presented in this chapter does not directly address the question of whether second marriages take on a different character from first relationships. Rather, we have been concerned with how individuals who have been married once before alter their conceptions of marriage and their conjugal patterns as they move from one marriage to the next.

We have observed the process which Berger and Kellner (1964) have called "nomos building," the construction of a common reality within the marriage which serves to organize and rationalize the couple's mutual expectations and understandings. Inevitably, marriage involves a nomic transformation whereby each partner, in the course of an intimate dialogue, abandons some preexisting notions of the world lodged in his or her own biography and arrives at a shared way of experiencing situations. The outcome of this marital conversation is always precarious. Should husband and wife begin to question each other's sincerity, good will, or judgment, the basis for developing and sustaining a common reality is seriously undermined and neither the marriage nor the self remains reliable or secure.

Divorce may be thought of as the disintegration of the common expectations accumulated in the course of a marriage. In the exit from marriage, individuals may come to question (sometimes quite rapidly) whether they were ever in love and may conclude that the understanding achieved in the former marriage was externally imposed. This is probably why so many of our informants believe that they were socially pressured into marrying the first time or that they were misled by youthful misjudgment into thinking that their previous partner was the right person for them.

Remarriage involves the delicate act of simultaneously repudiating the construction of reality developed in the first marriage and building a new set of understandings with a different partner. Predictably, individuals do not see the entrance into the second marriage as a recapitulation of what happened when they married the first time. From the descriptions of how couples met, fell in love, and decided to marry, it might appear that the process of remarriage has little in common with the process of first marriage. Undoubtedly, differences do exist. Individuals may use different criteria for selecting a mate, may be less subject to peer and family pressure to enter marriage, may adopt a more pragmatic than hedonistic view of love, and may enter marriage with less inflated expectations.

Even if the process of remarriage were not dissimilar, people marrying a second time have a strong interest in perceiving the event as different. In reentering marriage, individuals must build a common reality anew. And the task of doing so is far more complex the second time, for if those who reenter marriage believe that they were deluded before, how do they know that it will not happen again? We learned that the risk of a second mistake is a focal concern for many remarried couples. Believing that the process of entering marriage is different the second time is a reassuring notion. Even though they are no longer naive about the difficulty of achieving a successful marriage, they are prepared to assume the risk of remarriage because the conditions of marriage are different this time. Whether the conditions are in fact different is probably no more important to the outcome as whether there is a perception of a sharp disjuncture from the manner of marrying the first time.

Were it not this perception, remarried persons might enter marriage prepared to be disillusioned, suspicious of their mate's motives, and wary of making too large a commitment. We have seen some of these tendencies displayed in our sample; but, for the most part, individuals appear remarkably resilient in their capacity to construct a new and different reality which, to use Berger and Kellner's language, involves the replacement of one "maritally based subworld" for another.

In the preceding section we provided some of the details of how individuals manage this reconstruction. For some, there is very clearly a shake-up effect stemming from the destruction of their first marriage and the transition to divorce. There is considerable social permission for experimentation during divorce. Individuals are expected to change, grow, develop new capacities—in short, to reorganize themselves. As noted earlier, women in particular were likely to experience this period as a painful but often exhilarating time of self-discovery. Informants reflected with amusement on their reexperience of adolescence or, sometimes, belatedly experienced a period denied them when their youth was truncated by an early marriage. Sexual experimentation, new occupational initiatives, and therapy were common experiences seen as critical to personal development during the interim between the two marriages. (For a useful discussion of this process, see Vaughan, 1979.)

As a result of their attempts to deal with the shattering of their first marriage, individuals typically saw themselves as being in the midst of change before they became involved in their current relationship. A second marriage is almost never perceived as picking up where the first marriage left off. On the contrary, most individuals believe that they are capable of making a different kind of marriage because the experience of being married and divorced has made them more mature and realistic, better able to share, and less demanding and uncompromising. A number described the period of divorce as providing an opportunity to put themselves in touch with contemporary values.

Consistent with the perspective on marriage as a construction of reality, individuals strongly adhered to the view that things are different the second time, in large measure, because they married someone else. When asked how things would work out if they were to marry their former spouse now, less than one-fifth believed that the marriage would be any different. Central to the reorganization of their view of marriage is the belief that they have now married the right person. The attributes of the right person vary widely; nonetheless, most respondents when asked what they looked for in their current marriage partner made some reference to qualities of understanding, sympathy, and trustworthiness. Although it seems unlikely that these traits would not be highly valued in first marriages, they take on an overriding importance for persons entering marriage the second time because they are essential qualities for building a new and more secure set of marital expectations.

The definition of the right person as "someone who allows you to be yourself" recurred again and again in the in-depth interviews. Remarried people generally believed that they were not permitted to be their real selves in their first marriages. As they negotiated a new conception of reality in their new marriage, individuals became free—indeed almost obligated—to a new sense of self. Most respondents in our sample felt that remarriage changes a person emotionally although there is little evidence from the Central Pennsylvania data that individuals who remarried were any more likely to change on a number of measures of emotional adjustment and well-being than individuals who remained divorced (Spanier and Furstenberg, 1982). Thus, it seems likely that the perceptions of personal change are both part of the process of nomos transformation and a product of this transformation.

When individuals believe that they have changed and are now married to someone quite different from their former spouse, they have a license to construct a very different set of marital expectations. Significant shifts were reported in styles of conflict, decision-making patterns, and the division of labor. We have no sure way of knowing whether these perceptions would be evident to an outside observer, but they are certainly evidence of a new set of objectifications—the shared reality that underpins the new marriage.

This shared reality of second marriages assumes a typical form. The participants in our study generally claim to enjoy much better communication, to experience disagreements with a greater sense of trust and good will, to arrive at important decisions less unilaterally, and to allocate domestic chores more equitably. If there is a hyperbolic tone to these accounts, it is probably derived less from the respondent's desire to present his or her marriage in a favorable light (although our participants are certainly not immune to this tendency), than from using the first marriage as a baseline against which to judge the second. The second marriage usually benefits by comparison to the first. It is as if individuals moved from a dreary, unpleasant job to a better one. The expectation of progression, that a change is for the better, is part of the imagery of conjugal as well as occupational careers. The disagreeable features of the first marriage mean that individuals enter the second with modest expectations. If these expectations are satisfied, individuals experience an enormous sense of relief, which has the effect of heightening their sense of the differences between the first and second marriage.

The perception that things are better this time can be self-reinforcing, helping to sustain the marital dialogue. As individuals gain a sense of trust that their partner is in fact different, they can take personal risks and experiment with new conjugal styles. Thus, it seems likely that there is an objectively greater measure of communication and sharing, emanating from the belief that it is possible to do things differently in second marriages. The marital dialogue, the process of socialization in marriage, is shaped in no small measure, by a biography of failure in the past. The nonrecurrence of failure in and of itself provides a substantial incentive for each partner to invest effort in the new marriage.

Although little or no attention has been given to couples who experience serious difficulties in adjusting to remarriage, it does not take much imagination to see the potential fragility of the process of negotiating a new marital reality. The individuals in our sample readily admit to entering the second relationship feeling gun shy, still wounded, and vulnerable. We noted the tendency of many respondents to minimize their fantasies and thus to protect themselves from disillusionment in their second relationship. Most confessed to a need to monitor the state of the relationship to a greater degree than they had done in their first marriage. Many expressed the view that if things were not going well in their new relationship, it would take less to persuade them to divorce than was the case in the first marriage.

Thus, there can be another side to having a standard against which to judge the second marriage. There is the danger of history repeating itself—if not in an identical form, then at least as a variant of the past. When individuals already acquainted with the symptoms of marital breakdown begin to reexperience the loss of a common reality, disintegration can be swift. We shall elaborate on this theme in Chapter 9 when we account for the higher rates of dissolution in remarriages. For very real reasons, individuals who have been married before should be more apprehensive about failure. As we have seen, they have many ways to protect themselves from its recurrence; but, if these precautions prove ineffective, remarried persons are extremely vulnerable to the disintegration of their marital subworld. In the event that their second marriage appears to be a replay of their first, their commitment to the relationship is likely to drop precipitously. They will not tolerate a second time what they learned not to tolerate before.

Our data lead us to what may seem a paradoxical conclusion. It seems to us that the fundamental nature of first and second marriages is the same insofar as marriage can be perceived as a process of constructing reality. First and second marriers appear to have the same kinds of conversation in order to arrive at a common sense of the meaning of their partnership. Remarried people probably apply criteria rather similar to those used by first-married people in assessing the quality of their relationship. As we noted earlier, few studies have contrasted the conjugal patterns of couples in first and successive marriages, and our study is not designed to yield data on this question. We suspect that had we been able to contrast the marital expectations and behavior of first and second marriers, no dramatic differences would have emerged (see Weingarten, 1980).

Although remarried couples go through similar processes of marriage building and probably construct similar types of marriages, they experience the transition quite differently by virtue of their having done it once before. Their perception that their second marriage is quite different from their first is probably accurate to some extent; but whether true or not, this perception strongly influences how much they are willing to invest in their current relationship. When people build a marriage on the ruins of a previous relationship, that historical event creates a layer of experience that often works to their advantage but may also work to their detriment.

CHAPTER 4

Patterns of Parenting

Except for what has been learned from clinical studies and a handful of small-scale investigations, there is little information on how stepfamilies function (Walker et al., 1977; Furstenberg, 1979). Most existing studies are limited in scope, have problems with their samples, and are, for the most part, cross-sectional rather than longitudinal. That is, they do not follow the experience of adults and children as they make the transition from divorce to remarriage. Consequently, we do not have even the most rudimentary information on how remarriage alters the life situation of the parents or affects the well-being of their children.

Our objective in this chapter is to examine whether and in what manner parental roles change as individuals move from divorce to remarriage. Throughout the analysis, we will be contrasting the experience of custodial and noncustodial parents. However, since custody is confounded with the gender of the parent, we must try to separate the effects of the caretaking arrangement and the sex of the parent in considering the child-care patterns that evolve.

Custody Arrangements

No exact figures are available for the United States as a whole on the disposition of children at the time of divorce. Census information suggests that about 9 out of every 10 children in single-parent families are living with their mothers, and this proportion has been fairly constant during the recent period of rising divorce rates (Sanders and Spanier, 1979). However, as some single-parent families are created by the death rather than the divorce of a spouse and others result from out-of-wedlock childbearing, we cannot be certain how precise this ratio is for the specific population of divorced parents. Moreover, the census figures offer no clues as to whether these custody arrangements are stable or whether they shift over time when the husband or wife remarries or enters a new relationship. Finally these figures do not reflect the emergence of growing pressures for more cooperative child-care arrangements after divorce.

Although by no means based on a representative sample, the data from the Central Pennsylvania study provide information on the stability of custody arrangements during the two-year period of the study. We can also examine how changes in the respondent's marital situation affect his or her involvement in the parental role. In the analysis that follows, we shall first look at the custody arrangements over time and then examine the performance of parental responsibilities for men and women separately as their marital situations changed from the initial interview in 1977 to the follow-up two and a half years later.

Of the 181 respondents who participated in both interviews, 104 (57 percent) had children who were still under the age of 18 in 1979. As is shown in Table 4.1, 80 percent of the children were living with their mother at Time 1. In another 13 percent of the families, children were split between the father's and mother's care or were in the joint care of both parents. In 6 percent of the cases, the father had sole responsibility; while in the remaining 2 percent of the cases, the children were in the care of someone else, usually a close relative. Although the great majority of families maintained these arrangements in 1979, almost one-fifth of the respondents reported a change in custody arrangements.

Table 4.1 provides information on the direction of these shifts. Overall, there was a slight decline in the number of families in which the wife assumed sole responsibility for the children, down from 80 to 75 percent of the cases. There were no shifts in the six cases in which the husband had sole custody at Time 1, but 17 percent of the families in which children were living with their mother at the time of the initial interview made some change in custody by the follow-up. In most instances, one or all of the children went to live with the father. Among the small minority who had less orthodox custody arrangements at Time 1, there was a good deal of turnover. Most children who had been living in joint or split custody were with their mother at Time 2. Actually, these descriptions of the amount of flux in these families may be misleading because some of these children had in fact been living primarily with their mother at Time 1 even if they were described as being in joint custody.

What our data suggest is that joint or split arrangements may be either temporary accommodations to external pressures or makeshift attempts to resolve unsettled conflicts. Whether or not these arrangements are made for the child's benefit we cannot say from the data at hand. Clearly, the children experienced the greatest amount of residential instability when custody was not exclusive.

TABLE 4.1
Shifts in Custody Arrangements: Central Pennsylvania, 1977 and 1979 (in percentages)

	Children at Time 1 (1977) with				
	Father	Mother	Split Between Both Parents	Neither Parent	Total
Children at Time 2 with					
Father	*	5	8	—	10
Mother	—	83	62	*	75
Split between both parents	—	11	23	—	12
Neither parent	—	1	8	*	3
Total	6	80	13	2	100
(N)	(6)	(83)	(13)	(2)	(104)

* Percentage not presented due to small base of subgroup (N < 8).

It might be expected that shifts in marital status would upset child-care arrangements. Are custody realignments more likely to occur when the respondents and their former spouses reenter new relationships? The data from Central Pennsylvania provide some support for this expectation, but the picture is more complicated than we had anticipated. It was rare for both husband and wife to remain single throughout the study, but when they did, stability in the custody arrangement was relatively high: More than four-fifths of these previously married couples had the same arrangement at both interview points. Similarly, when both husband and wife remarried there was also a high degree of stability in the location of children. Again, roughly four out of five couples maintained the same arrangement.

Change occurred most frequently among families in which one spouse remarried and the other did not. Half of these families altered their custody arrangement in some way. Whether it was the husband or the wife who remarried seemed to matter less than the fact that only one changed marital status, for in both instances the wife was less likely to maintain responsibility for the children.

We know from the reports of the respondents that some of these shifts were voluntary on the mother's part. Difficult-to-manage adolescents were sometimes transferred to their fathers who offered more discipline than the mother felt capable of providing. It was also not unusual for a father to assume custody for a young son who was having emotional problems in the aftermath of divorce. In some instances, too, a male helped out when his overburdened ex-spouse returned to work by shouldering more of the child-care responsibilities. However, not all of the changes were consensual. When males remarried and females did not, males made a claim for a greater share of child care by arguing that they could offer a more stable environment to their offspring. When the wife married and the husband did not, men made the argument that continuity with the children should not be disturbed.

A detailed analysis of the small number of cases in which the wife forfeited custody of the child reflects the mixed motives involved. Women who retained custody of their children were more likely to express high levels of satisfaction than those who relinquished some or all of their children to their former spouse (76 percent of the former were very satisfied at the follow-up, compared to 45 percent of those who experienced a custody change). Obviously, however, one cannot characterize the custody changes with any sweeping generalizations. Some women clearly felt that the placement of a child with the father enhanced their own situations; others did so only with reluctance, as indicated in the quotation below.

> INTERVIEWER: Did the kids accept the [second] marriage pretty early or was that a difficult and slow process and is it still going on?
>
> MOTHER: Well, no. All three had accepted him but the oldest one which is in fifth grade did not accept him at all in the beginning and so therefore, he decided to live with his father. The other two, there was no problem at all. . . .
>
> INTERVIEWER: Was that part of the custody arrangement or was that something you worked out?
>
> MOTHER: We worked that out during our divorce proceedings but it was all voluntarily. I decided to let the child make his own decision and it has its ups and downs.

Overall, satisfaction with custody did not vary greatly over the course of the study. Parents who were living with their children usually were pleased with the arrangement at both the first and second interviews, while those living apart from their children were typically far less satisfied. As women usually retained custody of their children, they were more likely to be contented with the current child-care arrangement than were the men in the sample. The sex differences are negligible when the custody arrangement is taken into consideration. About three-fourths of both the males and females living with their children were very satisfied with the arrangement, while nearly two-fifths of the parents who were living apart from their children expressed discontent.

There seems to be remarkably little awareness of this disparity in the perspectives of the parents. When asked to report on their former spouse's satisfaction with the arrangement, most custodial parents reported that they sensed little dissatisfaction with the arrangement. As their former partners are not in the sample, we cannot check these perceptions against the actual reports of their former spouses. However, if we look at the sentiments of the noncustodial spouses—who are the counterparts of those former spouses—the evidence suggests that parents who have custody of their children generally underestimate the discontent of their former spouse. This disparity in perceptions may serve to reinforce the view held by the custodial parents that their former spouses are unwilling to shoulder their share of the responsibility—a view that will emerge as we present more of the findings from the survey.

Finally, we could discern no clear-cut differences in custody satisfaction between the respondents who remained single during the course of the study and those who remarried. Satisfaction was highest among the handful of couples where neither partner remarried, perhaps reflecting the stability of this arrangement; but the numbers are too small for us to be certain that this finding is not a result of random variation. And a change in marital status during the course of the study did not affect the level of satisfaction with the custody arrangements for either the parents living with their children or those living apart from their children. Therefore, we are inclined to conclude that remarriage usually does not alter custody satisfaction unless it alters the existing arrangements between the former spouses.

Contact and Closeness Between Parents and Children After Divorce and Remarriage

As might be expected, parents not residing with their offspring had less and less contact with their children during the course of the study. Table 4.2 shows this pattern of attrition over time. The response categories for the amount of contact are not exactly the same at Time 1 and Time 2, but the drop seems to occur primarily among parents who were seeing their children fairly regularly—a few times a month—rather than those who in effect maintained joint custody, seeing their children at least several times a week. By the follow-up, the proportion of parents who saw their nonresidential children several times a month or more had declined from nearly three-fifths to less than one-half if we rely on the respondent's self-report (when he or she is the noncustodial parent), and from 49 to 38 percent if we use the custodial parents' reports about the former spouse's frequency of visitation. At the point of the initial interview, there was a fairly wide disparity between these two figures; but at the follow-up the self-reports and reports about the former spouse were quite similar.

As 80 percent of the nonresidential parents are males and given the small size of the sample, it is difficult to tell whether there are any distinct sex differences in the amount of contact between noncustodial parents and their children. Combining both respondents' reports about themselves (when they are noncustodial parents) and about their spouses (when they are not) provides enough cases to examine interaction patterns separately for mothers and fathers who do not live

TABLE 4.2
Frequency of Noncustodial Parent's Contact with Their Children by Sex of Parent: Central Pennsylvania, 1977 and 1979 (Based on Self-Reports and Reports about Former Spouse; in percentages)

	1977					
	Self-Report			Report About Former Spouse		
	Total	Males	Females	Total	Males	Females
Daily	10	7	29	5	2	19
Few times a week	14	12	29	12	10	19
Once a week	22	26	—	15	15	12
Few times a month	12	10	29	17	17	19
Once a month	6	7	—	12	14	6
Less than once a month	22	24	14	20	20	19
Never	12	14	—	19	22	6
(N)	(49)	(42)	(7)	(75)	(59)	(16)

	1979					
	Self-Report			Report About Former Spouse		
	Total	Males	Females	Total	Males	Females
Daily	4	3	8	2	2	–
Few times a week	14	16	8	15	12	30
Few times a month	24	21	33	21	24	10
Once a month	10	10	8	12	12	10
Occasionally during year	28	32	17	28	26	40
Hardly ever	6	5	8	10	12	–
Never	10	10	8	12	12	10
Summer only	4	3	8	2	2	–
(N)	(50)	(38)	(12)	(61)	(51)	(10)

NOTE: Totals in this and following tables exceed 104 cases because of a small number of families with split custody.

with their children. The data reveal few differences in the behavior of male and female noncustodial parents regarding their contact with their children. While mothers have more contact with their children than do fathers, the differences are not sizable or significant. (A comparable analysis using national data revealed a similar pattern, though the differences were somewhat more conspicuous. See Furstenberg and Nord, 1982.)

To what extent does cohabitation or remarriage contribute to the general decline in contact between nonresidential parents and their children? The results from Central Pennsylvania are by no means definitive, but they suggest that remarriage may contribute to a reduction of contact between nonresidential parents and their children. In families where neither parent had remarried, two-thirds of the nonresidential parents continued to see their children at least a few times a month. In the intermediate situation—when one parent had reentered a relationship and the other had not—40 percent of the parents living apart from their children saw them several times a month or more. When both partners had remarried, only 34 percent of the nonresidential parents continued to see their children on a regular basis.

There are many possible reasons why new relationships may intrude on the maintenance of parental contact and responsibility. Residential movement is associated with a change in marital status, increasing the difficulty of regular visits. Individuals who remarry or live with a new partner may have less energy to invest in parental responsibilities because they may be called upon to put their resources into new relationships with their partner and stepchildren. The assumption of a new relationship may also make it possible to relinquish ties with children that have been problematic. These alternative explanations for the decline of parental responsibilities are further discussed in Chapter 5.

We might anticipate that the decline in contact would adversely affect the quality of the relationship between the parent and child. Unfortunately, the parent-child relationship was not measured at the initial interview in such a way as to provide a good baseline for assessing the change in intimacy over time. In the 1977 interview, a substantial minority of the nonresidential parents (42 percent) reported that their relations with their children had improved since the separation; far fewer (27 percent) respondents living with their children were so generous in their reports about the quality of the relations between the children and their nonresidential parent.

At the follow-up it was again true that a substantial, albeit smaller, minority of respondents reported that relations had improved between them and their nonresidential children; their opposite numbers—the residential parents—have harsher reports on the quality of relations between the nonresidential parent and their children. Whereas half of the females and three-fourths of the males report that they are very close to their children who are not living with them, none of the female respondents and only 12 percent of the male respondents who are living with the children assess their former spouse's relationship with their children as very close.

Neither view seems to us to be objective, but they do appear to capture a certain reality of family life after divorce. What is apparent is the wide gulf between the views of the former partners—a discrepancy that must make coparenting hazardous indeed.

We might wonder at the extent to which remarriage contributes to these separate and very different outlooks on the success of the nonresidential parent in maintaining closeness to his or her children. Consistent with our findings on visitation, we have discovered that in families where neither partner was married, both self-evaluations and spouse evaluations indicate a closer relationship between nonresidential parent and children. Where one or both partners remarried, the quality of parent-child relations was evaluated less favorably.

Given the small numbers involved and the crudity of the measure, these findings cannot be taken to be anything more than suggestive. Moreover, it is entirely possible that the pattern of deterioration in the tie between the child and the parent outside the home that we observe may be temporary. Whether remarriage significantly worsens relations and, if so, whether the disturbance is short-lived cannot be made completely clear from the data. Nevertheless, our data suggest the possibility that parents who take on new family responsibilities are less willing or able to sustain commitments to preexisting parental obligations.

Parental Responsibilities

We can examine this possibility more closely by looking at the evidence (however fragmentary) that parents not living with their children retreat from an active child-care role, particularly when they become involved in new relationships.

The disengagement from the parental role seems quite pronounced for both men and women who are living apart from their children. Data were not collected on the degree of involvement of the nonresidential parent at the time of the initial interview; however, a number of measures were included in the follow-up. Perhaps the best of these was a question asking the parents, both residential and nonresidential, to report on how nine child-care responsibilities are divided among possible caretakers. The question is reproduced in Table 4.3. Parents were given a card which listed themselves, their former spouse, various relatives, their current partner, and the children themselves. Using the nine items, a summary ratio was constructed indicating the contribution of the nonresidential spouse relative to that of residential spouse. If participation were equal, the overall ratio would be one. The lower the ratio, the less the involvement of the nonresidential spouse. In interpreting the results, it is important to remember about half of the sample are residential parents reporting on the behavior of their former mates and themselves; the other half are their counterparts, although not their actual spouses, who are nonresidential parents providing their perceptions of their experiences.

As we discovered about other measures, the views of residential and nonresidential parents do not coincide. Residential parents describe more limited involvement on the part of the former spouse than is indicated by the accounts of the nonresidential parents themselves. Table 4.4 shows just how large the disparity is. Whereas 40 percent of the residential parents reported that their former spouse had no

TABLE 4.3
Items Included in Ratio of Child-Care Responsibilities

In dividing up the various responsibilities of raising (name of child), can you tell me who generally does what?

a. Who usually contributes to their financial support?
b. Who usually supervises the children after school?
c. Who usually sees that they are doing their homework?
d. Who usually makes plans for their birthdays?
e. Who usually selects their summer camp or summertime activities?
f. Who usually arranges for them to see their relatives?
g. Who usually makes decisions about their religious training?
h. Who usually attends school conferences?
i. Who usually gets involved if there is a serious discipline problem?

NOTE: Response categories are: respondent, former spouse, respondent's relatives, former spouse's relatives, former spouse's current partner, respondent's current spouse/partner, the child(ren), someone else.

involvement in child rearing, only 8 percent of the noncustodial parents admit to being totally uninvolved. More than half report that their involvement is relatively high. (Ratios reaching .50 or greater were arbitrarily designated high involvement.)

This difference in perception of parental involvement reflects, in effect a "his and her" view because most residential parents are females and most nonresidential parents are males. However, the distortion is a result of the respondent's familial rather than gender role. Female nonresidential parents displayed the same enlarged view of their contribution as males. In short, custodial parents, with the principal responsibility of child rearing, feel that they do virtually all of the work; the noncustodial parent thinks he or she is making a fairly substantial, if not equal, contribution. In this respect, divorce may have the consequence of reenforcing traditional gender roles in the family because women typically retain custody of their children.

Some residential parents prefer to bear a heavier child-care burden because they wish to limit the involvement of their former spouse, but a substantial minority (40 percent) complain that the child's other parent assumes too little responsibility. Nonresidential parents, on the other hand, generally voice the feeling that they have too little responsibility. Here, a gender difference does appear. Male noncustodial parents reporting about themselves and female custodial parents reporting about their former husband generally concur that the male has too little involvement. By contrast, the small number of females living apart from their children feel their involvement is about right while male custodial parents complain that their former wives take too little responsibility. Possibly, females who give up custody find it more difficult to acknowledge their limited maternal role to an interviewer; alternatively, they may feel that they have already paid their dues. This small but very special subgroup deserves more examination because it may very well grow in number in the future.

As responsibility declines, influence over the children naturally decreases. When asked in the follow-up to report on the degree of influence that they exert on family decisions, about one-third of the parents living apart from their children reported having a minimal role; only one-fifth said that their influence was great. The reports by the residential parent accorded them even less decision-making authority; more than half assigned them little or no influence in decisions regarding children. Females perceived that they had, and were acknowledged by male residential parents to have, more influence than

TABLE 4.4

Extent of Nonresidential Parent's Participation in Child Care by Sex of Parent: Central Pennsylvania, 1979,[a] Based on Self-Reports and Reports About Former Spouse (in percentages)

	Self-Report: Ratio of Noncustodial Respondent's Care to Custodial Former Spouse's Care			Report About Former Spouse: Ratio of Noncustodial Former Spouse's Care to Custodial Respondent's Care		
	Total	Males	Females	Total	Males	Females
Index score						
.00	8	8	10	40	36	60
.01 to .49	36	40	20	44	46	30
.50 and above	56	52	70	16	17	10
(N)	(48)	(38)	(10)	(62)	(52)	(10)

a. See Table 4.3 for nine items from which the ratio was constructed.

b. Score of one indicates equal participation of both biological parents; the lower the ratio, the less involvement of noncustodial parent.

males when they did not maintain custody; but their role was not as great as they believed if we rely on the report of the male custodians. Moreover, nonresidential mothers perceived a sharper decline in their influence over their children during the two years preceding the follow-up than did residential fathers. Twice as many (50 versus 24 percent) women say their decision-making role shrank. Perhaps by virtue of their central position in the family prior to marital dissolution, it appears that mothers who do not retain custody assume a larger role in the child rearing in the period immediately following the divorce. Eventually, however, they experience the same drop in decision-making authority as do fathers who are living apart from their children. By the follow-up, the males seem already to have adjusted to their position as outsiders. Indeed, as many nonresidential fathers report that their role in the family increased as report that it decreased, suggesting that some leveling off may eventually occur in the allocation of responsibilities.

Are the decline of involvement and loss of influence of the nonresidential parent precipitated or merely hastened by remarriage? Keeping in mind the problems of sample size, there is some slight evidence that individuals who remarry take a less active part in child-rearing decisions. In the atypical families where neither spouse married again, respondents were somewhat more likely to give themselves if they were the nonresidential parent, or their former spouse if they were not, a higher rating on the ratio of participation in decisions about the children than was true at the other extreme—in families in which both parents remarried. However, it is the asymmetrical situations in which one spouse remarried and the other did not that provide the most interesting bit of evidence on shifting roles. Whether or not they were the custodial parent, respondents who entered new relationships while their former spouses did not were more likely to acknowledge that the nonresidential spouses had a larger role in making decisions than those in the reverse situation. More than half of the respondents who married when their spouse did not reported that the noncustodial parents had increased his or her influence over the past two years, as compared to only 13 percent of the respondents in the reverse situation.

It would appear as though the nonresidential parent retains a greater measure of parental responsibility by avoiding a rapid remarriage. Of course, it is entirely possible that individuals committed to playing a central role in raising their children are less likely to remarry or cohabit precisely because they are unwilling to face a competing set of demands. Thus, noncustodial parents who resist remarriage may do so because they are more committed to retaining ties to their children and are more aware of the difficulties of managing two families. Similarly, parents who retain custody may be initially reluctant to reenter marriage if they feel that by doing so their partner will gain a greater measure of control over the children.

Because a new relationship compels individuals to make emotional investments elsewhere, a shift often occurs in the balance of child-care responsibilities. This may either be interpreted as an abdication when the noncustodial parent marries; or, on the other hand, if the custodial parent marries the shift may seem more like a concession to permit greater involvement by the outside parent. Remarriage also alters the child-care pattern for another set of reasons, having less to do with time and energy and more to do with domestic politics. Parents who remain single when their spouse does not may retaliate by tightening their control over the children, as seems to have occurred in the case cited below:

> NONCUSTODIAL FATHER: I have a little boy, Junior. He is six years old.
> INTERVIEWER: How does that work out? How often do you see him?
> NONCUSTODIAL FATHER: I haven't seen him since we got married. Well, he was supposed to be in our wedding and then my ex-wife put the screws to that idea. I mean, she just started causing little problems and stuff like that. . . . She was trying to upset our wedding day.

Divorce, Remarriage, and Perceptions of Parental Competence

The final section of this chapter examines respondents' feelings about how well they are managing their parental responsibilities. The data we present should not be taken as a reliable indicator of the parent's actual skill in performing his or her role, but only as a subjective measure of parental self-esteem. Whether feelings of competence are related to actual performance is an open question, one that goes beyond the scope of this analysis. Although these items lack information on the child's behavior, they are still important because they provide an indication of the degree of gratification respondents are deriving from the parental role and of how the level of gratification is affected by divorce and remarriage.

Several indicators of perception of parental competence were drawn from a 1976 national study of well-being of children (Zill, 1984). Parents were asked how often they have felt worn out or exhausted from raising a family, whether there have been times when they have lost control of their feelings and felt that they might hurt their child, and how they rate their overall performance as a parent. Table 4.5 provides the distribution of responses to these questions in the national sample and in the Central Pennsylvania sample, and breaks down the Central Pennsylvania respondents by sex, custody arrangement, and marital situation. At first glance, it appears that the overall distribution of responses in Central Pennsylvania is remarkably similar to the distribution obtained in the national survey. In both the national survey and our study, three-fourths of the respondents gave themselves a good or excellent rating as a parent, slightly less than half said that they rarely or never felt worn out or exhausted, and nearly 90 percent hardly ever or never felt that they would lose control of their feelings to the point of physically hurting their child.

These general comparisons may, however, exaggerate the similarities between our respondents and the national sample of parents. Almost all the members of the larger sample were females, usually the biological mothers of the study children, while nearly half of the Central Pennsylvania sample consists of fathers, most of whom were not living with their children. When we examine only the residential mothers, sizable differences emerge on two of the three items. Central Pennsylvania mothers with custody of their children are more likely than mothers in the national sample to say that they feel worn out and to report that they sometimes lose control of their feelings. They are also less likely to feel that they are good parents. Our findings indicate that divorced and remarried mothers experience more difficulties in their parenting role than do mothers in general. (Zill found similar results when we compared the responses of parents who were and were not previously married using the same questions. See Zill, 1984.)

Not surprisingly, the findings presented in Table 4.5 reveal that parents who have custody of the children were far more likely than noncustodial parents to report being worn out at least some of the time (79 versus 21 percent) and were more than twice as likely to report that they sometimes lost control over their feelings to the point of physically endangering their child. At the same time, a higher proportion of the parents living with their children rated themselves as excellent or good in their parental role than the parents who were living apart from their

TABLE 4.5

Parental Competence by Sex, Custodial Status, and Marital History of Respondent: Central Pennsylvania, 1979 (in percentages)

	Totals from National Survey, 1976	Totals from Central Pennsylvania Survey, 1979	Sex		Custodial Status		Marital History	
			Males	Females	Custodial	Noncusto-dial	Single	Remarried
Frequency of feeling worn out from child raising								
all the time	2	4	2	5	5	3	—	8
most of the time	5	3	—	5	3	3	4	2
sometimes	48	50	23	69	71	15	50	50
rarely	30	27	37	19	19	38	33	21
never	15	17	37	2	2	41	12	19
(N)	(1747)	(101)	(43)	(58)	(62)	(39)	(48)	(52)

Frequency of losing control
and hurting child

often	1	1	—	2	2	—	2	—
sometimes	10	13	7	17	16	8	12	13
hardly ever	35	31	19	40	39	18	33	29
never	54	56	74	41	44	74	52	58
(N)	(1747)	(101)	(43)	(58)	(62)	(39)	(48)	(52)

Rating of performance as
Parent

excellent	12	9	12	7	3	18	10	8
good	63	64	55	71	77	45	69	59
fair	25	24	29	20	20	29	19	28
poor	1	1	2	—	—	3	—	2
terrible	—	2	2	2	—	5	2	2
(N)	(1747)	(98)	(42)	(56)	(60)	(38)	(48)	(49)

children (80 versus 63 percent). The picture that emerges from the Central Pennsylvania study is that noncustodial parents experience fewer strains associated with day-to-day child rearing, but they feel more deficient as parents, probably owing to lower involvement in the family.

Because women are typically custodial parents, our data show sharp gender differences that parallel the differentials reported above between residential and nonresidential parents. Women are significantly more likely to experience feelings of exhaustion and to report that they sometimes lose control of their feelings, but at the same time they rate themselves more favorably as parents. Unfortunately, there are not enough cases to explore the interaction between gender and child custody, but an inspection of the small number of cases of male custodial and female noncustodial parents strongly suggests that custody arrangements are more important than gender in shaping feelings about parental competence. There is the possibility, however, that females who have custody may experience exhaustion and loss of control more than do males, perhaps because males with children receive more assistance from their former spouse, relatives, and paid help.

To what extent does entering a new relationship ease some of the burdens borne by divorced parents? Subjectively, respondents who were remarried or cohabiting seem to feel that it does provide assistance. Nearly two-thirds of the respondents who had entered a new relationship in the preceding two years stated that it had become less difficult for them to "manage the various tasks of raising [their] children" since they started living with their current partner, while only 8 percent of the respondents replied that child rearing had become more difficult as a result of their domestic change.

Yet, we can find little evidence that people who were remarried at the follow-up actually experienced fewer strains in their parental role. Parents who had custody of their children and who had entered new relationships were actually more likely to report that they were sometimes or often worn out by the burdens of raising a family than those who remained single (87 versus 76 percent) although they were somewhat less likely to feel in danger of losing control over their feelings (13 versus 29 percent). Whether or not they had custody of their children, parents who remarried also had a somewhat lower evaluation of their parenting success although the differences between the single and remarried groups are not statistically significant. It may be that remarried parents feel more demands on their time and energy and feel somewhat less adequate as parents because of the strains of managing two families. At the same time, they seem to feel that having an additional parent in the home compensates for the added difficulties of managing two families.

Conclusion

The data from Central Pennsylvania offer a provisional view of the management of parenthood during the transition from divorce to remarriage. Our tentativeness derives from several limitations of the study: the nature of the sampling procedures, omissions in the information collected in the initial interview, and the difficulties of applying sophisticated analytic techniques given the small number of cases. Nevertheless, the data we have assembled provide a fairly clear impression of the pattern of parenting during the first few years after marital dissolution. We have looked at shifts in the degree of involvement of the biological parents in response to custody arrangements and rearrangements as they move from one marriage to the next.

As we have noted throughout the chapter, there are conspicuous gender differences in the management of parenthood after divorce and remarriage. The traditional division of labor, with women assuming most of the child-rearing responsibilities, becomes even sharper as males typically reduce their involvement in the family following divorce. If anything, remarriage seems to intensify this pattern because males frequently reduce their participation in their first family as they become involved in a new relationship—especially if their former spouse remains single. In general, we found that when individuals, male or female, defer marriage, they are more likely to share parental responsibilites more equally than when one or both remarry.

It was not completely clear from the data whether males withdrew from paternal responsibilities or whether they were effectively locked out by persistent strains with former partners who maintained a gatekeeping function. From a previous analysis we know that continued conflict between the formerly married couple strongly affects the level of paternal involvement. The inability of parents to resolve the disputes that led to the divorce has a powerful and persistent effect on the pattern of parenting after the marriage breaks up. On this issue Paul Bohannon (1970:54) has written the following:

> Coparental divorce created lasting pain for many divorcees I
> interviewed—particularly if the ex-spouses differed greatly on what
> they wanted their children to become, morally, spiritually,
> professionally, even physically. This very difference of opinion about
> the goals of living may have lain behind the divorce. It continues
> through the children.

Limited communication and divergent interests between the custodial and noncustodial parent, usually the child's mother and father respectively, often lead to two separate perspectives on parenting. Parents living apart from their children feel closer to them than they are believed to be by custodial parents. Noncustodial parents also feel that they perform a larger share of child-rearing responsibilities and have relatively greater parental influence than they are given credit for by their former spouse. The "his and her" view that prevails in marriage thus may be widened by divorce.

The "his and her" perspective on divorce is not, strictly speaking, a product of gender differences but rather emanates from the divergent situations of the parent who has custody and the parent who does not. When fathers get custody, they adopt an outlook that is very similar to that of most of the mothers in the sample. When mothers relinquish custody, they have much more in common with the males who are living apart from their children.

Our data pick up the story too late for us to draw any definitive conclusions about the causal impact of custody arrangements, but they suggest the possibility that exclusive custody may contribute to a decline of involvement on the part of the absent parent—further complicating the difficult process of coparenting. A legal system that sharply circumscribes the rights and responsibilities of one parent in favor of the other inevitably creates divergent interests, which are bound to result in disparate perspectives on family roles.

However, we must make note of gaps in our knowledge that limit our ability to recommend an alternative to the clearly deficient system now in place. In the first place, we understand too little about how divorce alters preexisting divisions of labor in the family. Only longitudinal research, beginning before divorce occurs, can answer the question of how marital dissolution affects the assignment of parental responsibilities.

We also do not know enough about the conditions that affect the couple's ability to negotiate with one another about child-rearing practices after divorce. A significant minority of our sample reported changes in custody arrangements following the divorce that were not explicitly sanctioned by the courts. Often these changes involved the movement of one or more children to the noncustodial parent, usually the child's father.

We have touched upon the complications created by the remarriage (or cohabitation) of one or both of the former partners. The presence of stepparents or surrogate parents does not noticeably contribute to worsening relations between the formerly married couple, but neither does it necessarily dampen conflict. Evidence from the qualitative case studies conducted after the structured interviews leads us to suspect that the net effect of new relationships on coparenting patterns is not conspicuously positive or negative, but in particular cases the addition of a new spouse can have either very beneficial or very destructive effects on the balance of relations between the former spouses. As our study spans only the early years after divorce, we cannot draw any firm conclusions about the long-term impact of remarriage on parenting patterns. The slight tendency of nonresidential parents who enter new relationships to withdraw from their children may signal a transitory disruption or, alternatively, may reflect an incipient trend toward fuller disengagement.

The most elusive but intriguing question introduced by these data—one that figures centrally in reconsiderations of custody arrangements—is whether or not remarriage alters conceptions of parental responsibility. At the heart of this issue is the relative weight of biological and sociological parenthood and the degree to which blood ties or legal ties count in the determination of parental rights and obligations. Is it possible that if conjugal succession becomes commonplace, parenthood in the future will be governed more by legal than by biological status?

At present we can detect little indication that biological parents who reside away from their children are willing to cede parental rights to their former spouse's current partner. As males become more involved in parenting, they will probably become even less inclined to relinquish their parental claims following divorce and remarriage. Ironically, in the course of marriage and divorce men may develop a genuine interest in breaking down traditional gender roles—even if only as a means of guaranteeing enduring ties to their children.

CHAPTER 5

Renegotiating Parenthood

In the preceding chapter, we described a series of significant changes in patterns of parenting that take place after marital dissolution. Our results showed that parents living outside the home gradually disengage from child-rearing responsibilities. The remarriage of nonresidential parents further diminishes the likelihood of their participation, but remarriage is not as significant a deterrant to a continued relationship with the child as we had anticipated. Other conditions such as the quality of relations between the formerly married couple, lack of geographical proximity, and the age of the child are often more important determinants of continued contact between the child and the parent living outside the home. Interestingly, however, the gender of the noncustodial parent was not strongly related to the pattern of parenting after divorce and remarriage. Women who do not live with their children were about as likely as men to limit their parental involvement in the Central Pennsylvania sample.

Data from the National Survey of Children reveal that many of the patterns discovered in Central Pennsylvania appear to persist over a longer span of time and can be generalized to the wider population of children whose parents separate or divorce. Indeed, the curtailment of contact between the noncustodial parent and child becomes even more marked as time passes (Furstenberg et al., 1983a; Furstenberg, 1982b). From the NSC we learned that about half of all children who are living apart from their biological fathers have not had any personal contact with them in the past year. Fewer than one in six have contact as often as once a week. Over time, fathers not living with their children are less likely to keep up their contact than are mothers who do not have custody, suggesting that the relatively high patterns of contact observed in the Central Pennsylvania study between fathers and their children will be subject to severe attrition as geographical dispersion occurs, as fathers fail to meet financial obligations to their children, or as they withdraw emotionally from the responsibilities of child rearing. In analyses of the NSC data, we learned that there is no single explanation for why fathers disengage but rather a varied set of reasons for retreat from paternal involvement.

As we saw in the previous chapter, noncustodial parents have very different accounts from their former partners as to how much they actually had retreated from their parental obligations and why their participation in child rearing was not greater. While noncustodial parents were often criticized for their lack of parental interest, they countered by pointing out that relations with their children were thwarted if not actively sabotaged by their ex-spouses.

In this chapter, our interest is not to determine which of these realities is the more accurate but rather to explore the causes and consequences of the disparate perceptions. We believe the key to understanding these divergent accounts resides in the recognition that divorced parents frequently adopt a different image of parenthood from the prevailing one. We will address some of the difficulties that coparents face in renegotiating this new definition of parenthood after divorce.

Parents generally derive their status from two basic sources: their function as progenitors and their function as providers. Traditionally in American society the biological and sociological functions of parenthood are fused. Divorce makes sociological parenthood problematic, and remarriage increases the possibility that the two bases of parenthood will become disconnected. Thus, the process of negotiation after divorce often assumes the form of a contest—the residential parent emphasizing the obligation of the other parent, typically the father, to live up to the responsibilities of providing emotional and material support. The nonresidential parent in turn is likely to advance his or her claim to parenthood based on biological connection to the child.

Moreover, the two parents are likely to disagree on what constitutes a sufficient display of commitment to parenthood. The custodial parent, frequently overburdened with the responsibilities of being the principal caretaker, tends to minimize the involvement of the former spouse. By comparison to the period before the marriage ended, the former spouse's material and emotional contribution to the family has generally declined; and, by comparison to what the residential parent does, it may even appear trivial. Thus, the residential parent is predisposed to find that the former partner's performance does not measure up to accustomed expectations of sociological parenthood. Not infrequently, residential parents complained that the child's noncustodial parent expected to be treated like a father or mother but did not conform to the norms of parenthood.

> CUSTODIAL MOTHER: I feel very trapped. I feel like it's my responsibility to provide those girls with the best life that they can possibly have. I can't count on him [noncustodial father] for anything—nothing.

Nonresidential parents see the world quite differently. As their inability to live up to full-fledged sociological parenthood becomes more conspicuous, the significance of the biological connection to the child becomes more salient. Nonresidential parents who see their children irregularly often reserve their visits for such occasions as birthdays or holidays, as if to underscore the symbolic importance of their blood ties to the child. As we shall discuss in the following chapter, nonresidential parents pressed extended kin into service, partly as a way of reminding the child of his or her place in a family lineage. Continued relations with grandparents, as we shall see, are a concrete means of strengthening tenuous bonds between nonresidential parents and their children.

The nonresidential parent who became more marginal as time went on often turned to the child for reassurance that his parental prerogatives would not be violated. The child's definition of the situation was critically important as a means of validating the status of the absent parent. Tangible displays of parental concern in the form of presents, shopping trips, or outings were common mechanisms for preventing an erosion of the child's attachment, which might undermine the parent's already precarious role.

> CUSTODIAL MOTHER: Money does a lot of things and when Jason is down there, he's really king.
>
> CUSTODIAL STEPFATHER: They go to shows. Something every night.
>
> CUSTODIAL MOTHER: Every weekend they go down, you know it's like . . .
>
> INTERVIEWER: Like going on vacation?
>
> CUSTODIAL MOTHER: Well it is. I mean, from Henry's point of view, he says well, I hardly get time to spend with my son and when he comes down I want to do things with him and he takes him.

Needless to say, custodial parents were likely to view such attempts as seductive efforts to win the child over or buy the child off. They saw the nonresidential parent as having an unfair emotional advantage by being able to treat parenthood as all play and no work. This perception— understandable though it might be—sometimes resulted in further competition between the parents, with each accusing the other of bad faith.

Data from both parents and children in the National Survey of Children indicated that this pattern of compensatory part-time parenthood was widespread. We discovered that parents who only saw their children occasionally devoted their time almost exclusively to recreational activities, rarely helping out with the more mundane tasks of child rearing such as supervising homework or directing the child in household tasks. Part-time parents generally seemed to be more concerned with maintaining friendly and gratifying relations with their children. They were less likely to acknowledge that they had definite rules for the children and more lax about implementing the rules that they claimed were in effect than were parents who resided with their children. There appeared to be more than a grain of truth in the popular assertion that noncustodial parents are more like pals than like parents, especially when contact with the child was irregular and infrequent. (For a fuller discussion of the findings from NSC, see Furstenberg and Nord, 1982.) As a consequence, custodial parents often expressed resentment toward their being put in the position of being the heavy in matters of discipline.

Remarriage and the entrance of a stepparent into the deliberations sometimes enlarged the arena of conflict between the formerly married couple, at least temporarily. The stepparent poses a direct threat to the biological parent, especially one who plays a limited role as a sociological parent. If the absent biological parent becomes largely a ritual figure—like a grandparent—as several informants described their position, there was a strong possibility of further disengagement. Some noncustodial parents, uncomfortable with their marginal role to begin with, were inclined to retreat from significant involvement with the child altogether when a stepparent entered the scene.

The alternative of trying to enlarge the coparenting system was rarely accomplished without a certain amount of rivalry between the noncustodial and stepparent. An especially sensitive barometer of this rivalry was the child's use of names to refer to new parental figures. The child almost never stopped referring to his biological parent as Mom or

Dad regardless of how little contact was maintained with the noncustodial parent. On the other hand, there was far more variation in the assignment of names to the stepparents.

The qualitative case studies provided evidence that naming was a kind of political act, signifying a degree of acceptance of the stepparent as *a*, if not *the*, sociological parent. Residential parents, for the most part, encouraged their children to refer to their new partners as Mom or Dad although most insisted that they did not push their children to adopt these terms if they chose not to. Stepparents had differing views about the desirability of being designated as Mom or Dad. Some resisted the idea of their replacing the missing parent while others were delighted about the prospect of doing so. Obviously the age of the child was an important consideration in the naming practices that emerged. It was also far more common to promote a kinship designation when the child had little or no contact with the biological parent living outside the home. Noncustodial parents frequently were alarmed to learn that their children were referring to their stepparents by a term that they felt should be reserved for a biological parent. A number actually prohibited the child from referring to their stepparent as Mom or Dad.

> CUSTODIAL STEPMOTHER: . . . I think she [noncustodial mother] is jealous of me. . . . Now she just told me that I'm doing all the things that she should be doing, but she never thought of it until I started doing them. . . .
> INTERVIEWER: So she feels that you are taking her place?
> CUSTODIAL STEPMOTHER: Yes. She has forbidden them to call me "Mom" when she's around. I am "Betty" and will never be anything else.
> INTERVIEWER: So they observe that rule, but when they are with you alone, what do they call you?
> CUSTODIAL STEPMOTHER: "Mom."
> INTERVIEWER: I mean you have no objection to their calling both you and her "Mom?"
> CUSTODIAL STEPMOTHER: No. I told them that they didn't have to call me "Mom" if they didn't want to. They could call me whatever they wanted to.

The data from Central Pennsylvania do not provide a reliable basis for assessing how often nonresidential parents adopted a competitive rather than collaborative style of dealing with their former spouse's new partner. Moreover, even if we had a reliable way of determining the frequency of various styles of coparenting, the styles would certainly shift over time. The reinterview caught most individuals who had remarried in the earliest stages of their new relationships. Many were still trying to resolve long-standing custody differences or to adapt to changing family circumstances (as our earlier data attest), and it is highly likely that the patterns we observed will change over time.

Further data that bear on this question were collected in the National Survey of Children (Furstenberg and Nord, 1982). We were surprised to discover rather little evidence of continued conflict between biological and stepparents. Apparently jealousy subsides over time. Formerly married biological parents have less and less contact over time, and their spouses see one another rarely if at all. What little information is passed back and forth is often carried by the child or conducted in a businesslike manner over the telephone. The low level of contact between the residential and nonresidential parents dampens potential conflicts although the lack of communication sometimes does not serve the child's interests particularly well, especially when problems arise at home or at school. The great majority of residential parents report that they rarely or never discuss childrearing matters with their former spouses or with former spouses' new partners. Even when the outside parent or parents maintain fairly regular contact with the child, close to half of the custodial parents report little or no communication.

But there are some individuals who manage to maintain viable coparenting arrangements. Turning back to the case data from Central Pennsylvania, let us mention some of the considerations that arise in fashioning a viable agreement and draw out some implications for a variant model of parenthood that may become more common in the future.

The idealized portrait of the successful coparenting arrangement usually includes a high degree of coordination between the parents, frequent communication, residential propinquity, and mutual trust between the parents—in short, the conditions that make for a successful marriage also figure in successful coparenting. Needless to say, most formerly married couples have some difficulty living up to this standard.

In the Central Pennsylvania study, authentic joint custody situations were extremely rare although somewhat more common than occurred in the national survey. Only a tiny fraction of the sample reported that the child regularly resided in two households or had daily contact with both parents, and these rare cases declined by half during the course of the study. However, the number of coparenting situations in which the noncustodial parent maintained weekly contact with the child remained fairly constant for about a third of the sample.

No doubt, part of the stability that does emerge is attributable to legal agreements which specify the visitation rights of the noncustodial parent, but our qualitative case studies suggest that more often than not couples informally negotiate an agreement that involves regular participation in childrearing by the noncustodial parent. These collaborative arrangements were most common in families where both parents worked and where the residential parent—typically the mother—had an interest in a high level of paternal participation.

Routinization was a critical mechanism for achieving successful collaboration arrangements. When arrangements became highly predictable, the formerly married couple was usually able to conduct the business of coparenting with a minimum of conflict. Rearrangements that involved extensive negotiations generally produced resistance and mistrust.

No formula seemed to exist for specifying the right balance of involvement by the coparents. More important than any particulars was the existence of an arrangement itself, a reflection of what Emile Durkheim referred to as the "non-contractual elements of contract."

Contrary to what might be expected, several informants reported that physical distance helped to promote collaboration. The residential parent was less likely to feel threatened by elevated demands for participation, while the nonresidential parent experienced less ambivalence about maintaining a low level of contact. In such cases, the couple could afford to be generous to one another.

CUSTODIAL STEPFATHER: Nobody's at anybody's throat now. And everybody is able to, you know, . . . we haven't gone out anywhere . . . we've gone shopping while we were down there and taken all the kids and all four of us. We'd go walking and stuff.

CUSTODIAL MOTHER: It was for the boys.

INTERVIEWER: Do you think there would be a lot more contact if they lived closer by?

CUSTODIAL MOTHER: Probably.

CUSTODIAL STEPFATHER: At that point, if we'd have more contact then probably friction would be there. The way it is now, it's just nice because there isn't any friction.

INTERVIEWER: Uh huh. So the distance preserves a certain . . . ?

CUSTODIAL STEPFATHER: Right.

CUSTODIAL MOTHER: Yes.

CUSTODIAL STEPFATHER: I prefer the way it is myself [laughs].

INTERVIEWER: And that's your feeling too, Nancy?

CUSTODIAL MOTHER: Oh, definitely. I think Jim would get under my skin very rapidly once more.

Established routines were sometimes upset when one or both parents entered a new relationship. We have already described the threat raised when a stepparent is added to the family constellation. But in some situations, new parents produced just the opposite effect: Problems between the formerly married couple subsided. This reduction of tensions seemed more likely to occur when both parents acquired new mates.

New spouses were able to be constructive in several different ways. The most obvious one is their occasional ability to dampen longstanding conflicts between the formerly married couple by accelerating the process of emotional disengagement. Individuals felt less need to hold onto feelings of bitterness or enmity once they became involved with someone else. Indeed, as we have reported in Chapter 3, the process of second marriage can involve a reorganization of the self that is sometimes quite dramatic and far-reaching. Accordingly, individuals sometimes developed capacities for dealing with their former spouse that did not exist when they were married. The lessening of tensions between the formerly married couple sometimes paved the way for a more collaborative style of coparenting.

In relationships that were emotionally impacted, the intercession of a new party—the current spouse—occasionally served to provide new solutions to old problems. Child-care arrangements, for example, were sometimes worked out between the residential parent and the nonresidential stepparent. In our small sample there were even instances of negotiations taking place between the residential and nonresidential stepparents, who could assume a more disinterested and conciliatory role. Of course, such cases were hardly the rule; but they indicate the possibility that remarriage can broaden options for coparenting, especially when biological parents are willing to cede certain parenting rights to stepparents.

We do not know enough about the conditions that make it possible for alliances to form between biological and stepparents. Obviously, the social situations and personalities of the various parties affect the likelihood of coalitions across remarriage chains. But we suspect that underlying conceptions of parenthood also affect the possibility of parental alliances. Some stepparents indicated a willingness to play only a peripheral role in child rearing based on their conviction that the child's biological parent should assume the major responsibility; others felt that they were entitled to full parental rights if they contributed more material and emotional resources than did the child's biological parent. Similarly, some biological parents adhered to the belief that based on blood ties, they retained absolute claim to parental authority; but others felt far less convinced of their blood rights.

Unfortunately, our study was not set up to examine these beliefs in any detail. We do know that our respondents divided quite evenly when asked whether they agreed or disagreed with the statement, "Stepparents can't really take the place of a natural parent in the child's emotional life." Similarly, about half concurred with and half rejected the statement, "It is generally harder to love a stepchild than to love one's own child." Finally, our respondents were also split on whether "Stepparents are better off if they think of themselves more as a friend to their stepchildren than as a parent." These statements are only crude indicators of conceptions of parenthood, but they suggest that there is little consensus among our respondents on a model of parenthood for blended families.

This finding should not be surprising, for this family form is a contemporary creation. A key question is whether, in the course of divorce and remarriage, couples are forced to redefine their notions of parenthood in ways that take into account the realities and potentialities of their new family arrangements or whether parental conceptions remain unchallenged by life experience.

If it turns out that family reconstitution does significantly alter conceptions of parenthood, this raises the possibility that some general shifts in the relative importance of biological versus sociological parenthood may be taking place in our culture as conjugal succession becomes a more common pattern. While in the recent past biological and sociological parenthood were inextricably bound, in the future they are more likely to become distinctive strands, leading to more complex socialization arrangements. Assuming these trends continue, we may be witnessing profound changes in the arrangement and the meaning of parenthood.

CHAPTER 6

Intergenerational Relations

Complicating our ability to describe and account for the variability of kinship patterns in contemporary society is the flux within the current system. Some observers believe, for example, that the general decline in fertility and the increase in childlessness in particular may be altering the availability of kin resources. Similarly, other researchers speculate that the growth of welfare institutions may be weakening the basis of intergenerational exchange (Elder, 1974; Hareven, 1978; Sawhill, 1978). Whether, or how, particular demographic, economic, and political developments have modified American kinship practices has not been established with any degree of precision. Even assuming that patterns of kinship behavior have been altered by the profound institutional transformations that have taken place in contemporary American society, it does not necessarily follow that fundamental understandings about kinship have been revised as well (Schneider, 1980). Evidence is lacking on whether shifts occurred in classifications of kin, notions of closeness and distance, or expectations attached to specific kin relations in response to organizational changes within the family.

The extraordinary increases in divorce and remarriage rates present an interesting opportunity to explore conceptions of kinship, rules of kinship behavior and the possibility of change in either of these two domains. This chapter examines the ways in which patterns of divorce and remarriage may restructure our notions of kinship and the functioning of the kinship system in American society.

Implications of Remarriage for Kinship Relations

To the extent that we have thought about the significance of demographic trends for the working of the kinship system, our attention has largely focused on their meaning for children—particularly regarding their intellectual and social development (Herzog and

Sudia, 1971; Hetherington et al., 1978; Longfellow, 1979; Zill, 1984). There has been far less interest in exploring the implications of these changing patterns of marriage on adults in the middle and later years of life.

We have already observed that many adults will have the experience of rearing children who do not reside with them or of residing with children who are not their offspring. In the previous chapter, we speculated on how these new arrangements will alter the concept of parenthood. The question of the changing meaning of parenthood becomes even more intriguing when considered from a temporal perspective. How are generational linkages affected by divorce and remarriage? A key feature of the conjugal family in our society is that it is the principal domestic unit. The meaning of close family must derive in part from spatial proximity as well as from conceptions of close genetic or blood ties, as David Schneider (1980) has pointed out. To what extent does the residential separation of parents and children in early life attenuate their emotional bonds in later life?

If information is lacking on the effect of divorce and remarriage on close family relations, we know even less about the impact on kinship bonds that span more than a single generation or cut laterally across a generation. Does the universe of relatives expand because individuals retain both their old and new relations? Or does it contrast because they lose their earlier relatives and cannot cement ties to kin acquired in later life?

Previous Research on Kinship Relations After Divorce

When the problem of how kinship relations are restructured after divorce and remarriage was first considered, the literature on divorce and remarriage was reviewed. One point of departure was textbooks on marriage and the family. Although this analysis of the existing literature was not exhaustive, it produced almost no references to remarriage in recent family texts. If they mentioned the subject at all, most writers dwell on the prospects of conjugal success in a second marriage. By and large, family sociologists ignored the implications of remarriage for kinship relations (Furstenberg, 1979).

Previous research has largely ignored these questions. Several reviews of the literature note the paucity of research on this subject (Bohannon, 1970; Cherlin, 1978). For example, Walker et al. (1977:

281) in the most extensive survey of the literature on remarriage, observe that "an additional shortcoming in the research literature is the lack of a focus on relationships of remarriage family household members with relatives and friends connected through a former marriage. Very few studies examine step-relationships with the extended and friendship network outside the remarriage households."

One of the rare exceptions to the generalization in Walker et al. is a perceptive essay by Paul Bohannon (1970) on the aftermath of divorce (see also Mead, 1971). In a brief comment on the complex social configurations resulting from remarriage, Bohannon introduces the notion of a "divorce chain," the social links that are created by successive marriages. Bohannon contends that this arrangement might be viewed as a new extended family form, the modern equivalent to the multigenerational family unit. Unfortunately, Bohannon said little about the implications of this kinship constellation for the individual or society.

Several investigators—Adams (1971), Sussman (1976), and Troll et al. (1979)—have reviewed the existing studies in some detail but uncovered little of relevance to the subject of family reconstitution. In fact, Lillian Troll and her colleagues (1979) commented on the strategic importance of conducting research on the way that kinship patterns are affected by divorce and remarriage. The problems that ensue are not restricted to young married couples; their middle-age parents and even their grandparents must relinquish old relations and incorporate new ones in adjusting to family changes.

Marvin Sussman (1976), noting the sharp increase in divorce and remarriage, speculates on how these changes may affect patterns of intergenerational exchange. Like Troll, Sussman reasons that multiple marriages inevitably enlarge the pool of potential kin, just as is true in large extended families. "The promise of an inheritance," Sussman writes, "may provide motivation for family members to invest in a relationship with the elderly person," while the elder in turn "has a greater field of relatives from which to choose." In effect, Sussman is making an argument similar to the one advanced by Bohannon. Remarriage enriches the kinship network and may, to some extent, offset the impact of declining fertility on the stock of effective kin.

Interestingly enough, the few empirical investigations of how kinship relations are restructured after divorce and remarriage have failed to consider this possibility. Indeed, each has emphasized the reduction of kinship contacts and the diminution of intergenerational exchange, probably because they focused on the period immediately after divorce. Rosenberg and Anspach (1973) in a study of working class kinship patterns in Philadelphia discovered that formerly married participants maintain, if not increase, contact with close kindred (parents, siblings, and spouses of siblings) following a divorce. By contrast, they interacted with significantly fewer members of their former mate's kindred (affines) in the period after divorce. Approximately one-quarter of the widows and one-fifth of the divorced listed their former spouse's kin in the pool of available relatives, compared with three-fifths of the currently married. Following Schneider, the authors argue that the recognition of affinal relations as "kin" is optional in American society. So the dissolution of the marriage usually nullifies kinship consciousness, weakening effective ties (see Weiss, 1975).

There is one serious shortcoming in this study: Kinship links are traced exclusively on an individual basis, ignoring those contacts that might appear if the family were taken as the unit of analysis. Specifically, the Rosenberg-Anspach thesis that the maintenance of affinal ties depends on the preservation of the conjugal bond excludes the possibility that children constitute another link that is less easily erased. After all, children remain members of their absent partner's kindred. Accordingly, a potential conflict arises between the interests of adults and their children. The extinction of former relations places children in jeopardy of being disconnected from a significant portion of their kindred.

Another study of kinship interaction after divorce, conducted by Spicer and Hampe (1975), highlights this point. While based on a smaller and less representative sample exclusively of divorces, the findings strongly corroborate the results obtained by Rosenberg and Anspach. Divorced men and women reported distinctly less contact with the relatives of their former spouse after the break of their marriages (based on retrospective accounts). At the same time, contact with consanguineal kin increased slightly, especially among women who presumably relied on their parents and siblings for material and emotional support after divorce. The data collected by Spicer and Hampe reveal a tremendous amount of variation in amount of contact among respondents and their former in-laws.

A critical question left unanswered by both of these two studies is what, if any, changes take place in the event of remarriage? Does a second marriage result in a further withering away of kinship contacts with affines from the initial union? If so, are any provisions made for continuing the links between children and their kindred or are these ties replaced by stepkin, the blood relations of the child's residential stepparent? Only one study could be located that even addressed these questions; it is an investigation by Donald Anspach (1976) which is billed as a preliminary study to generate hypotheses.

Anspach interviewed a sample of mothers in Portland, Maine, of whom 47 were divorced, 37 were remarried, and 35 were in their first marriages, collecting information on the number of available kin, contacts with these relations, and perceived changes in kin contact following divorce and remarriage. In line with the findings of the previous two studies, divorced and remarried persons perceive a decline in social relations with their former spouse's close kin although approximately a third of each group reported seeing at least one member of their ex-husband's family in the preceding week. Significant for our discussion, Anspach also discovered that the patterns of interaction with the present spouse's family among women in their first and second marriages were identical. About three-quarters of each had seen a family member. In short, the remarried were like the divorced in regard to their previous spouses and like the once-married women in regard to their current spouses.

In attempting to explain the variation in contact with paternal kindred, Anspach observes that the role of the absent father is critically important. When the parents break off or drastically curtail interaction after divorce, relations with paternal kin decline accordingly, resulting in an imbalance in a child's kinship network. By withdrawing from his role as the child's sponsor, the father weakens the child's link to his or her paternal kin. Anspach's data show that maternal kin are much more likely to be favored when the father is seen infrequently. They figure more equally when the father maintains his ties to the family.

This study, like the two previous investigations, emphasized the disadvantage to the child whose parents are divorced, especially in the event that the nonresidential parent (typically the father) severs contact and fails to link the children to the nonresidential parent's kin. But a less dire interpretation can be fashioned from the existing data. To a surprising extent, bilateral kinship ties are maintained after divorce and even after remarriage. Although divorce unquestionably restricts the child's access to relatives on one side of his or her family (usually the father's), this result is far from inevitable. Moreover, when remarriage occurs—and this event is highly likely—the child appears to enjoy a certain advantage. Ties with both parents' families can be maintained even after new links are established with the stepparent's family.

The impact of divorce and remarriage on the senior or grandparent generation may also have favorable as well as unfavorable consequences. Of course, the situation for the relatives of the residential parent is not problematic, at least regarding the level of exchange. If any shift occurs at all, it is probably in the direction of intensifying interaction as the divorced parent is forced to rely more heavily on the support of kin in the aftermath of divorce. By contrast, the relatives of the nonresidential parent may stand to lose out when the parent is not present in the home to serve as a direct link to the child. However, we have seen that relatives of the nonresidential parent frequently maintain contact with the child, especially when custody of the child is shared to some extent. The preliminary data assembled by previous researchers may have in fact understated the extent of interaction between children and the relatives of their noncustodial parent because they did not expect to find much contact occurring.

In the next section of this chapter, we will examine in greater detail the mechanisms that preserve the generational ties between the child and his or her relatives and the pressures brought to bear on residential parents to deal with their former in-laws (that is, their children's kin). We shall try to illustrate the stake various parties hold in maintaining existing kinship ties.

At the same time, another set of incentives operate on the family of remarried persons, leading to the incorporation of new relations into the kinship network. Specific pressures are brought to bear on the extended family to reach out to step-in-laws and their children. The case studies we shall present suggest that extended kin may find it difficult to maintain close ties with relatives who remarry if they insist on treating their newly acquired relations as non-kin. Just as refusing to recognize a kinperson's spouse as a relative may impair bonds within the kindred, slighting the stepchild may produce a similar rupture within the bloodline. Studying the pressures brought to bear on the extended family to incorporate the new spouse and his or her children provides a fascinating example of how individuals pass from strangers to kin.

As part of the process of preparing for the follow-up survey, we carried out a series of 24 qualitative case studies of couples living in Philadelphia who had remarried recently. It is these cases to which we refer in the latter part of this chapter. The subjects of this pilot study were located from marriage records in Philadelphia. It should be clear, however, that the people with whom we talked are neither representative nor typical of remarried couples in general. They are a self-selected sample of persons who are willing to share their experiences. They are predominantly middle class and well educated, a fact that should be kept in mind throughout the following discussion.

When conducting the interviews, we resisted the dictates of our discipline and deliberately refrained from asking structured questions. Rather we conversed with the subjects about a wide range of topics relating to the transition from divorce to remarriage. Most participants, relieved of the burden of answering structured queries, responded rather fully and sincerely—sometimes even enthusiastically—to what were often nebulous questions. The collaborators in this pilot study may be thought of as informants in the sense in which anthropologists are accustomed to using the term.

Preserving Kinship Ties

Certain organizational features of our family system might predispose members of a conjugal network to retain ties with one another after divorce. Schneider and Cottrell (1975) make the point that the boundaries of kinship are flexible; that is, relationships are to a very large extent discretionary. There is, as they put it, no specific "rule of closure." The optional nature of the system means that divorce can occur without necessarily nullifying existing kinship ties based on a preexisting marriage. Individuals have, therefore, a choice of whether or not to be related when they are no longer connected by an intact marriage. In the discussion that follows, we try to show why individuals, especially if they are parents, have a stake in preserving relations with affines (relatives by marriage) following a divorce. We will argue that when children are involved, there are certain structural pressures working to preserve ties between former family members even when sentiments might dictate the discontinuation of relationships.

Let us look first at the mechanisms operating to preserve kinship ties with the family of the nonresidential parent as well as some of the circumstances that undermine the continuity of relationships. When asked about the amount of contact they had with their former in-laws, most informants explained that they saw less of them, often because they were no longer living in the same locality. However, during other parts of the interview, it became clear that members of their former spouse's family had figured critically in their lives in the very recent past.

CASE 1

This is part of an interview with a formerly married husband and his second wife, married for the first time. The man, whom we call Robert, had one child (Robbie) who lived with his former wife (Irene), who had remarried and subsequently separated. During Irene's marriage, she left the country, leaving the child with her mother.

> HUSBAND: I don't see that she's [his former wife] changed so much.
>
> WIFE: Can you believe that she never wrote to him and said that she was sending that child home, alone?
>
> INTERVIEWER: How did you find out?
>
> WIFE: His grandmother called Robert. Robbie's grandmother. Irene's mother. His mother-in-law called him.
>
> HUSBAND: And she said she was going to Washington to pick him up.
>
> INTERVIEWER: That suggests that you have maintained some kind of relationship with her . . . at least she's still reponding to you as a family member.
>
> WIFE: . . . for the child. They legitimately like him [referring to her husband] see, and it's because of her that I think it's been a much more communicative type of thing about Robbie. . . . What information you get about Robbie comes from his mother-in-law.
>
> HUSBAND: [after some further clarification]. . . . they [his in-laws] want to be very friendly. And I think Robbie's grandmother has been in some ways more concerned and more motivated to take care of him than his mother has. [Husband goes on to describe how the grandmother and the estranged parents went to see a psychologist to coordinate plans for the child.]

CASE 2

This is a portion of an interview with a remarried husband and his second wife, who had not been previously married. The couple live with children from the husband's first marriage who came to live with them after their mother was hospitalized for emotional problems.

HUSBAND: [recounting the period when he assumed custody of the children] Then there would be periods when she would want to see the kids every third weekend or something . . . that was fine with me. She really tried to be a good mother, within the limits of what she was capable of doing. She frequently took them to her parents, and they are pretty decent people, so I had confidence that they were going to be ok. I was honestly glad to get rid of them for the weekend, it was great occasionally.

Both of the informants quoted above depict the grandparents (their former in-laws) as the child's protectors, a characterization that we suspect is not unusual in families that have experienced a divorce. Particularly if relations with in-laws were amicable before the breakup of the marriage, the grandparents or sometimes the child's uncles or aunts (the parents' siblings) can serve as emotional intermediaries between children and their separated parents. In Case 1, the mother-in-law plays a central role in bringing the father back into the family constellations. (Interestingly, the present wife, after searching for a term, finally resorts to the designation of mother-in-law even though that same term could also be used to describe her own mother's relationship to her husband). The grandmother, by virtue of her own relationship to the child, is in an especially strategic position to intercede on behalf of the child, reminding the absent parent of his rights and obligations. And once the father assumed a more active presence in childrearing, the child began to have more contacts with the father's family as well.

In the second case, the grandparents are serving a surrogate role for the mother, incapacitated by illness. By doing so, they relieve the father of exclusive parental responsibilities and at the same time provide a direct bridge between the children and their maternal relatives. It was through visits with the grandparents that the children maintained contact with their uncles and aunts.

The patterns described above do not apply to all the families we studied. One woman, for example, who experienced a bitter separation from her husband reported that her parents would not permit her ex-husband near their home even though he had custody of the children. She agreed with her ex-husband that her parents were being "asinine," but our informant explained that her parents did not want to expose their children "to a face from the past." Even though her family avoided contact with their former son-in-law, the daughter arranges for them to see their grandchildren when they visit her.

Children are, as anthropologists have reminded us, a form of social property. Except under rare circumstances, custody arrangements recognize the interests of both parents (and indirectly, their families) although the division does not typically stipulate an even share. Involvement of extended kin may serve to impress upon the various parties a sense of mutual rights and obligations. The grandparents assume an especially critical role in preserving family claims after the marriage contract between the parents is terminated. They often represent the interests of the absent parent, reminding both their former in-laws and their grandchildren that ties to the absent parent endure. The grandparents are often in an especially advantageous position to link the child to other family members of the kindred. Thus, by threatening to break lineage ties a divorce may have the paradoxical consequence of invoking family ties. Grandparents may become guardians of the family line.

Quantitative studies of patterns of visitation unless explicitly designed to discover accommodations are likely to miss the part of the action that takes place among family members formerly related by marriage. As children retain consanguineal ties to both parents and hence to their retrospective families, the estranged couple are predisposed to acknowledge some type of relationship to their former affines although the precise nature of this relationship remains unspecified. In a few cases, the bond between the parent and his or her former in-laws continues as though the divorce had never occurred. More typically, relations between the two parties are more perfunctory, maintained merely for the children's sake.

All the principals involved, the parents, their respective close kindred, and the children have a stake in not disrupting the generational ties. The parents, whatever the degree of enmity between them, are usually willing to concede that it is in the child's best interests not to destroy kinship connections that might be emotionally and materially important to their offspring both at present and in the future. Informants who had little good to say about their former spouse frequently acknowledged the legitimate rights of his or her family to see the child. And often they went out of their way to promote continued relations with the extended family, arranging weekend or vacation visits.

Of course, the grandparents serve the residential parent's interests in another way as well. In many cases they continue to lend assistance, relieving the parent of some of the burdens of child care. Several informants who were residing with their children explained that they tended to see their former in-laws when they dropped their children off for a visit. In several instances, it appears that their in-laws' house was a neutral zone where the previously married couple could carry on their common business of parenting. Because of the benefits derived by the parents, the grandparents (and other relatives as well, by inference) held a secure position within the family so long as they performed a helping role.

Interestingly, the helping role that the grandparents performed for their former son-in-law or daughter-in-law and their grandchildren probably served to strengthen their bond to their own child. Grandparents who have only an ancillary part to play in the family when the couple is married become much more important to their children when a divorce takes place. Men turn to their parents for child-care support; women may do likewise; and both may seek financial aid as well. Divorce increases the level of exchange as it serves the parents' interests to involve the older generation.

All of this is not to say that divorce necessarily promotes harmony in the extended family. On balance, divorce, as we shall demonstrate in Chapter 7, complicates relations between the generations, especially between adults and their former in-laws. Strains are particularly likely to occur when the in-law relationship was weak to begin with, or when the senior generation took an active part in the divorce process. What we have tried to suggest is that there may be a response within the family system offsetting these potential rifts that works in the opposite direction, promoting continued relations between the generations. In sum, divorce does not inevitably disadvantage the senior generation either vis-à-vis their grandchildren, their own children, or even their former in-laws. Considering the latter instance, it is possible that when in-laws provide help to an estranged spouse, she or he may respond with devotion and gratitude, thus strengthening long-term family obligations.

Augmenting the Kinship Network

Relationships with new kin are not mandatory, but they are permitted and even encouraged. Although children have no blood ties to their stepparent's kindred, they are connected to them by marriage. Culturally, they are permitted to think of these relations as equivalents to their blood relatives; and the evidence that we have collected thus far indicates that they frequently do. Our kinship system allows for an unlimited number of siblings, uncles, aunts, cousins. With the possible exception of marriage, there are no closed sets in our kinship categories. While we are accustomed in our society to having only two parents and four grandparents, these categories, too, are potentially elastic. We quote at some length below a section from an interview with a remarried woman, describing the situation of her daughter, who is living with her remarried father. She is telling about the child's initiation into a new kinship network.

INTERVIEWER: What about other relatives; I mean, she now has a fairly extensive set of . . .

WOMAN: Yeah, she loves that. She loves it. Like they went to Minnesota for a week, and she got to meet 15 different relatives, and now, I don't know what that makes, 4 or 5, 10 sets of grandparents I think, and I don't know how many sets of aunts and uncles, and she would describe every single one of them to me and how nice they were and what they gave her and what they did. She loves it. She loves the attention.

INTERVIEWER: So . . . she has four sets of grandparents now?

WOMAN: Well, she would, wouldn't she? I mean, if she's got four parents . . . my parents are alive and Art [present husband] has a father alive but not a mother. Jerry [former husband] has both his parents alive and Carol [former husband's wife] has both her parents alive, so she really has seven.

INTERVIEWER: Does she have a relationship with Art's father?

WOMAN: Yeah, and I think it's pretty nice. Not . . . we don't see him that often, but he's very good to her and she's very friendly to him, and they have a sort of tickle kind of relationship.

INTERVIEWER: What does she call him?

WOMAN: Well, we're working on that. Sometimes it's Pop-pop, and Grandpa, it comes out most, but not Samuel, not by his first name or anything like that . . . I think it's kind of nice to have

the name of grandpa or grandfather or something like that. And I
guess she has enough of those [laughter].

INTERVIEWER: And then she sees something of Carol's family?

WOMAN: They all went up there for a family reunion at
Christmas time, but at Thanksgiving, Henny [the child] went to
Syracuse just to see them, Pop-pop and Nana or whatever, I can't
remember what it's called now.

INTERVIEWER: And does Art have any brothers and sisters
around?

WOMAN: Leslie, Art's sister . . . Henny's very fond of Leslie, sort
of a female kind of relation . . . big-sister sort of a thing and she
sends her special things and stuff. [She goes on to describe a more
distant relationship that her child has with a brother of her
husband whom he doesn't see very often.] Well, she didn't acquire
too much with Art and I. No. But with Jerry and Carol, I mean,
they lived together for a year or two before. But they didn't
branch out into all the familial kind of stuff until they'd really
gotten married. So, really, since April, she's met everybody in the
chain. So that is a real onslaught of people.

INTERVIEWER: Has that meant any decline in her contact with
your family, or . . .

WOMAN: I think so . . . because, well, it's not like my parents
are her only grandparents so they're very special and sort of a
sacred entity or something. I mean, she can go to any level for
love and attention now, that kind of attention.

INTERVIEWER: Do your parents feel any sense of diminution in
their relationship with her?

WOMAN: No . . . you see, my mother and father have three new
children [her mother remarried 12 years ago] so it wasn't a real
grandmother situation, I mean.

This conversation serves to illustrate a number of themes that came
up in the interviews when subjects were questioned about how
remarriage had altered their own and their children's kinship networks.
It was generally assumed that they and their children would annex the
current spouse's family so long as the new parent had active ties with
his or her relatives. With respect to family, the rule seemed to be that
what is mine is thine. Accordingly, children were encouraged if not
required to adopt kinship designations for their new relatives—most
importantly, the grandparents. In turn, there was some active pressure
put on elders to treat the children as grandchildren. Even with the
stepparent's active sponsorship, the process of incorporation was not

automatic. One stepparent described with a certain trace of bitterness how her parents slipped her stepson some money for Christmas while giving their biological grandchild a toy. Although she felt it was understandable in view of the limited contact that had taken place between the child and her parents, the informant was determined not to allow the situation to be repeated in the future.

This particular case notwithstanding, there is little question that from the point of view of the child the process of family augmentation is usually a real boon. As in the case quoted previously, the child has additional doting grandparents, uncles, and aunts, and additional cousins. To convert Bohannon's phrase, a "remarriage chain" develops which can become quite complex. In the case we have cited, it later surfaced in the interview that Carol (the stepmother) had been previously married as well. Henny, it turns out, went along with her stepsister on the weekends when Carol's child visited her grandparents. Our informant casually mentioned that "those grandparents have been actively involved in Henny, too." We also discovered that both Carol's former husband and his father were doctors and had treated Henny during a recent illness. Apparently remarriage chains extend the children's networks, spanning across a number of families, and creating indirect connections among a large universe of individuals. As we shall elaborate in the conclusion of this chapter, the ties established through remarriage chains establish a support system for the children even when kinship is not directly invoked or acknowledged.

Moreover, a much larger pool of relatives exists for the child from which gratifying and supportive relations may be selected. As suggested by the case just mentioned, some of these relatives may drop out of the child's kinship world due to conflicting obligations or geographical distance. Second-order affinal relations may also be more fragile and especially vulnerable to dissolution if and when second marriages end. For example, a set of siblings whom we interviewed shortly after the breakup of their mother's second marriage, were divided on whether they considered their stepfather (whom they had never even lived with) a relative. The oldest replied that she thought he was a relative but the youngest thought he was more like a "a friend"; and, he added, "I guess 'cause you don't see him as much as you see Katherine" (his stepmother who now lives with him). Interestingly, at a later point in the interview this same child when asked to list his relatives included the parents of his stepfather as his grandparents.

Acknowledgment of kinship may never develop or may be rescinded if the marital link is broken and contact ceases. This pattern is evident in many of the black families who participated in the study of adolescent childbearing. Ties with the biological father frequently survived limited contact, whereas relations with stepfathers were transient unless the man resided in the home or had done so for an extended period of time (Furstenberg, 1976; Furstenberg and Talvitie, 1980).

Our data are far too sketchy at this point to supply any detail about the process involved in acquiring new relatives through marriage. Most of the parents we spoke to did not view the situation as highly problematic, and the few children we interviewed confirm this impression. When asked how it feels to get new relatives, one child explained, "You just press a button and it's there all of a sudden." At the same time children are sensitive to the distinctions between old and new relations, sometimes using the term real to describe their consanguineal kin. When speaking of her stepmother's siblings, a teenager explained that "their children aren't as much cousins as like friends." She went on to explain, "We've only known (them) like two years of our lives so we can't be like intimate, you know, like our real cousins."

It would appear that relations acquired by marriage are automatically eligible to be relatives—"like pressing a button"—but may not be considered as kin unless there is some intimate contact over an extended period. In this respect, the same general rules are applied in deciding whether persons are relatives when remarriage takes place as might occur when any marriage takes place (Schneider, 1980). In making the determination, the child is not acting entirely independently. As we indicated earlier, there is pressure on extended relatives to incorporate the child in the family; so, too, we might expect parents to exert pressure on their children to "adopt" the same persons whom they consider as relatives. In effect, the children are encouraged to acknowledge the conjugal ties between the biological and stepparent. If they refuse to regard their stepparent's kin as their relatives, the children are implicitly denying their own ties to their stepparent and ultimately rejecting the legitimacy of the marriage that brought about their new family situation. Should this occur, it would no doubt create a serious rift between parent and child, forcing the parent to choose between cognatic and conjugal loyalties.

There was no case in the pilot study in which a child refused to acknowledge his or her stepparent's relations. Probably such instances are more likely to arise when the children are older and hence less willing to adopt a new family. In general, we suspect it happens less frequently than is portrayed in popular treatments of reconstituted families. The permissive feature of the system, which allows the child to add on new relatives without relinquishing ties to existing relations, undoubtedly dampens the potential of conflict and rivalry between the old and new families. This is not to say that competition between families does not develop but that the absence of a zero-sum rule means that existing relatives will not necessarily lose out except perhaps on specific ritual occasions such as Thanksgiving or Christmas day. We shall have more to say about how time is allocated among extended relatives in the next chapter.

Not only is the kinship system elastic, it is also relatively unspecific in defining the nature of family obligations outside the nuclear unit. Thus, for example, there are no exact requirements prescribing how often relatives must see one another. Contact between kin can be infrequent without jeopardizing their status as relatives (probably more so than among friends). As is suggested in the conversation quoted earlier, remarried couples may initially take some pains to sponsor their children in their own families and invent special kinship designations for significant relations. However, it probably does not require more than episodic visits to reinforce these family ties. This means that the child can absorb and be absorbed by a fairly substantial number of relations. If he or she already has cousins, there is a place for more cousins. If not, the child can rather quickly learn what it means to have a cousin.

One feature of contemporary American families that probably makes the adaptation to remarriage relatively easy for both adults and children is the declining birth rate. The fact that fewer children are being born and intervals between the generations are lengthening should promote greater receptivity to the acquisition of new relations. Older people, particularly if their offspring are childless, might be expected to welcome the addition of grandchildren even if they arrive by an unconventional route. Similarly, children may appreciate supplemental grandparents, especially if their own are not easily accessible. As we shall amplify in the conclusion, remarriage has the consequence of distributing a diminishing pool of children among a larger circle of adults. For children, it means being connected—albeit sometimes only weakly—to a great number of adults who are prepared to treat them as kin.

To be sure, remarriage complicates the child's world. One point that arose in several interviews is that generations become blurred by remarriage (more so than is the case in first marriages). An 11-year-old slyly announced with some amusement that his new uncle was younger than he. "I mean, they're too young to be uncles," his sister explained. The 11-year-old volunteered that he was good friends with his new relative, whom he regarded more like a "cousin." Age boundaries normally associated with kinship categories were being violated.

In many respects, remarriage recreates a kinship configuration that disappeared several generations ago. Higher death rates prior to this century created the necessity of family augmentation; kinship networks were made up of family fragments as individuals were incorporated into a household after the premature death of a parent or spouse. This frequently resulted in breaking down sharp generational boundaries. Similarly, large family size had the effect of widening the age range within families as siblings (if not stepsiblings) were typically spaced years apart. As family size diminished and siblings' ages became more uniform, cross-age contact within the family became less common. The growing pattern of divorce and remarriage may be reversing this trend by making family arrangements more complex and age-heterogeneous again. As generations become less distinct in the everyday world of family life, the salience of generational boundaries in the larger society may decline as well.

Discussion

In this chapter, we have explored the likely effects of divorce and remarriage on relations among extended kin generally and, more specifically, on interaction between generations within the family. The observations that we have offered should be treated as suggestions, not conclusions. They have not been substantiated by empirical investigation, and the data provided in the chapter are intended only for purposes of illustration. With these qualifications in mind, we would like to pull together some of the comments about the implications of remarriage for kinship relations that were scattered throughout the chapter and suggest some promising directions for future research.

It is worth reiterating that the upsurge of divorce and remarriage is a relatively novel trend. It could wane and become less prominent in the future. Even if it does become a relatively permanent feature of our kinship system, it is not clear that it will retain the form it has today. One development that may be occurring already is a change in custody arrangements. In the twentieth century (although not in previous times) children have generally resided with the mother when marriages were voluntarily dissolved. Although it is not yet evident from official statistics (U.S. Bureau of the Census, 1979), a trend toward shared custody may be emerging that could have profound implications for kinship relations after divorce. Much of the imbalance in kinship networks can be traced to the disappearance of the nonresidential parent, the child's main link to that side of his or her family. If both parents actively participate in raising the child, the child may not suffer any loss of parental sponsorship in the wider kinship network. Indeed, we have argued that marital disruption may promote active kinship ties outside the nuclear family as parents look to extended relatives for assistance and support in child care. The pattern of reliance on older family members for child-care assistance could create long-standing obligations to the senior generation, obligations that might be paid off in the later years of life. When grandparents have functioned as caretakers for their grandchildren, they may enjoy greater contact with kin in their later years of life (see the situation of the black family, Stack, 1974; Jeffers, 1967; Hill, 1977). Thus even when divorce is not followed by remarriage, it does not necessarily have dire effects on relations among extended kin—the inference commonly drawn from the handful of existing studies.

Divorced people usually remarry. Contrary to some scholars who believe that remarriage replaces former kin with a new set of relatives (Mead, 1971), we believe that children will often and parents will sometimes hold on to old relatives and at the same time acquire new ones. Our kinship system permits the augmentation of kin without relinquishing existing relations. And we have argued that it is generally in the interests of everyone to retain as many relatives as possible. The result is a structure that Bohannon labeled a "divorce chain" but that might more properly be referred to as a "remarriage chain." Whatever it is called, this configuration links (primarily through the child) former and present conjugal partners and their relatives.

This family chain has some potentially interesting features for the position of the child in the larger society. Of course to the extent that they are connected to close kin and their relatives, children will be afforded a good deal of support and assistance. Presumably, children with three or more parents and five or more grandparents as well as additional kin in other categories have an advantage over those with fewer close relatives.

Granovetter (1973) argues that "weak ties"—that is, social relations that are based on acquaintance rather than emotional intensity—are highly functional for the flow of information. All other things being equal, the more extensive the kinship network, the better situated a person is with respect to social and economic opportunities. An individual with a large number of social relations has connections that are potentially useful resources—not only for times of crisis but also for meeting routine challenges such as looking for a job, finding housing, or obtaining the name of a good dentist. The chain of relationships established by remarriage works to the benefit of both child and adult. With the increase of weak ties to a larger number of relatives, each stands to gain information and material resources. Instead of—or in addition to—knowing a friend of a friend, each person in the remarriage chain may know a relative of a relative.

When looked at from the vantage point of the larger society, the social structure generated by extensive remarriage has the consequence of increasing kinship ties and creating a network that offsets to some degree the decline in family size that has occurred in recent decades. People may have fewer relations by blood, but they may acquire a greater number through marriage. Another way of viewing this change is to say that a smaller number of children are, in the aggregate, being shared by a greater number of adults. This, of course, raises the possibility that relatives will compete for the rights to the children, but it also means that a greater number of kin will feel obligated to care for and protect the child. The extent to which this added measure of adult input in the socialization process may result in a more favorable learning environment deserves examination in future studies.

Remarriage establishes a greater number of intergenerational connections between children and their adult relatives and between parents and the senior generation. The interviews that we have conducted reveal that children's relations within their own generation were also expanded. Youngsters acquired stepsiblings, cousins, and sometimes uncles and aunts who were approximately their age peers; they may serve as generational intermediaries for the child. This new system of allies may reduce the potential for sharp cleavages along distinct generational lines.

In considering the consequences of divorce and remarriage for kinship relations, we have not addressed several problems that deserve mention. Our emphasis throughout has been on recently remarried couples in their childbearing years. In contemplating the impact of family reconstitution on intergenerational ties, we have only alluded to a series of interesting questions that might arise were we to view the problem from a longitudinal perspective. For example, individuals might retain ties to former in-laws for a relatively short period after divorce but curtail relations sharply in the later years of second marriage. Relatives may relinquish claims gradually as contact diminishes—a pattern that would not show up unless the data were examined longitudinally. However, to use the language of exchange theory, relatives who played an instrumental role at the time of divorce may build up credits that are not quickly forgotten. The parent who provides her divorced daughter-in-law with emotional and material support until she is remarried may receive assistance from her and her children many years later. Clearly, then, researchers must be prepared to examine the process of family reformation over time if they are to do justice to the dynamics of divorce and remarriage.

In this chapter, we have dealt almost exclusively with the consequences of second marriage for kinship patterns among families still in their childbearing years. This is not a totally arbitrary decision because the great majority of couples who remarry do so in their younger years. (More than three-fourths of all remarriers and four-fifths of those who remarry after divorce are under 45.) Nevertheless, it is both theoretically interesting and policy-relevant to examine remarriage later in the life course. We have focused on the impact of the attrition and addition of relatives on the senior generation, pointing out certain reasons why their role may be enhanced when divorce and remarriage occurs. But can we expect a reciprocal effect when it is the elderly who divorce and remarry? Certainly, this question deserves more attention than it has been accorded by gerontologists.

We have also not elaborated on the specific types of exchange that may be altered in the event of divorce and remarriage. For example, it is entirely possible that contact may be greatly disrupted by divorce and remarriage without a significant change in the flow of material resources; that is, inheritance patterns may remain unchanged. Similarly, we have contended that remarriage widens the child's kinship world; but it is conceivable that this widening occurs at the expense of diminishing the intensity of emotional contacts.

This leads us to a final caveat. Although it may have appeared so at times, it has not been our intention to depict divorce and remarriage as an attractive feature of family life in America. In considering the response to family reconstitution, we have stressed the potential for adaptation in our kinship system, arguing that remarriage presents advantages as well as problems for family members.

CHAPTER 7

The New Extended Family

As we have shown in the previous chapter, a couple's divorce affects their children and their children's grandparents, resulting in possible alterations in generational ties. Our analysis now takes up continuities and discontinuities in intergenerational ties between grandparents and grandchildren following divorce and remarriage. Our aim is both to describe the impact of divorce and remarriage on relations between the first (oldest) and third (youngest) generations and to speculate on the broader meaning of these contacts for the functioning of the kinship system. This chapter supplies some empirical data to test a hypothesis proposed earlier that the pattern of conjugal succession has the consequence of enlarging the child's network of kinship ties.

The potentially unsettling effects of divorce and remarriage on intergenerational relations have not gone completely unnoticed. Several gerontologists have observed that increases in divorce may disturb the flow of assistance between young and middle-aged adults and their parents, and may jeopardize the maintenance of ties between the senior generation and their grandchildren (Brody, 1978; Sussman, 1976). The two most widely cited studies, one by Rosenberg and Anspach (1973) and the other by Spicer and Hampe (1975), examine the frequency of contact between divorced parents and their close relations (parents and siblings). They demonstrate rather convincingly that relations between blood relatives intensify somewhat following a divorce, while relations between in-laws are severely curtailed following the dissolution of the marriage.

Although the contact between the grandparents and the grandchildren has not been studied directly, the implication drawn from these two studies is that a similar pattern of attrition occurs between the child and his or her grandparents on the side of the noncustodial parent. If the child's mother, for example, ceases relations with her former parents-in-law, then it is assumed that the child will suffer a similar loss of contact with the grandparents. However, this assumption has not been tested adequately. But even if intergenerational relations are in fact adversely affected by divorce, it does not necessarily follow (as previous researchers have generally concluded) that marital disruption shrinks the child's pool of available kin. As we have noted, divorce is generally a transitional rather than a terminal event. If and when remarriage occurs, the child is exposed to a new set of relations who may or may not become active figures in the child's life.

Little or no attention has been paid to the problems for the elderly of incorporating new relations after remarriage. In their comprehensive summary of the family situation of older people in contemporary society, Troll and her colleagues remark (1979: 126-127) as follows:

> Most writers refer only to the in-law adjustment problems of young married couples; few note the adjustment problems of middle-age parents and even older grandparents to the new families introduced into kin networks upon each new marriage in the family.

After reviewing the existing literature on the impact of remarriage on kinship patterns, Troll and her associates conclude, "We know so little about kinship relations among reconstituted families that we cannot even speculate about them."

Few studies, then, have examined the impact of remarriage on kinship bonds. In a small study of women still in their first marriages, divorced women, and remarried women, Anspach (1976) discovers that all three marital subgroups enjoy about the same contact with their own parents. Divorced and remarried women had little contact with their former in-laws, although approximately a third of each group continued to maintain regular relations with their ex-spouse's family. Both women in first marriages and those in remarriages had nearly as much contact with their (current) spouse's family as with their own kin. In short, remarried persons were in an especially advantageous position in the kinship network—able to draw support from members of their own family, from their present in-laws, and to some degree from their former in-laws. As in the other studies referred to earlier, the implications for grandparent-grandchild relations are unstated. But it would seem reasonable to conclude that to the extent that children continued to see the family of their noncustodial parent, they might experience an enlargement of kin as a result of divorce and remarriage.

Of course, such a conclusion is conjecture at this point for it is not substantiated by direct data on the extent and quality of relations between children and their grandparents (biological and affinal). It may well be that children have only a fixed amount of time to spend with grandparents. If they spend more time with one set, they will have to reduce their interaction with another. Moreover, it is possible that even if children do continue to see their grandparents on the noncustodial parent's side, relations may be strained as a result of the divorce. Conversely, it is possible that affinal grandparents may not develop the same emotional commitment to the child as do biological grandparents.

In our exploratory case studies we learned that the rules of our kinship system permit a great deal of discretion to adults and children regarding the decision of whether or not to maintain ties with former in-laws and, specifically, with the child's grandparents on the side of the noncustodial parent. Similarly, the flexibility of the kinship system facilitates the incorporation of new relations into the individual's kinship network. Children, for example, seemed to experience no difficulty in adding on new sets of grandparents, uncles, aunts, and cousins. An accordion seems a better metaphor for the kinship system than does a pie.

Whether these case studies provide an accurate reflection of the experiences of the more general population of individuals who divorce and remarry was explored further in our surveys. The data we have collected, while not definitive, go a long way toward extending our knowledge of the impact of divorce and remarriage on grandparent-grandchild relations. (An ongoing study by Cherlin and Furstenberg is applying these findings to a national sample of disrupted families.)

The data from Central Pennsylvania confirm the impressions of previous investigators that relations between divorced adults and their former in-laws decay rapidly. While we have little firm information on the amount of contact between these parties prior to separation, there is no reason to believe that relations were generally strained. Only a small minority of the respondents (20 percent) reported that their in-laws had been opposed to their marriage; and two-thirds said that family relations were not a source of frequent disagreement during their marriage. The question did not distinguish between blood and affinial ties, but only a minority of the respondents reported that their in-laws had endorsed the breakup of the marriage (and not all because they sided with their son or daughter). Yet, at the time of the first interview less than a third of the sample said that they had received any form of assistance from their in-laws since the time of the separation—a period of about a year, on the average. Table 7.1 shows that slightly more than a quarter of the respondents reported that their parents-in-law had provided moral support; financial aid or services such as errands or assistance in the home were even less common.

These figures probably represent at least some drop-off from the level of aid provided by in-laws prior to the dissolution of the marriage. In any case, it is clear from the table that the modest amount of support provided by former in-laws trickled away almost entirely during the course of the study. By the follow-up, only 7 percent of the sample had received any form of assistance in the weeks prior to the interview.

Data on patterns of contact were not collected in the initial interview, but we did ask the participants in the follow-up to report how often they saw their in-laws. The amount of interaction is consistent with the flow of assistance. Fewer than 1 in 10 reported that they saw their former in-laws more than occasionally during the year. Information on support from and contact with other members of their ex-spouse's family revealed a similar pattern of disengagement.

Assistance from parents, particularly around the time of the separation, stands in stark contrast to the meager support provided by in-laws. It was found that 8 in 10 parents provided moral support, and nearly half lent financial aid and helped out by providing household services after the separation. We have no way of knowing whether assistance increased during the period immediately following the breakup of the marriage, nor can we trace precisely the slope of exchange during the initial interview and follow-up. Unfortunately, the questions in the first interview did not contain a fixed time interval but rather asked whether any support had been provided since separation. Consequently, we cannot assume that the drop-off of support reflected in Table 7.1 is more than an artifact of differences in question wording.

Even if we cannot discern changes in patterns of parental support over time, the table makes clear the differences between the extent of assistance provided to the divorced respondent from parents and from former in-laws. In the previous few weeks, most parents had provided some form of assistance. Financial aid was being supplied by 1 out of 7; more than 1 out of 4 furnished home services; and more than half were lending moral support. More than a third of the respondents saw their parents on at least a weekly basis (not shown), and half visited with them on the average of a least once or twice a month. Most of those with infrequent contact were separated geographically from their parents. While lack of proximity also created a barrier to frequent contact between respondents and their former in-laws, the relationship between proximity and interaction was not so clearcut. Many former in-

TABLE 7.1
Provision of Three Types of Support to Respondents by Parents, Former Spouse's Parents, and Current Spouse's Parents: Central Pennsylvania, 1977 and 1979

	Parents		Former Spouse's Parents		Current Spouse's Parents	
	1977	1979	1977	1979	1979	
Support						
Services	49% (205)	28% (164)	12% (205)	1% (165)	14% (83)	
Financial Aid	44% (205)	15% (164)	6% (205)	2% (165)	8% (83)	
Moral Support	82% (205)	55% (164)	28% (205)	5% (165)	27% (83)	
Index of Aid						
0 types	15% (205)	35% (165)	68% (205)	93% (166)	63% (84)	
1 type	25% (205)	37% (165)	20% (205)	5% (166)	25% (84)	
2 types	29% (205)	19% (165)	9% (205)	1% (166)	11% (84)	
3 types	30% (205)	8% (165)	2% (205)	0% (166)	1% (84)	

NOTE: For all respondents, for Centre County in 1979, the percentages of those having contact at least once or twice a month with parents, former spouse's parents, and current spouse's parents are as follows: with parents—56% (165); with former spouse's parents—10% (166); with spouse's parents—44% (84).

laws who lived close to one another had infrequent contact. Thus, it appears that social taboos and emotional distance rather than physical space separated individuals once related by marriage.

This conclusion is reinforced by one additional finding from the follow-up interview. When asked whether they still thought of their former spouse's parents as relatives, less than a quarter of the sample replied affirmatively. In response to a question addressed in the open-ended interviews, it was clear that divorced persons—although generally reluctant to acknowledge a kinship bond with former in-laws—had difficulty disassociating themselves completely from these former family members. "They are sort of related to me," we were sometimes told, "but I don't consider them to be my relatives."

The following exchange indicates the kind of detachment that occurred in many cases:

> INTERVIEWER: Were they [former in-laws] like friends to you . . . or . . . like . . . relatives or . . . what?
>
> WIFE: They were definitely relatives, they were terrific to me.
>
> INTERVIEWER: Yes, but now . . . ?
>
> WIFE: Now, they are nothing, but I don't want them to. . . . I don't really know if it's appropriate for them to . . . like send me a Christmas present. I don't and they didn't last year and I don't think they will. . . . I would say they are more like friends, but I don't really foresee any kind of continued relationship with them.

Most respondents had difficulty continuing to think of their former in-laws as part of their family. The length of their association, as measured by the duration of the respondent's marriage, was related to whether in-laws were considered to be relatives. Approximately a third of those married more than seven years, compared to 6 percent married less than seven years, still thought of their in-laws as kin. This relationship is partly explained by the fact that those married longer are more likely to have children. Only 11 percent of the childless respondents still thought of their former in-laws as relatives, compared to 32 percent of those with children.

Some respondents reasoned that even if their former in-laws were no longer related by marriage, they were still related, albeit indirectly, by blood.

> INTERVIEWER: What about your relationship with his parents?

> WIFE: I see them occasionally. They usually spend their winters down South and their summers here, but they travel in the summer and I don't get to see them often, although we do talk on the telephone.
>
> INTERVIEWER: Do you consider them still relations?
>
> WIFE: Well, I consider them as the kids' grandparents, you know.

Of the sample 85 percent reported that their children still regarded their noncustodial parent's family as their relatives. Except in rare instances when the dissolution of the marriage completely obliterated relations between the child and noncustodial parent, the affiliation of children with the family line of their nonresidential parent remained unbroken. Acknowledging these indirect ties, some respondents described their former in-laws as "my children's grandparents." In the next section, we shall explore what this affiliation actually implied in the way of contact with and support from the child's grandparents.

Relations Between Grandparents and Grandchildren After Divorce

Before describing the patterns of association between grandparents and grandchildren, we should take note of the fact that our data were supplied by divorced parents who, in some cases, could only estimate the incidence of the child's contact with their former spouse's kin. This is especially true when the parent and child were not living together or when the child's visits with the noncustodial parent's kin occur only when the child is already with that parent. Consequently, we suspect that our figures probably understate the true amount of interaction for parents may not always have been aware of times when their children got together with their grandparents.

The figures provided, even though imperfect, give us some insight into the impact of a divorce on the grandparent-grandchild relationship. The upper two rows of Table 7.2 show the amount of contact between the respondent's children and the children's two sets of grandparents, the parents of the custodial and the noncustodial parent. The data, all based on reports from a divorced individual, are presented separately for the children who live with the respondent and those who live elsewhere. (As the data only pertain to children under the age of 18, virtually all the children not living with the respondent are living with

TABLE 7.2
Amount of Contact Between Grandparents and Grandchildren, by Child's Residential Situation: Central Pennsylvania, 1979

	With R's Parents		With R's Former Spouse's Parents		With R's Current Partner's Parents*		With R's Partner's Former Spouse's Parents*	
	1	2	1	2	1	2	1	2
Children living in household	39% (72)	92%	4% (70)	64%	25% (40)	80%	—	—
Children living outside household	14% (57)	74%	35% (58)	90%	3% (38)	47%	—	—
Stepchildren living in household	18% (33)	79%	—	—	30% (34)	82%	3% (35)	63%
Stepchildren living outside household	3% (39)	4%	—	—	10% (39)	77%	—	—

* Includes both current spouses and current partners.

NOTE: Column 1 is the percentage with contact at least once a week, and column 2 is the percentage with contact at least occasionally (ritual contact).

the child's other parent.) As might be expected from national data, more than four out of five of the children living in the household were living with their mothers. (An even higher proportion of the mothers had been awarded custody but had permitted the child to reside with the father because they believed it to be in the child's interest.)

Although the sizes of the cells in Table 7.2 are not large, the results for the most part assume a consistent form. Children have more regular contact with the grandparents on the side of the parent who has custody than with those of the parent who does not. Almost 4 in 10 of the children see the former set of grandparents at least once a week and more than 9 in 10 see them at least occasionally during the year. Parents report roughly the same patterns of contact with the two respective sets of grandparents for children living outside the home (with their ex-spouse) as for those who live with them, thus offering some reassurance that their reports are not subject to substantial bias.

The pattern of contact between the child and his or her grandparents on the noncustodial parent's side indicates that separation and divorce definitely restrict the child's relations with extended kin. (Patterns of interactions with uncles and aunts closely parallel relations with grandparents.) Only a small minority of children maintain frequent contact with their noncustodial parent's family—that is, see them on at least a weekly basis. There is a distinct difference in the levels of grandparent-grandchild relations, which presumably results from the loss of active sponsorship from the parent who moves outside the home. Later on, when we take up the sources of variation in contact between grandparents and grandchildren, we shall examine the causes of attrition more directly.

Despite the obvious difference evident in the figures presented in Table 7.2, we should not overlook the important finding that most children regardless of their custodial status continue to see their grandparents at least occasionally during the year. Somewhere between two-thirds and three-fourths of the children see their noncustodial grandparents a few times a year or more, and about a third see them at least once or twice a month. Thus, divorce rarely breaks the ritual ties between the first and third generations although it usually removes grandparents from day-to-day or even week-to-week contact with grandchildren.

In the 1979 follow-up, we asked the parents who assumed responsibility for various child-rearing activities such as planning for summertime activities, supervising the child's homework, and so forth. In almost no instances were grandparents or other kin listed as significant caretakers, regardless of the parent's marital situation or the child's residential status. The only significant role assumed by grandparents— and then in only a small minority of cases (roughly one in 10)—was the contribution of financial support to the child. Grandparents on both sides of the family were about equally likely to lend such assistance. It seems that the curtailment of contact resulting from divorce may not severely slow the flow of material resources to the child from the senior generation, but that conclusion requires further consideration with a larger sample.

Although it would seem that divorce limits a grandparent's access to the child when the youngster is living with a former in-law as opposed to a daughter or son, the level of contact maintained and the amount of support furnished by the senior generation is considerable in light of the fact that relations between the first and second generation are so limited. Apparently, it is deemed appropriate for grandparents to see their grandchildren even when the grandparents have little or no relationship with the child's other parent. Whereas only 10 percent of the respondents report seeing their former mother- and father-in-law as much as once or twice a month, 36 percent say that their children visit with their grandparents that often.

From the open-ended interviews, we learned that some of these contacts occur when the child stays with his or her noncustodial parent. But frequently we were told that the residential parent makes independent arrangements for the children to see this set of grandparents on weekends, holidays, or during the summer. Parents often stress the importance to the child of maintaining ties with both lineages even when they themselves no longer feel any ties to the former spouse's family.

Remarriage and the Extension of Kinship Ties

Up to this point, we have spoken only of the contraction after divorce of intergenerational relations, specifically those with the noncustodial parent's parents. But as we noted earlier, most divorced persons remarry generally no more than a few years after the occurrence of a divorce. At the follow-up, 35 percent of the sample had remarried and another 13 percent were living with someone of the opposite sex. In the analysis that follows, we shall combine the individuals who cohabit with the remarried persons. Specific break-downs examining these subgroups revealed that their behavior was usually quite similar with respect to relations with extended kin. Indeed, the cohabiting couples had, if anything, more frequent contact with extended family members than did the remarried couples—perhaps because they often had younger children residing in the household. Consequently, we felt justified in treating the two groups similarly in the analysis.

Returning to Table 7.1, the lower panel of which presents data on relations between the respondent and her (or sometimes his) current spouse's or partner's parents, we discover that contact is only slightly lower with new in-laws than with biological parents. Of course, the specific nature of the interaction may not be adequately captured by these various measures. For example, it is possible that this pattern of relatively high interaction may be unwelcome or may be viewed with ambivalence by the respondents who may experience some stress in acquiring new kinship obligations. We can test this possibility by examining the response to a particular question included in the interview which asks chiefly about the process of assimilation into the family.

> People describe the process of meeting new family members in different ways. Would you say that meeting (spouse or partner's) relatives has been mostly comfortable and pleasant, somewhat uncomfortable, or unpleasant?

Only 16 percent of the sample replied that the process had been somewhat uncomfortable or unpleasant, an astoundingly low proportion in view of the fact that a goodly proportion are not even (yet) married to their partner and all were previously divorced. When asked to comment on how easily their family had accepted their spouse or partner, almost exactly the same proportion—17 percent—reported complications. Comments from the open-ended interviews corroborated the impression of a relatively smooth process of incorporation into the new family. One case study yielded the following account:

> INTERVIEWER: Was it easy for you to become a member of his family or is that something that is still going on? Do his parents accept you as a daughter-in-law?

WIFE: Oh, yes. They accepted me pretty much right away. We had no problems at all. I'm part of their family and I pretty much was so from the very beginning.
INTERVIEWER: What do you call them?
WIFE: Mom and Dad.
INTERVIEWER: And your relationship with her family [to husband]?
HUSBAND: Rather quickly. There was a little more difficulty because the kids were involved and there were a lot of questions as to whether the kids were being hurt by the divorce and I was part of that uneasiness, so some people took a little longer. By her mother, I think I was accepted rather quickly and by Bob, her stepfather, likewise. Some of the aunts and her one brother were skeptical because of the kids' situation.

It appears from all indications that most divorced persons who reenter relationships encounter little resistance from their new partner's family and the great majority appear to accept new family members quickly. When asked to list the persons closest to them, 14 percent of the persons who had reentered marriage or were living with someone mentioned an in-law, even though few had been in the relationship for as long as two years. As rapidly as relations were dissolved between former in-laws, they seem to have been established with their current partner's relatives. When it comes to family ties—the operating principle of marriage, no less so in second than in first relationships—is: "What is thine, becomes mine." In-laws seem to be replaceable and substitutable from one marriage to the next.

Relations Between Children and Their Stepgrandparents

We have already noted that the rules of kinship after divorce operate somewhat differently for children than for their parents. While children suffer some loss of contact and support, their relations with extended kin are not dissolved. Because children remain linked by blood to the family of the noncustodial parent, there is, in short, no expectation of replacement or substitution. Instead, the evidence points to a different principle at work: augmentation and expansion.

Looking again at Table 7.2, the lower two rows present information on the amount of contact between children and their stepgrandparents, the parents of their mother's or father's new partner. While not quite as high as the level of interaction among consanguineal grandparents and grandchildren, relations among affinal grandparents and grandchildren are nonetheless quite active. Of the respondents 3 out of 10 report that their stepchildren see their current partner's parents at least once a week, and slightly less than one-fifth say that their own parents have that much contact with their stepchildren. Only a small fraction of the respondents report the absence of at least ritual ties between their children and their partner's parents. Considering the fact that many couples in the sample are newly married or have only recently begun to live together, the amount of interaction is impressive.

Again, the data on contact may be a poor indicator of the nature of the relationship which develops between children and their stepgrandparents. It is possible that even though contact is high, the emotional relationship may be strained or perhaps somewhat forced. A substantial minority (35 percent) of the total sample (not shown) concurred with the opinion that "there are often problems in getting grandparents to accept stepchildren." However, those respondents with children who had actually remarried or had begun to live with their partners were less likely to subscribe to this view than those who remained divorced. This may indicate that the adjustment for children is less problematic than parents fear. In general, the remarried respondents are more optimistic about parenting and conjugal relations in remarriage than the still-divorced respondents.

Moreover, when asked to report on their children's experiences in meeting their partner's family, the respondents overwhelmingly described the process as comfortable and pleasant. Only 1 in 10 gave any indication of serious complications. Even more persuasive evidence of this relatively easy process of assimilation was the parents' testimony in the open-ended interviews.

> INTERVIEWER: So you've been pretty well accepted into his family?
>
> WIFE: Yeah. His mother has a chain around her neck of the letters that spell out her grandchildren's names and it was not very long before she had Rick's and Tim's spelled on there too. That indicates to me that his family has accepted us. You see, his mother plays the violin and she has given my son one of her violins and he was so very proud.
>
> INTERVIEWER: I see. So they are really treated like grandchildren?

WIFE: Oh, absolutely!

HUSBAND: And . . . her mother treats my boys in the same way and remembers them on their birthdays and when the boys have a chance to go up to Rockport with us, they'll go along and be very cordial to her mother.

INTERVIEWER: . . . you are parents and your father lives close by . . . so what's his relationship to [new wife's] kids?

HUSBAND: Well, all the kids call him Grandpap.

WIFE: The boys asked him . . . I guess they asked me first what they should call him. I said "you can call him whatever you want to" and they just said "well maybe he doesn't like us. We can't call him Pap like Hal and Ben [natural grandchildren] do." I said, "well, he does too like you. You guys ask him what you're allowed to call him." So they went down there and they were scuffing their feet along the floor and had their heads hung down and they [said] "what do we call you?" And he said "well, you can call me Pap." That made them really happy . . . He's very nice to them and he bought Christmas presents for them and everything. You can tell that there is still a coolness there. He does like them but it's not quite as close [as with his own]. It takes time. I think he is coming round.

In our earlier analysis of case studies, we learned that children did not experience a great deal of difficulty in accepting the notion that they could have more than two sets of grandparents. With some alacrity, they invented new kinship terms for the grandparents whom they annexed when remarriage occurred. While it was clear that emotional relations with these new adult figures did not run as deep as with the adults with whom they had long-standing relations, it is also the case that they seem to be able to make room for additional family.

To test whether children might feel any conflict as a result of the augmentation of their kinship network, we examined the pattern of associations with the different sets of grandparents. If there were a zero-sum principle at work here, we might expect to find a negative correlation in the patterns of contact: the more contact with biological kin, the less contact between stepkin. However, no evidence for this pattern emerged. Indeed, there was a slight positive association between the levels of visitation with the two sets of biological grandparents (on both sides of the family) and between the levels of contact with biological and affinal grandparents. If anything, what is implied by the data is a rule of equity, ensuring all grandparents access to the child.

The more any set of grandparents sees the child, the more others were afforded the same privilege. Obviously, in extreme situations, the child could be at risk of over-exposure to relatives. But we obtained little evidence that children were suffering from the effects of having to celebrate too many Thanksgivings or Christmases.

Sources of Differentiation in Grandparent-Grandchild Relations

The data presented thus far distinguish levels of grandparent-grandchild contact according to the child's residential location and, by implication, physical and emotional distance from his or her grandparents—biological and affinal. In this section we will look more directly at the conditions which govern the level of contact between the first and third generations, hoping to discover some of the sources of variation in intergenerational relations. Unfortunately, the size of our sample is so small that the results we shall present are only suggestive, and the reader should bear in mind the provisional nature of these findings.

We have already reported that participants in the Central Pennsylvania study expressed the belief that their children's relationships with their grandparents should be preserved even when they, themselves, ceased to have contact with their former in-laws. They continued to hold that view even when they or their former spouses entered a second marriage. We looked for differences in intergenerational contact among families where one or both parents remarried and those where the parents remained divorced until the follow-up. The marital status of the parent seemed to have little or no effect on the likelihood of either regular or ritual contact between the children and their grandparents.

While the parents' marital status had little consequence for the child's future relations with his or her grandparents, the nature of the parents' ties with one another and with the child was an important factor determining the child's kinship contacts. The inability of parents to establish a workable coparenting relationship seemed to interfere with intergenerational relations. As is shown in Table 7.3, children had less contact with their noncustodial parent's family when their parents had little contact with one another. The data at hand do not permit us to determine whether such parents were denying their former spouse's family access to the child or whether relations were so strained as a result of the divorce that the family made no attempt to maintain contact with the child. In either case, the child's relationship to the noncustodial parent's family withered because of a bitter divorce.

As one would expect, the absence of contact between the parents is associated with low levels of contact between the nonresidential parent and his (or sometimes her) child. Low contact between the children and their parents was the major reason children were unable to maintain ties with their grandparents. Over half of all children who saw their noncustodial parents on a regular basis (two or more times a month) had at least two visits with their grandparents per month on the noncustodial parents' side; one-fifth of those who had only occasional contact or no contact at all with the noncustodial parents visited with their grandparents that frequently (Table 7.3). For both practical and emotional reasons, extended kin are generally unable to bridge the gap created by the divorce without the sponsorship of the child's parent (their son or daughter). The absent parent relies heavily on his family at those times when he sees the child. Often the grandparents provide a site for visits with the child and lend assistance to the parent who may lack the wherewithal to care for the child. Thus, extended family are inevitably drawn into a significant supportive role when their child experiences a divorce and continues to assume childcare responsibilities. In the event that the parent abdicates his (or her) role, the grandparents are effectively shut out of a relationship with the child. In short, the fate of grandparent-grandchild relations is directly linked to the patterns of parent-child relations that evolve after divorce.

TABLE 7.3
Children's Contact with Nonresidential Parents by Contact Between Parents (Former Spouses), for Respondent's Residential and Nonresidential Children: Central Pennsylvania, 1979

	Parents' Contact	
	Twice a Month or More Often	Once a Month or Less Often
For residential children: Percentage of children seeing grandparents twice a month or more often	54%	26%
	(22)	(34)
For nonresidential children: Percentage of children seeing grandparents twice a month or more often	56%	20%
	(18)	(25)

Still, there were some circumstances in which the grandparents were able to overcome the lack of sponsorship by the nonresidential parent. From the case studies, we learned of instances in which in-laws maintained exceptionally close ties. More than a few respondents said that their in-laws had sided with them rather than their own child at the time of the divorce and thus avoided a breach of relations with their grandchildren (whether unintentionally or intentionally).

Physical proximity was an important condition affecting the overall level of contact. When the divorce resulted in residential movement of the former daughter- or son-in-law household, grandparents were much more likely to lose contact with their grandchildren. As Table 7.4 reveals, residential propinquity is an important determinant of the level of contact between grandparents and grandchildren. The data follow the same pattern we observed in Table 7.3, with a sharp difference occurring in the level of intergenerational contact according to the residential situation of the child. Nonetheless, it is clear that when the child's grandparents on his noncustodial parent's side live close by (within an hour of the respondent), they continue to see the child with some degree of regularity. When they do not, almost half lose even ritual contact (at least "occasional" contact). By contrast, the custodial parent's family rarely relinquishes ritual contact with the grandchild even when they are separated by physical distance.

Part of the reason that physical proximity is such an important predictor of continued intergenerational contact is that propinquity is also linked to preservation of ties between the child and the noncustodial parent following a divorce. If the respondent's family lived in the Centre County area, he or she was less likely to relocate following the divorce. When the noncustodial parents remained in the community, they were more likely to see their child on a regular basis and the grandparents, accordingly, had more access to the child. Our sample is not sufficiently large to explore with any quantitative precision the anomolous cases of noncustodial parents who had grown up in Central Pennsylvania but had moved away following the divorce, leaving the custodial parents living close to their former in-laws. Would physical proximity override the emotional distance created when the parent was not present to sponsor relations with his (or her) family? The handful of families in this situation revealed that the emotional distance created by divorce is a more significant barrier to the maintenance of intergenerational contacts than physical distance. Children tended to see the family of the noncustodial parent no more often than they saw the parent.

TABLE 7.4
Amount of Contact Between Grandparents and Grandchildren by Child's Residential Situation and Marital Status of Respondent, Controlling for Proximity of Grandparents: Central Pennsylvania, 1979

Within an Hour

	Contact with R's Parents				Contact with R's Former Spouse's Parents				Contact with R's Current Partner's Parents	
	R Unmated		R Mated		R Unmated		R Mated		R Mated	
	1	2	1	2	1	2	1	2	1	2
Children living in household	61% (18)	0%	74% (23)	4%	13% (16)	13%	5% (19)	32%	47% (19)	5%
Children living outside household	25% (16)	19%	13% (15)	13%	0% (12)	53%	13% (15)	7%	7% (15)	47%
Stepchildren living in household			46% (13)	0%					71% (14)	0%
Stepchildren living outside household			5% (20)	40%					0% (19)	26%

Outside an Hour

	Contact with R's Parents				Contact with R's Former Spouse's Parents				Contact with R's Current Partner's* Parents	
	R Unmated		R Mated		R Unmated		R Mated		R Mated	
	1	2	1	2	1	2	1	2	1	2
Children living in household	0% (10)	10%	0% (16)	17%	0% (12)	42%	0% (23)	48%	5% (21)	7%
Children living outside household	0% (7)	29%	11% (18)	44%	22% (9)	11%	20% (20)	15%	0% (23)	57%
Stepchildren living in household			0% (19)	37%					6% (17)	12%
Stepchildren living outside household			0% (16)	75%					10% (19)	32%

* Includes both current spouses and current partners.
NOTE: Column 1 is the percentage with contact at least once a week, and column 2 is the percentage with contact at least occasionally (ritual contact).

Suggestive as these findings are, however, they are based on too few cases to settle the matter.

Our final finding concerns the conditions which promote or inhibit the establishment of relations with stepgrandparents. As we noted earlier, the diminution of contact with the noncustodial parent's kin is more than made up for—at least in quantity—by the augmentation of new family members when the custodial parent enters a new relationship.

In looking for conditions that determine the level of contact between children and their stepgrandparents, we were struck by the absence of a difference between the remarried families and those couples who were cohabiting. We had expected that children would have far more contact with stepgrandparents than with parents of unmarried partners. No sizable differences were evident. We did find, however, that whether or not marriage occurred, the child was more likely to see his new relatives on a regular basis when the relationship was a long-standing one. Still, our data show a remarkable amount of contact even among families where the relationship was newly established—that is, in the previous year. These results substantiate the impression obtained from the case studies that extended relatives, and parents in particular, reach out to a stepgrandchild as a way of displaying support for or endorsement of their blood relation and help to reinforce his or her conjugal commitment.

As Table 7.4 shows, this process occurs more rapidly when the respondent's new in-laws are living close by. When distance is taken into account, children have almost as much contact with affinal grandparents as they have with biological grandparents. This fact is a remarkable testimony to the flexibility of the kinship system in adapting to divorce. Again, we must bear in mind that our measures do not permit us to draw any conclusions about the quality or emotional intensity of these contacts when they occur. Nevertheless, our data seem to support the contention that children whose parents divorce *and* remarry are likely to experience a rapid increase in extended kin. The tables only show part of that network. They do not indicate the child's contact with his affinal grandparents on the side of his noncustodial parent when that parent also remarries.

Conclusion

The data from Central Pennsylvania show that divorce disrupts ties between grandparents and grandchildren, particularly when such marital dissolution separates parents from their children. Physical and emotional distance between parent and child lessens the likelihood that relations will continue between the first and third generations. Except in rare instances when a noncustodial parent continues to preserve intimate bonds with his or her in-laws, grandparent-grandchild relations are almost entirely dependent on the custodial parent's mediating role.

Generally speaking, most noncustodial parents did continue to see their children on a fairly regular basis, and hence children had access to extended kin. Indeed, we discovered, in the open-ended interviews conducted in conjunction with the survey, that noncustodial parents—typically fathers—relied heavily on their parents for child-care assistance. These grandparents played a critical role in helping parents to manage unfamiliar or difficult child-care tasks when divorce occurred.

Accordingly, we might have anticipated relations between the first and third generations on the noncustodial parent's side to decline after remarriage. But there was no indication that grandparents were squeezed out of the picture when the crisis of divorce was over. So long as parent-child relations continued, which was often the case, the grandparent's position was not jeopardized by a second marriage. In fact, it might even be argued that extended kin, by their continued interest in the child, helped anchor the relationship between parent and child, although we have no specific data to test this supposition.

What remarriage does is not to subtract but to add on relatives. Contrary to our expectation, contact with biological and contact with affinal grandparents were not inversely related. Contact with stepgrandparents did not diminish the child's interaction with the family of his or her noncustodial biological parent. Earlier we speculated that parents may have felt committed to a principle of equity whereby all relatives have, at least theoretically, an equal claim to the child.

If such a principle exists, it would be of some importance to study its application in blended families. How do children manage relations with such an abundance of kin? Do grandparents perceive themselves as at a competitive disadvantage when the child has more than two family lines? How do parents reconcile the potentially conflicting claims on the child? These questions take us beyond the scope of our limited analysis, but the answers would furnish a wealth of information about changing kinship practices in American society.

David Schneider, in his seminal study of American kinship (1980) has suggested that an important feature of our system is its discretionary quality. Individuals have the option but never the obligation to define people as relatives when they are not closely related by blood. Kinship is often achieved rather than ascribed. Remarriage illustrates this principle by creating an enlarged pool of potential kin. To a large extent, it is up to the various parties involved to determine the extent to which potential kin will be treated as actual relatives.

Earlier, we observed that from a societal perspective remarriage has the consequence of distributing a small pool of children (given low rates of fertility) among a larger network of relatives. The family in the latter part of the twentieth century is extended more by marriage than by blood. Kinship relations may be more extensive if most people marry more than once, but they may also be more transitory if conjugal relations are ephemeral. Will this development alter the meaning of kinship and, in particular, lessen the intensity of kinship bonds? Only time and a good deal more empirical investigation will answer that question.

CHAPTER 8

Remarriage and Well-Being

Typically individuals who divorce undergo a range of social, psychological, and economic adjustments. Dozens of studies conducted over the last decade have confirmed Goode's (1956) earlier finding that divorce poses threats to the well-being of a substantial proportion of persons whose marriages are disrupted (Bloom et al., 1979; Chiriboga et al., 1978; Hetherington, Cox, and Cox, 1978; Rubin, 1979; Spanier and Casto, 1979; Thompson, 1981; Weiss, 1975). Despite the strong and consistent evidence of risk to such persons, little is known about the circumstances that may help moderate such risk. This chapter seeks to ascertain whether remarriage appears to be helpful in enhancing one's well-being following marital disruption.

Much of the growing body of research on divorce focuses on the immediate post-divorce transition; little information is available on long-term adjustment patterns. The well-documented range of problems encountered by those who divorce has not been examined in the context of changing personal and social circumstances after divorce. Many researchers and clinicians, as well as those who experience divorce, assume that remarriage following divorce may be a significant—if not *the* most significant—alteration in social circumstance influencing enhanced well-being. Our data allow for a reasonable assessment of the transition from divorce to remarriage.

Following a brief description of the transition from divorce to remarriage in our Central Pennsylvania sample, we seek to determine whether those who remarry relatively soon after a divorce fare better on several indicators of well-being than those who delay marriage for a longer interval or, in some cases, indefinitely following their divorces. The data also allow for comparisons of persons who have remarried, those who have not remarried, and those who are not remarried but are cohabiting. Additional comparisons are made by gender, presence or absence of children in the household, the quality of the marriage shortly before divorce, and by which member of the couple initiated the divorce.

Marital Status and Well-Being

The concept of well-being has not been defined adequately in the literature on divorce adjustment, but has come to serve as a general term, encompassing such concepts as happiness (Glenn, 1981), trauma (Goode, 1956), adjustment (Kitson and Raschke, 1981), impact (Thompson, 1981), health status (Renne, 1971), and stress (Chiriboga et al., 1978). Several studies have assessed various aspects of well-being by considering a range of indicators (Bachrach, 1975; Bloom et al., 1978; Campbell et al., 1976; Weingarten, 1980). In this study, we have chosen to use a rather general concept of well-being as our interest is to examine changes in an array of social, psychological, and health indicators. In addition to its longitudinal scope, the study is an advance over earlier work in that it assesses changes in reports of eight variables that collectively explore a broad spectrum of well-being.

Previous cross-sectional studies have presented inconsistent data as to whether remarried individuals are happier, better adjusted, or have a more positive health status than do individuals who have been divorced but have not remarried. In her probability sample of several thousand adults in California, Renne (1971) sought to examine Bernard's (1956) hypothesis that remarried persons are better adjusted than persons still divorced. Bernard speculated that individuals who fail to remarry are more likely to be physically ill or disabled, emotionally unstable, isolated or withdrawn, or prone to problems relating to the opposite sex. Bernard and Renne both argue that this is a reasonable speculation as remarriage is the preferred alternative (as evidenced by the fact that most persons remarry) and so those who do not remarry may be "unusual or abnormal in some way" (Renne, 1971: 345). Renne's data show, however, that people who had remarried were either more likely or as likely to report physical health problems as those who were still divorced.

Glenn (1981) draws on data from several social surveys conducted by the National Opinion Research Center and concludes that there is a remarkably high level of well-being among persons remarried after divorce. His findings are consistent with many other more specialized studies that have compared the well-being of individuals in different marital statuses. It should be pointed out, however, that Glenn's conclusion is based on a comparison of remarried with never-divorced, married individuals. The cross-sectional data used in his analysis were not specifically arranged for a comparison analogous to Renne's. Glenn is able to argue, nevertheless, that there are few long-term negative effects on the well-being of persons who remarry after divorce. Similarly, using data from another national cross-sectional survey, the National Survey of Modern Living conducted in 1976 at the University of Michigan, Weingarten (1980: 555) found little "to suggest that first-married and remarried people are substantially different in their *current* well-being and adaptation to marriage and parenting."

Despite the absence of empirical support from previous studies, there is nevertheless a widespread belief that well-being is greater among the remarried than among the divorced who have not remarried. Cross-sectional studies that allow for comparisons of married, divorced, and remarried samples unfortunately cannot be sufficiently sensitive to the complexity and range of transitions experienced by individuals who divorce. What appear to be transitional effects may in fact be attributable to initial differences in characteristics between remarried and still-divorced individuals. Furthermore, such studies may be misleading. The remarried group in cross-sectional samples may be from different first-marriage cohorts than the married or still-divorced groups. Such cohort differences can be influential when transitions pertaining to marriage, divorce, and remarriage are concerned (Spanier et al., 1975).

There is other evidence in the literature that suggests that some large-scale surveys using cross-sectional designs may not be picking up the diversity of experience related to divorce and remarriage, perhaps because of varying time intervals from the point of marital disruption. For example, Goode (1956) reported that 37 percent of the women he studied could be described as low trauma, 21 percent as medium trauma, and 42 percent as high trauma (the trauma index assessed behavioral deviations assumed to be sensitive to emotional and behavioral upheaval, such as poor health, sleeping difficulty, and low work efficiency). Spanier and Casto (1979), using a global assessment of post separation problems, found that 22 percent of their sample experienced severe problems while 78 percent had only mild or no problems.

Other writers point out that marital dissolution can provide relief after a stressful marriage, as well as opportunities for positive growth (Bloom et al., 1979; Brown, 1974; Rubin, 1979). Nager, Chiriboga, and Cutler (1977) show that there are periods of relative distress and relief following marital separation and that people vary in intensity, timing, and duration of their response.

Thus, as Kitson and Raschke (1981) point out, many questions about the dynamics of divorce adjustment have been raised but the "lack of longitudinal data on the divorce process has made the cause and effect relationships difficult to determine." The present study represents the first attempt to draw on longitudinal data—admittedly limited by the size and selectiveness of the sample—to assess the relative impact of remarriage on well-being.

Measures

Eight measures of well-being are used in this study. A range of indicators was selected for purposes of triangulation and because well-being is a broad and complex concept not adequately gauged by measures that tap single variables. Complete data were obtained on all measures of well-being for all 180 respondents. Six of the indicators of well-being—life satisfaction, satisfaction with health, suicide propensity, Cantril ladder life satisfaction, self-esteem, and affect balance—were explored in both the initial and follow-up interviews. A change score was computed for these measures. Two additional indicators of well-being—psychosomatic symptoms and changes in habits—were asked about in 1979 and were designed to elicit a retrospective report of change since the first interview.

For all eight variables, responses were collapsed and trichotomized into three categories: increase in well-being, no change in well-being, and decrease in well-being. The relative proportions of the respondents in each category vary, in part because of the total possible number of uncollapsed response categories. For example, the proportion of respondents showing no change in self-esteem is small compared to the proportion of respondents showing no change in suicide propensity. Most of this difference is accounted for by the substantially greater range of responses possible in the self-esteem measure. Such differences are an artifact of recommended coding procedures and in no way reflect on the adequacy of the findings or subgroup comparisons for each variable.

Life satisfaction was measured by the following item: "Taking all these things together (the work you do, where you live, your way of life, the things you do for enjoyment, your health), how would you say things are going for you these days? Would you say things are very good, pretty good, so-so, not too good, or not good at all?"

Satisfaction with health was assessed by this question: "Now we'd like to know how satisfied you are with your day-to-day life. Please tell me how satisfied you are with your health—extremely satisfied, somewhat satisfied, or not satisfied?"

Suicide propensity was measured by the item: "Sometimes people think about suicide after a divorce or separation. During the past two years, did you ever (1) make an attempt to take your own life? (2) make plans about how you would go about taking your life? (3) reach the point where you *seriously* considered taking your own life? (4) *think* about doing this even if you would not really do it?" Respondents answered yes or no to each item. This measure was designed as a Guttman scale item and scored by summing the number of affirmative responses.

To examine *psychosomatic symptoms,* the following item was presented: "I am going to read you a list of common conditions that people experience. Please look at this card and for each condition I mention, tell me whether this has increased, remained the same, decreased, or whether you never had this condition at all in the last two years: sleeplessness? nervousness? being tired? headaches? indigestion? allergies? colds, flu or fever? irregularity? moody spells? depression?" The number of affirmative responses determined the total psychosomatic symptoms score.

Changes in habits was measured by asking the following: "Please tell me if the following activities have increased, remained the same, decreased, or whether you never did this activity at all in the last two years: gambling? drinking with friends socially? drinking when you are alone? smoking? taking drugs with a physician's orders? taking drugs without a physician's orders?" An increase was coded as "+1," a decrease as "−1," and no change or "never engaged in the activity" as a "0." The six scores were summed to establish the total scale score.

In addition, three measures of well-being widely cited in the literature were used in this study: a scale of satisfaction developed by Cantril (1965), Bradburn's (1969) affect balance scale, and Rosenberg's (1965) self-esteem scale.

The Transition from Divorce to Remarriage

In what way do those who have remarried within four years of their separation differ from those who have not? There appear to be no significant relationships between marital status at the follow-up and age, income, occupational status, education, religion, religiosity, or gender. Furthermore, in our sample the presence or absence of children in the home is not related to marital status at the second interview. Of those with no children 30 percent had remarried by the second interview compared to 33 percent of those with children. The presence of children as an incentive for remarriage was found in a national survey analyzed by Koo and Suchindran (1980) but was not confirmed in the present study, undoubtedly because of the more restricted age range in our sample.

One variable in the present study does play a role in influencing marital status at the follow-up—attributions of who initiated the divorce. Of those who stated that they initiated the divorce 42 percent were remarried by Time 2 compared to only 30 percent of those who stated that their spouse was responsible for initiating the divorce. This finding may suggest that those who are surprised by the initial proposal to separate or who were less willing to see the marriage end may require a longer period of time before they are willing to consider remarriage. Alternative explanations—that the spouses who first suggest divorce are likely to have a potential new partner already identified, or that those who remarry relatively soon are stronger psychologically—are not supported by other analyses from the same data set (e.g., Spanier and Margolis, 1979).

During the first interview, respondents were asked how they felt about remarriage. Of those who said they had definite plans to remarry, 31 percent had not yet remarried by the second interview. Only 22 percent of those who were eager to remarry had done so, compared to 30 percent who said they were reluctant. Of the respondents who stated that they probably would never remarry 19 percent had done so by the time of the second interview. This finding suggests that the transition to remarriage is not generally planned or foreseen by many of the individuals who reenter matrimony, an observation we also made in Chapter 3.

It is evident from our data that there is exceptional diversity in the transition from marriage to divorce to remarriage. This is highlighted by the variations in living arrangements for both the children and adults involved. Some respondents had no children born during the first marriage living with them, have not remarried someone with children, and have borne no children following a remarriage. But other respondents may acquire children in any one of these three ways. In addition, there may be children from a previous marriage or stepchildren from a previous marriage of a new spouse or partner who do not live in the same household as the respondent. As we pointed out in Chapter 2, this complex array of parent, stepparent, custodial, or noncustodial relationships makes it difficult to characterize marital disruption and its aftermath easily. As the presence of children in the household may be especially relevant for understanding remarriage and because the dynamics of divorce and remarriage are known to affect men and women differently, the analysis in the next section considers variations by household living arrangements and gender.

Remarriage and Well-Being

Table 8.1 shows that divorced persons in general tend to report enhanced well-being following their divorce. Data for the total sample demonstrate that for four of the indicators studied—life satisfaction, Cantril ladder, self-esteem, and psychosomatic symptoms—there are significant improvements in well-being from Time 1 to Time 2. For three of the measures—satisfaction with health, suicide propensity, and changes in habits—no changes were evident over time for the sample as a whole. For one variable—affect balance—there was a decrease reported across the sample. Thus, although there is variability across indicators, the overall evidence available suggests a tendency toward enhanced well-being during the recovery period following divorce.

As it is plausible that changes in well-being might vary by age, perhaps suggesting the need for control for age in the analyses, age was correlated with each measure of well-being at the first interview and each measure of well-being at the second interview. The correlations were found to be uniformly low, with only one of eight correlations significant for Time 1 variables and no correlations significant for Time 2 variables. This finding argues against the need to control for age in subsequent analyses.

Our principal interest in Table 8.1 is on the differences between those who have remarried and those who have not within three to four years following their divorce. While there are some minor fluctuations from indicator to indicator, overall there is remarkable similarity between the distribution of percentages of increase, no change, and decrease for the remarried and formerly married respondents on each variable. A series of two-tailed t-tests were performed comparing the remarried and

TABLE 8.1
Summary of Changes Over Time in Selected Measures of Well-Being for Divorced Persons by Remarriage Status (in percentages)*

Well-Being Measure	Changes in Well-Being Between Time 1 and Time 2		
	Increase	No Change	Decrease
Life satisfaction			
Total sample (N = 180)	31.8	49.7	18.5
Remarried (N = 62)	33.9	48.4	17.7
Not remarried (N = 118)	30.8	50.4	18.8
Single (N = 94)	31.1	52.7	16.1
Cohabiting (N = 24)	29.2	41.7	29.2
Satisfaction with health			
Total sample	17.8	63.9	18.4
Remarried	11.4	70.5	18.0
Not remarried	20.3	61.0	18.6
Single	19.2	60.6	20.2
Cohabiting	25.0	62.5	12.5
Suicide propensity			
Total sample	22.8	56.7	20.5
Remarried	20.9	54.8	24.2
Not remarried	23.6	57.6	18.6
Single	23.5	59.6	17.0
Cohabiting	25.0	50.0	25.0
Cantril ladder			
Total sample	41.8	25.1	33.0
Remarried	50.0	25.8	24.2
Not remarried	37.6	24.8	37.6
Single	39.8	24.7	35.5
Cohabiting	29.2	25.0	45.8
Self-esteem			
Total sample	54.2	11.3	34.5
Remarried	51.7	13.3	35.0
Not remarried	55.5	10.3	34.2
Single	55.3	8.5	36.2
Cohabiting	56.5	17.4	26.1
Affect balance			
Total sample	41.8	10.6	47.6
Remarried	43.9	11.9	54.2
Not remarried	46.0	9.9	44.1
Single	48.3	7.9	43.8
Cohabiting	36.3	18.2	45.5

TABLE 8.1 (continued)

Well-Being Measure	Changes in Well-Being Between Time 1 and Time 2		
	Increase	No Change	Decrease
Psychosomatic symptoms			
Total sample	49.7	23.5	26.8
Remarried	54.1	19.7	26.2
Not remarried	47.5	25.4	27.1
Single	50.0	25.5	24.5
Cohabiting	37.5	25.0	37.5
Changes in habits			
Total sample	29.1	43.0	27.9
Remarried[a,b]	34.4	45.9	19.7
Not remarried	26.3	41.5	32.2
Single[a]	25.5	41.5	33.0
Cohabiting[b]	29.2	41.7	29.2

*All measures are coded so that a high score represents high well-being. Thus, those who show increases have improved on the measure of well-being.

a,b. Similar superscripts indicate instances where t-tests revealed differences significant at the .05 level.

formerly married groups on each measure of well-being. None of the tests was significant at the .05 level. Thus, we must conclude that there are no noteworthy differences in well-being changes between respondents who have remarried and those who have not.

To further elaborate this finding, we subdivided the unmarried respondents into two groups: those who were single but living with another adult of the opposite sex, and those who were not cohabiting. Analyses were repeated, comparing the remarried with the single group and the remarried with the cohabiting group. Only one significant difference was found among the eight indicators of well-being in each analysis. In both cases, the t-test was significant for the variable "changes in habits" ($p < .05$). The weight of the findings, however, again leads to the conclusion that there is virtually no relationship between remarriage status and changes in well-being.

As previous studies have suggested potential differences in the response to divorce according to gender and presence or absence of children in the household, the relationship of these circumstances to well-being was also examined. We speculated that if remarriage status were not predictive of changes in well-being (or vice versa) then perhaps there were other influential variables which alone or in concert with remarriage status played a significant role.

In our comparison of males and females, presented in Table 8.2, one is again struck by the consistently narrow differences across variables between males and females. No significant differences emerged in the series of t-tests. It should thus be concluded that men and women did not evidence significant differences in changes in well-being at the end of the postseparation period studied in this research.

When comparisons were made between individuals with and without children in the household in 1979, a consistent pattern was revealed, which suggests that there is no significant relationship between household composition and marital status. For only one variable— changes in habits—was there a significant difference, with individuals with children in the household reporting greater well-being than those with no children in the household.

These findings were elaborated further by cross-tabulating presence or absence of children in the home with each measure of well-being while controlling for marital status at the follow-up interview. Because it is conceptually unclear how cohabiting respondents should be treated in such a comparison, separate analyses were performed including cohabitors with single respondents, with remarried respondents, and as a distinct group. Thus, a total of 48 cross-tabulations was performed. It was shown that when marital status is controlled no consistent relationship exists between presence or absence of children in the household and well-being. None of the 48 cross-tabulations were significant at the .05 level, using a chi-square statistic. Our data therefore suggest that the presence of children in the household following divorce neither detracts from nor enhances well-being.

Exploring Other Influences

In addition to examining the role of remarriage status, sex, and presence or absence of children in the home on well-being, an exploratory analysis was conducted to seek leads as to other possible variables that might predict variations in well-being following marital dissolution. Zero-order Pearsonian correlation coefficients were calculated between each of the change scores for the indicators of well-being and five additional variables that tapped potentially influential demo-

TABLE 8.2
**Summary of Changes Over Time in Selected Measures of
Well-Being for Divorced Persons by Gender and Presence or Absence
of Children in the Household at Time 2 (in percentages)***

Well-Being Measure	Changes in Well-Being Between Time 1 and Time 2		
	Increase	No Change	Decrease
Life satisfaction			
Total sample (N = 180)	31.8	49.7	18.5
Males (N = 83)	31.3	50.6	18.1
Females (N = 97)	32.3	49.0	18.8
Children (N = 126)	30.4	51.2	18.4
No children (N = 54)	35.2	46.3	18.5
Satisfaction with health			
Total sample	17.8	63.9	18.4
Males	20.5	65.1	14.5
Females	14.6	63.5	21.9
Children	16.8	63.2	20.0
No children	18.5	66.7	14.8
Suicide propensity			
Total sample	22.8	56.7	20.5
Males	22.9	61.4	15.7
Females	22.7	52.6	24.7
Children	21.4	54.8	23.8
No children	25.9	61.1	13.0
Cantril ladder			
Total sample	41.8	25.1	33.0
Males	32.6	30.1	37.3
Females	50.0	20.8	29.2
Children	42.4	25.6	32.0
No children	40.7	24.1	35.2
Self-esteem			
Total sample	54.2	11.3	34.5
Males	53.1	8.6	38.3
Females	55.2	13.5	31.3
Children	53.6	9.6	36.8
No children	55.8	15.4	28.8
Affect balance			
Total sample	41.8	10.6	47.6
Males	34.7	9.3	56.0
Females	47.3	11.6	41.1
Children	43.3	10.0	46.7
No children	38.0	12.0	50.0

(continued)

TABLE 8.2 (continued)

	Changes in Well-Being Between Time 1 and Time 2		
Well-Being Measure	Increase	No Change	Decrease
Psychosomatic symptoms			
Total sample	49.7	23.5	26.8
Males	54.9	23.2	22.0
Females	45.4	23.7	30.9
Children	48.4	22.2	29.4
No children	52.8	26.4	20.8
Changes in habits			
Total sample	29.1	43.0	27.9
Males	30.5	42.7	26.8
Females	27.8	43.3	28.9
Children[a]	31.7	42.1	26.2
No children[a]	22.6	45.3	32.1

*All measures are coded so that a high score represents high well-being. Thus, those who show increases have improved on the measure of well-being.

a. Similar superscripts indicate instances where t-tests revealed differences significant at the .05 level.

graphic and social correlates of well-being. Age, education, work satisfaction, kin support, and marital adjustment were considered. Marital adjustment was measured by asking the respondents to complete the Spanier (1976) dyadic adjustment scale in relation to the months shortly before their final separation. Kin support was measured by a composite index assessing overall support from kin following the separation. Education and work satisfaction used reports given at the time of the second data collection.

None of the five variables were related consistently to changes in any of the measures of well-being. Only 2 of the 40 correlations examined were significant—an inverse relationship between education and self-esteem ($p < .01$), and an expected positive relationship between work satisfaction and life satisfaction ($p < .01$). No other relationships were significant at the .05 level, suggesting that none of the five variables examined is related to well-being following marital disruption. In contrast to the present findings, previous studies (Koo and Suchindran, 1980; Spanier and Glick, 1981) have reported significant variations in divorce-related experiences by age. We again suspect that the absence of such a finding in the present study may be related to the relatively narrow age range of the sample.

Finding no apparent predictors of change in well-being, we explored additional possible explanations for these findings. It is plausible that individuals who report that they initiated the divorce could be expected to report greater well-being both during the initial postseparation period and at the time of the follow-up interview than those who reported that their spouse initiated the divorce. In a cross-tabular analysis that excludes the 13 percent of the sample who reported that the decision to divorce was a mutual one, this hypothesis found little support. Only two cross-tabulations between who initiated the divorce and a well-being indicator were significant, using a chi-square statistic (psychosomatic symptoms at Time 1 and life satisfaction at Time 2). The weight of the evidence therefore suggests that who initiated the divorce is not a useful predictor of well-being.

Irrespective of *changes* in well-being, we sought to determine whether an individual's well-being shortly following the final separation might predict his or her likelihood of remarriage by the second interview. Cross-tabulations were performed between each of eight measures of well-being at the first interview and marriage status at the follow-up interview. Significant relationships, using a chi-square statistic, were found in three cases. Individuals who were more likely to remarry were those who at Time 1 reported higher life satisfaction ($X^2 = 11.4$, df = 2, p < .01), greater affect balance ($X^2 = 13.6$, df = 2, p < .01), and a higher Cantril ladder score ($X^2 = 4.8$, df = 1, p < .05). Thus, limited evidence allows us to suggest that although well-being does not appear to change following an alteration in one's marriage status, the likelihood that one will remarry following divorce may be related to one's well-being during the immediate postseparation period.

For those who had remarried, we examined two other questions: Is length of remarriage related to well-being at the second interview, and is the quality of the remarriage related to well-being? Using zero-order Pearsonian correlations, we find that length of remarriage is not significantly correlated with any measure of well-being. With regard to the quality of the remarriage, however, we find substantial evidence that well-being and marital quality (measured by the dyadic adjustment scale) are significantly related. As shown in Table 8.3, six of eight measures of well-being are positively related to marital adjustment. Thus, we conclude that among individuals who have remarried reports of well-being are greatest for those whose marriages are well adjusted.

TABLE 8.3
Zero-Order Pearsonian Correlations between Marital Quality and Eight Measures of Well-Being for Remarried Respondents at Second Interview

Variable	Correlation with Marital Quality	Significance
Life satisfaction	.55	.001
Satisfaction with health	.15	*
Suicide propensity	.28	*
Cantril ladder	.42	.01
Self-esteem	.45	.01
Affect balance	.40	.01
Psychosomatic symptoms	.29	.05
Changes in habits	.30	.05

*Not significant at .05 level.
NOTE: N = 47

Conclusions

These data show that well-being is not significantly altered following the dissolution of a marriage by any circumstances that can be identified readily. Clearly, there is considerable individual variation in well-being during the postseparation period. This study demonstrates, however, that remarriage alone is not significantly related to enhanced well-being. Most individuals report greater well-being three to four years after their final separation regardless of their marital status at Time 2. Moreover, there appear to be no significant differences between men and women or between individuals with children in the household and individuals without children in the household.

Undoubtedly, then, variation in well-being during the postseparation period must be attributed to as yet undiscovered influences that await further study. Our data at least allow us to question earlier reports and a belief that may have become a common wisdom—remarriage following divorce is, in general, a precursor to enhanced well-being.

An important serendipitous finding, however, indicates that the likelihood of remarriage following divorce may be related to one's well-being during the postseparation period; individuals with the greatest well-being were most likely to be remarried three to four years after their final separation.

Furthermore, among those who remarry the quality of the remarriage is positively related to well-being. This discovery may help account for the absence of an overall difference in well-being between divorced and remarried persons. Our findings strongly indicate that remarried persons are heterogeneous, as is the remarriage experience. When second marriages are successful and rewarding, individuals typically fare better, it appears, than they would if they remained divorced. The individual's marriage experience is viewed through the lens of his or her past biography of failure, and the current evaluation of well-being is enhanced. Just the opposite effect may occur when a remarriage experience is unrewarding. An individual's sense of initial failure is reinforced and, in all likelihood, his or her sense of well-being is reduced. Thus, the remarriage experience may have a conditional impact on personal adjustment. Although it cannot be said that remarriage generally enhances psychological well-being, it clearly does so in certain cases. This may account for the popular impression that remarriage improves a divorced person's psychological well-being. We suspect that for every person who benefits from a remarriage, there is another whose psychological status is adversely affected by an unsuccessful remarriage.

It can be reasoned that some cross-sectional studies have shown remarried persons to have greater well-being than divorced persons because (1) the remarried may have had a longer time to recover from the divorce; (2) many of the unsuccessful remarriages have already ended in divorce and are thus not reflected in the data on remarried persons; and (3) remarriage tends to be selective of the psychologically healthier persons. This line of reasoning would permit an interpretation that suggests that persons who remarry after divorce and have successful remarriages have a remarkably high level of well-being, whereas those who fail in the remarriage are in the typical case likely to fare very poorly in terms of their psychological and social well-being.

One final point should be made in regard to our observation that divorced individuals, whether remarried or not, generally experience a greater sense of well-being over time. Individuals who remain divorced no doubt compare their current social and psychological state to their immediate postdivorce experience. By contrast to their former situation, they are likely to sense an improvement. Most experienced considerable distress initially and, over time, have come to see certain advantages in their present situation compared to their previously unhappy marriage.

In sum, divorced persons and remarried persons may themselves use different reference points to judge their current well-being. Divorced persons may compare themselves to a low point just after they separated, while remarried individuals may use as a baseline the period before remarriage when they were still divorced. In some sense, then, this makes their experiences not entirely comparable. It is also important to note that divorced people today, in contrast to the population studied a generation ago, probably experience less distress over time. They inhabit a world where singlehood is no longer as disreputable a status as it was a generation ago.

CHAPTER 9

The Risk of Dissolution in Remarriage

Why are the individuals who remarry following divorce more likely to experience marital dissolution than persons in their first marriages? In an imaginative synthesis of existing research evidence, Andrew Cherlin has proposed an explanation (Cherlin, 1978, 1980). The higher rate of instability in marriages following divorce, he believes, can be traced to the "incomplete institutionalization of remarriage," or to the absence of commonly understood guidelines for coping with problems of married life. According to Cherlin,

> problems are created by a complex family structure which cannot occur in first marriages. Because of the lack of social regulation, each family must devise its own solutions to these problems. The work of establishing rules increases the potential for conflict among family members, and the increased conflict, in turn, increases the likelihood of divorce [1980: 640].

Cherlin's explanation is an attractive one, for it nearly avoids a commonplace assumption that has eluded empirical confirmation—that the causes of conjugal breakdown are to be found in the malfunctioning personalities of the marital partners. Instead, he reminds us of the essential wisdom of C. Wright Mills's observation that "the problem of a satisfactory marriage remains incapable of purely private solutions" (1959: 10). Moreover, in drawing together findings from the slender empirical literature on reconstituted families, Cherlin is able to identify a number of specific areas of normative confusion: the absence of a commonly accepted terminology for members of the kinship network; the lack of guidelines for interaction between former spouses and among former and current partners; the overlapping and competing interests of parents; and the problem of controlling the possibility of incest among members of the stepfamily.

All of these special difficulties, he argues, impose strains on the reconstituted family, increasing the risk of conjugal breakup.

Although widely cited in the recent literature on remarriage, Cherlin's thesis has received little direct empirical scrutiny. In this chapter, we examine Cherlin's argument and present some preliminary data testing the hypothesis linking the "incomplete institutionalization of remarriage" and the higher rate of redivorce among couples in second marriages. Our findings do not support Cherlin's interpretation, and we offer a different explanation to account for the differential patterns of divorce between first and second marriage.

Examining the Hypothesis of Incomplete Institutionalization

Cherlin's hypothesis is constructed from three discrete observations. First, he points out that there is incomplete institutionalization of remarriage after divorce. Second, there is a distinctly greater risk of divorce for higher order marriages than for first marriages. Third, the risk of divorce following remarriage can be traced to the stress created by "problem[s] unknown to other types of families." In the discussion that follows, we do not dispute the first observation and generally concur with the second, although (as we shall show) most accounts of the magnitude of differences between divorce probabilities for first versus subsequent marriages are somewhat exaggerated. Our major criticism deals with the third observation—specifically with the evidence supporting the *link* between the incomplete institutionalization of remarriage and higher rates of divorce among previously married couples.

We believe that it is essentially correct to conclude that reconstituted families are confronted with a great deal of normative confusion. Until very recently, family researchers scarcely noticed the reconstituted family. When they did, with few exceptions, they failed to see its unique properties, preferring to believe that remarried families more or less reproduce the form of the nuclear family. Recent research belies this image (Furstenberg, 1979).

As we reported in Chapter 3, couples in the Central Pennsylvania study typically experience a fundamentally different process when they marry a second time owing to the fact that they must distance themselves from their first spouse, must revise marriage expectations and, frequently, in the event that they have children, must live in close proximity to their former spouse. In the qualitative case studies, almost all remarried couples are shown to believe that their biography of marital failure had an important bearing on their approach to marriage. More suspicious of romantic love, more cautious in selecting a mate, and more willing to enter marriage with less lofty expectations, many remarried people are inclined to believe that they are a breed apart.

Conceptions of parenthood and patterns of parenting also underwent considerable change in the process of moving from one marriage to the next. The complexities of coparenting were evident enough for separated and divorced couples; remarriage introduced further complications, sometimes disturbing fragile arrangements that had been painfully worked out at the time the marriage was disrupted. In addition to compelling some formerly married couples to renegotiate child-care understandings, remarriage ushers in a new set of actors who share, to a greater or lesser extent, the responsibilities and rewards of parenting. The data from Central Pennsylvania presented in Chapters 4 and 5 provide a great deal of support for Cherlin's assumption that stepfamily relations can be confusing and anomalous.

As cultural guidelines governing dealings between a biological and a sociological parent are lacking, the parties in the study were left to their own devices for developing a workable division of labor. The most conspicuous pattern was that there was no prevailing pattern. In some cases, the nonresidential parent migrated from one family to the next, severing emotional ties to biological children and investing instead in relations with stepchildren; in other families, the noncustodial parent divided loyalties, balancing obligations to biological children and to stepchildren; in still others, the outside parent played a marginal role as a stepparent and continued to devote primary attention to the children from the former marriage. As pointed out in an earlier chapter, tensions and misunderstandings over these arrangements were common between former partners as well as within current marriages because decisions could not always be made in concert with all interested parties.

Another potential source of strain in stepfamilies can be traced to the restructuring of kinship ties that inevitably takes place after divorce and remarriage. Again, the operating principle appears to be that individuals may retain or relinquish kin after divorce on a discretionary basis. Whether they continue to treat former in-laws as relatives is likely to depend on whether children continue to link ex-affines, how long the marriage endured, and how close the kinship connection was before the marriage was dissolved. It is clear that a significant minority of persons retain some relationship with their former in-laws, both for the sake of the children and because they do not wish to sever long-standing ties. Potentially, these affiliations could jeopardize the development of strong bonds with kin acquired by a new marriage; in fact, however, this seemed to occur rarely. Nonetheless, the size and complexity of kinship networks among remarried persons presented certain problems in managing the child's various responsibilities to several sets of grandparents, uncles, aunts, and cousins. The kinship world surrounding stepfamilies is complex and places parent and child in an arena of competing demands which can be emotionally exhausting.

In sum, there seems to be little reason to question Cherlin's assumption that remarriage makes family life more difficult if only because it is more intricate, less predictable, and far more variegated. As an emergent family form, remarriage inevitably provides less order, security, and certainty than the initial entry into marriage, which itself has become less institutionalized in the past decade. Thus, it is hard to dispute Cherlin's claim that individuals living in blended families face challenges not ordinarily experienced by members of conventional nuclear arrangements.

But do these challenges inevitably raise the risk of marital dissolution? At first glance, it would certainly seem so. As Cherlin points out, several estimates of the lifetime probability of divorce comparing couples in first marriages and remarriages consistently reveal that first marriers have a lower rate of divorce than remarriers, but the differential is modest. A recent estimate by James Weed (1980) using divorce registration data shows that 47.4 percent of first marriages eventually end in divorce compared to 48.9 of remarriages.

These relatively trivial differences conceal the true story, for remarried couples have less opportunity to divorce because of a higher mortality rate due to the fact that they are older when they begin marriage than couples entering marriage the first time. If death were not a possibility, the difference in Weed's study would be somewhat larger: 46 percent of first marriages would end in divorce by the twenty-fifth anniversary compared to 53.5 of remarriages. Still, these differences are not very great. (These figures correspond rather closely to estimates by Paul Glick, 1983, based on data from the 1980 Current Population Survey. Glick calculates that 49 percent of men and women will divorce, and 54 percent of women and 61 percent of men who remarry will divorce a second time.)

The pattern of divorce among the two populations is, however, strikingly different. Remarriages break up far more quickly than first marriages. Five years after entry in marriage, formerly married persons have almost a 50 percent greater probability of divorce; at 10 years, the risk of divorce among remarriers is 20 percent greater; by 25 years, it is less than 10 percent greater.

Cherlin might interpret this pattern as confirmation that the initial shock of living in an anomalous family situation creates a rapid and intolerable strain on the marriage, accounting for the rapid disintegration of the relationship. Later in this chapter we shall offer an alternative explanation to account for the differentials in the timing of divorce between first marriages and remarriages.

Other existing evidence on quality of first and second marriages can be consulted to establish whether remarriage is more hazardous. Some studies of marital happiness have revealed slightly higher rates of disenchantment among previously married individuals than among persons in their first marriage (Campbell et al., 1976; Glenn and Weaver, 1977; Renne, 1971; Weingarten, 1979). However, when careful controls are introduced in such studies measuring marital happiness, the differences that remain are usually insignificant and persist only for certain subgroups of the population. For example, women tend to be less happy in second marriages while men are more content (Glenn and Weaver, 1977; White, 1979).

In sum, while the overall pattern favoring the stability and quality of first marriages can be documented, the magnitude of the differences suggests that contrasted with such factors as age at marriage, premarital pregnancy, and economic status, previous marital history is a weak predictor of marital stability. Indeed, given the added stresses placed on the reconstituted family, it is surprising that remarried couples are not even more prone to dissolution. This point anticipates an observation that we shall return to in our conclusion: There may be some advantage to looking for the adaptive mechanisms in reconstructed families rather than focusing exclusively upon their higher risks of marital failure.

The crux of Cherlin's argument, however, rests not so much on the overall difference in divorce rates between first and previously married couples but rather in the presumed difference between previously married couples who are childless and those who bring children with them as they enter their second unions. As Cherlin (1978: 642) tells us,

The lack of institutional support is less serious when neither spouse has a child from a previous marriage. In this case, the family of remarriage closely resembles families of first marriages, and most of the norms for the first marriage apply. But when at least one spouse has children from previous marriage, family life often differs sharply from first marriages.

Thus, Cherlin expects to find sizable differences in the probability of divorce between persons in second marriage who begin their remarriage with ready-made families and those who remarry without children.

On the face of it, his reasoning is quite persuasive. In fact, any distinctive features of reconstituted families are not evident unless children bind the previously married couple together. Both qualitative and quantitative information from the Central Pennsylvania study reveal that social, psychological, and economic relations are much more likely to continue when the previously married couple has young children than when they are childless or have grown children.

Yet, the evidence that children from a previous marriage heighten the risk of divorce in second marriages is not very compelling. The data Cherlin cites from the National Longitudinal Surveys of Mature Women (Cherlin, 1977) produce only qualified support for the prediction. But as he notes in his initial analysis, he was unable to distinguish whether the children present in the household were from the previous or the current marriage or both.

In support of his hypothesis, Cherlin relies heavily on a finding reported by Becker et al. (1976, based on a reanalysis of the Survey of Economic Opportunity) that the presence of children from a previous marriage increased the probability of redivorce while children from the current marriage had just the opposite effect. The findings of Becker and his colleagues seem to fit nicely with Cherlin's argument that stresses will be significantly greater when the new marriage retains existing children.

Without dismissing the results reported by Becker et al., it is important to note a couple of limitations in their analysis. The data were collected in 1967 and do not include the experiences of more recent cohorts of remarriers; the objective conditions and subjective meaning of divorce and remarriage may be changing as divorce and remarriage become more common. A more serious difficulty is that the analysis by Becker and his colleagues does not control for relevant variables that might influence the direction of the results. For example, older women with many children may fare less well in the remarriage market and may have to settle for spouses with lower earning potential. Finally, the regression coefficients presented by Becker et al. essentially mask the critical question addressed by Cherlin. If children from a previous marriage engender conflict and increase the probability of conjugal strain, then the mere presence or absence of any children—not the number of children—ought to be the more crucial condition. Ideally, we would prefer to see a breakdown that reflects this critical distinction rather than a regression coefficient that gives equal weight to each additional child in predicting marital success and thus conceals more than it reveals.

James McCarthy (1978) provides such data. In a reanalysis of the 1973 National Survey of Family Growth, McCarthy shows comparisons of the probability of dissolution in first and second marriages,

TABLE 9.1
Cumulative Probabilities of Dissolution of Marriage by Presence of Children at Start of Second Marriage (for whites)

	Years	No Children Present	At Least One Child Present
Cumulative probability of separating after marriage: By years of marriage and presence of children	1	.023	.045
	2	.049	.091
	3	.079	.115
	4	.130	.145
	5	.174	.201
	10	.248	.282
Cumulative probability of divorcing after separation: By years of marriage and presence of children	1	.663	.551
	2	.821	.744
	3	.821	.815
	4	.864	.868
	5	.934	.868
Cumulative probability of divorcing after marriage: By years of marriage and presence of children	1	.012	.024
	2	.025	.049
	3	.052	.083
	4	.090	.104
	5	.146	.137
	10	.197	.236
(N)		(3,408)	(34,658)

SOURCE: From McCarthy, "A Comparison of the Probability of Dissolution of First and Second Marriages," *Demography*, Vol. 15, pp. 345-359, © 1978 by Population Association of America. Reprinted by permission.

subdivided by relevant demographic characteristics. Among the variables McCarthy examines is the presence or absence of children in the home at the start of second marriage. McCarthy constructs a series of life tables—one of which we have reproduced as Table 9.1—showing separately the probability of separation and divorce for remarried couples who were childless and those who had at least one offspring living in the home when they remarried.

As is apparent from an examination of McCarthy's life tables, the results provide only weak support for Cherlin's hypothesis. The probability of separation and divorce is only slightly higher in households with children at the start of the second marriage compared to those without children. Moreover, the differences appear to be concentrated in the first few years of remarriage; thereafter, the differential either disappears or is greatly attenuated. One might argue, nonetheless, that children from previous unions do not deter separation and divorce as do children from a present marriage and may slightly heighten the risk of conjugal dissolution; however, such an effect is barely noteworthy.

Further Tests of the Hypothesis

Additional evidence casting doubt on Cherlin's hypothesis that second marriers with children run a greater risk of separation and divorce is available from the June 1975 Current Population Survey, in which marital histories were obtained. The information available does not permit the construction of life tables, but we are able to present cross-tabulations showing the current marital status of remarried women by the number of children ever born. Although these data do not allow us to determine whether the children were from a first or second marriage, the comparisons between childless women and women with children are nonetheless informative. As shown in Table 9.2, childless women were just as likely as women who had children to separate and/or divorce after a second marriage. Moreover, this pattern of similarity, shown by age in Table 9.2, also holds up for various education and race subgroups. Given the short intervals between remarriage and redivorce and the generally lower levels of fertility in second and higher order marriages, it is likely that the great majority of the children ever born to the women whose marital histories are presented in Table 9.2 were produced before reentering marriage

TABLE 9.2
Current Marital Status Among Women Ever Remarried by Children Ever Born and Mother's Age
(numbers in thousands)

Age of Mother	30-39				40-49				50-59			
Number of Children	0	1	2	3+	0	1	2	3+	0	1	2	3+
Married	78	256	399	780	131	225	364	846	193	283	338	689
(percentage)	82.1	82.1	84.9	80.6	81.3	80.1	75.5	77.3	69.4	73.5	71.7	73.1
Widowed	0	2	8	17	8	8	13	1052	38	35	55	114
(percentage)	0	0.6	1.7	1.8	5.0	2.8	2.8	4.8	13.7	9.1	11.7	12.1
Separated/Divorced	17	54	63	171	22	48	102	196	47	67	78	139
(percentage)	17.9	17.3	13.4	17.6	13.7	17.1	21.7	17.9	16.9	17.4	16.6	14.8
Total	95	312	470	968	161	281	469	1094	278	385	471	942
(percentage)	100	100	100	100	100	100	100	100	100	100	100	100

SOURCE: June 1975 Current Population Survey, U.S. Bureau of the Census.

(Spanier and Glick, 1980a), especially among the older women in the sample. And yet, the rate of divorce and separation from second marriages was not elevated for women with children, paralleling the results obtained by McCarthy.

A preliminary indication of the strain created by the presence of children from a different marriage on conjugal relations in the new marriage is provided by the data collected in Central Pennsylvania. We were able to compare the quality of marital relations among individuals who were childless at the time of their remarriage with those who brought children into their second marriage. We subdivided the latter group into two family types—a simple form in which the remarried couple is parenting *only one* set of children (his *or* hers), and a complex form in which the couple is raising at least *two* sets of children (his *and* hers, and sometimes theirs as well).

Although the number of cases is small, we were unable to detect any sizable or significant differences in the degree of marital happiness reported by the three nonparent and parent subgroups in our sample of remarried persons. Individuals who began their second marriages with children were just as likely as those who did not to express high levels of satisfaction with their second unions.

The result was the same when we examined the specific subscales of the measure of marital quality that tapped conflict and disagreement in the marriage. As Table 9.3 reveals, conjugal conflict was not less evident in childless families or in the less complex family type than in the more complex blended families. The strains of married life do not, then, appear to be aggravated by the presence of stepchildren.

Several other findings lead us to the same conclusion. All respondents, regardless of their family situation, were asked their views on the difficulties of raising stepchildren. The results revealed no consistent differences. People actually facing the challenges of living in reconstituted families were no more likely to subscribe to the view that it was more stressful to raise children in stepfamilies compared to those who answered the questions hypothetically.

The table also shows that parents of children younger than 18 did experience more fatigue than childless respondents. But no differences appeared on this item between the two parent subgroups. Parents dealing with two sets of children—their biological children and stepchildren—were no more likely to say that they were tired and worn out than those who were raising only one set of children. Further, parents in complex families were just as likely to evaluate their

TABLE 9.3
Indicators of Marital Quality and Child-Rearing Attitudes,
and Assessments by Family Type,
Central Pennsylvania, 1979 (in percentages)*

				Stepfamily Type	
			No Children under Age 18	Simple: One Set of Children	Complex: Two or More Sets of Children
A.	Indicators of marital quality (from Spanier's dyadic adjustment scale)				
	Marital satisfaction	(low) 0	33	43	21
		1	33	28	41
		(high) 2+	35	30	38
	Marital disagreement	(low) 0	32	24	13
		1	16	29	20
		2	32	19	27
		(high) 3+	20	27	40
	Reported conflict in marriage	(low) 0	21	14	7
		1	17	26	17
		2	17	22	30
		3	25	31	27
		(high) 4+	21	8	20
B.	Attitudes about stepparenting (percentage in agreement)				
	"Generally, remarried persons have more difficulty disciplining their spouse's children than their own children."		68	60	76
	"Remarried parents usually favor their own children over their spouse's children."		50	62	41
	"Remarried couples often have problems raising children because they don't share the same standards."		36	48	57
	"Raising children part-time is much more difficult than raising them full-time."		66	78	77
	"It is harder to be a stepparent than to be a natural parent."		60	67	60
	"Children frequently play their natural parents and their stepparents off against each other."		76	67	66
	(N)		(43)	(61)	(30)

(continued)

TABLE 9.3 (continued)

	Stepfamily Type	
	Simple: One Set of Children	Complex: Two or More Sets of Children
C. Assessment of child-rearing experience in stepfamilies		
Extent of fatigue from the burdens of raising a family:		
most of the time	8	10
sometimes	39	43
rarely	28	40
never	25	7
Inability to control feelings with risk of hurting children:		
sometimes	12	3
hardly ever	31	37
never	56	60
Self-evaluations as parents:		
excellent	8	0
good	57	77
fair	35	23
(N)	(61)	(30)

*Cases with missing information or "don't knows" were excluded from the calculations producing minor variations in the size of the subgroups.

parenting skills as good or excellent as parents in simple families. And finally, parents in blended families were slightly less likely to say that they lost control of their feelings to the point where they thought that they might hurt their child. In sum, it does not seem to be the case that remarried persons with complex child-rearing demands experience a higher amount of family strain.

Perhaps the fact that many of our couples were still in the early stages of remarriage might account for the absence of the effect that Cherlin predicts. Yet, recalling the data on the pattern of divorce presented earlier, the strains resulting from child-rearing difficulties ought to be immediately visible if they are an important determinant of marital instability because the difference between first married and remarried couples is greatest in the first few years of marriage. In any event, controlling for the length of the current marriage did not alter any of the results reported above.

Until further evidence becomes available, it would be prudent to view Cherlin's hypothesis with skepticism. Most of the available data do not seem to confirm his prediction that second marriages with children from first marriages are markedly less likely to succeed. But if he is incorrect in his specific hypothesis, what can be the explanation for the general findings that second marriages are somewhat less likely to survive than first marriages?

An Alternative Hypothesis

We believe that the answer lies not in the incomplete institutionalization of remarriage but instead in certain qualities of those who remarry and the remarriage process. In a critical response to Cherlin's article, Terrence Halliday (1980) argues that the pools of first marriers and remarriers are not the same—principally because first marriers include a substantial (although unknown) number of individuals who are "stayers," people who are opposed to divorce on the basis of their religious beliefs. By contrast all remarriers can be classified as "movers," if only because they have demonstrated their willingness to move from one marriage to another.

Replying to Halliday's argument, Cherlin concedes that religious beliefs and opposition to divorce are correlated with patterns of marital disruption although the correlation is not nearly so great as Halliday contends. Yet, given the modest differential in the risk of divorce, the composition of the two marriage pools would not have to be very great to account for the difference.

Our argument goes one step beyond Halliday's. We believe that people who have divorced not only may be less committed to marital continuity for its own sake but also that the experience of divorce makes individuals more averse to remaining in an unhappy marriage or remarriage. Stated differently, the diverse population of remarried individuals shares at least one characteristic in common; namely, they have demonstrated a willingness or at least a capacity to consider divorce as an alternative to continuing an unhappy marriage. Although many previously divorced individuals resisted their divorce, this does not change the fact that they had to incorporate the status or label of divorced person into their self concept. Many never-divorced persons, by contrast, have marriages of exceptionally low quality but either would not consider divorce or would consider but reject it as a solution. They are resigned to what has sometimes been referred to as "holy deadlock."

In examining the process of remarriage in our Central Pennsylvania study, we learned that many individuals altered their views of marriage after their divorce and in the course of returning to matrimony. As we observed in Chapter 3, remarriage often involves revising conjugal conceptions—in particular the notion that marriage is a lifetime contract to be tolerated irrespective of the circumstances.

In our unstructured interviews, we were continually struck by the admissions of many of our informants that they were prepared to dissolve their second marriage if it did not work out. Regardless of how unattractive they considered this eventuality, the great majority indicated that after having endured a first marriage to the breaking point they were unwilling to be miserable again simply for the sake of preserving the union. In the quotations that follow, several respondents express the view that the experience of the first marriage changed their view of marriage:

> I think we also went into our second marriage with the attitude that if she woke up one morning and said "I'm not in love with you anymore (or) it's not the same for me anymore—I've met someone else," I'd say, "God bless" without any animosity.
> I would try my damnest [to make the marriage work] and hope that he would try the same way, but if we couldn't work it out, then we wouldn't stay together . . . it's a little different from what I thought the first time.
> I think the way you look on . . . the next relationship—you know, that these things can be terminated—that's a matter of historical record, so there's an illusion that's gone.

These comments suggest the possibility that the divorce experience itself may alter the prevailing—although possibly waning—standard that a marriage should be preserved "until death do us part." When asked, for example, whether they agree or disagree that "remarried couples are less likely to stay married if they are not happy together than people in their first marriages," nearly two-thirds of the remarried individuals replied affirmatively. Only one-fourth rejected the notion that second marriers hold a standard different from that of persons in their first marriage. Significantly, those who by the time of the follow-up had remarried or were living with a partner were just as likely to endorse the principle of "conditional commitment" as those still separated or divorced. This finding suggests that reentrance to marriage does not amend the view, shared widely among individuals who divorce, that marriage is not a permanent contract.

Indeed, we were struck by how ever-present the fear of marital failure is among persons who remarry after divorce. Despite an intense desire to prove that they are not incapable of achieving a successful marriage, many of the couples we interviewed were unwilling or unable to take for granted the eventual success of their marriage. Marriage had become much more of an achieved rather than an ascribed status, to use a familiar sociological distinction.

Given their level of vigilance, it is not altogether surprising that remarriages dissolve more quickly when a couple begins to experience conjugal dissatisfaction. Over half of the respondents in the Central Pennsylvania study believed that people often make the same mistake in marrying a second time. The apprehension that history might repeat itself and the knowledge of the symptoms of marital breakdown heighten the likelihood that marital disintegration will be swift in the event that serious problems arise. If it becomes clear that the second marriage appears to be a replay of the first—even if in a somewhat different version—commitment to the relationship is likely to drop precipitously. Remarried people will not endure an unhappy second marriage when they could not endure an unsuccessful first marriage.

Conclusion

Although the evidence we have furnished is by no means conclusive, it does suggest an alternative explanation for the difference in marital stability between first and subsequent marriages. If this alternative hypothesis is correct, remarried couples may not run a greater risk of marital failure because of the problems they face in dealing with situations for which clear cultural guidelines do not exist, as Cherlin suggests. Rather, couples in their second marriages may be somewhat more predisposed to leave an unhappy relationship than those in their first.

We do not deny that the situation in which remarried couples must operate is more ambiguous and perhaps more stressful. To acknowledge this point may seem like a contradiction in our argument. However, we do not believe that institutional ambiguity, which Cherlin rightly observes, necessarily results in marital dissolution. In fact, if remarried couples are adaptive and resourceful in dealing with anomolous and problematic situations, special dividends may accrue to their marriages.

In assuming a one-to-one relationship between stress and negative outcomes, social scientists are inclined to ignore the complex process of problem solving, coping, and adaptation that builds resources as well as dissipates them. In a review of the remarriage literature, Furstenberg (1979) discovered a preoccupation among family sociologists with marital risks. Researchers seemed remarkably uninterested in the informal and inventive ways in which individuals responded to culturally uncharted situations. Their underlying assumption may be a tacit but conscious acceptance of what Dennis Wrong referred to some years ago as the "oversocialized conception of man." Critics of this view tend to point out that individuals are creators and destroyers of social institutions, not merely conveyers and obeyers of social understandings.

Sociological notions such as "role strain," "marginality," and "sociological ambivalence" indicate the problematic and sometimes stressful features of social life but need not imply deviance, maladaptation, or dysfunction. The contradictions inherent in social institutions allow flexibility and room for maneuvering—in short, opportunities for negotiation that may be more difficult to come by when normative consensus is high.

Thus, it may be useful to view institutionalization less as a fixed state than as a continuously changing process. In this respect, remarried couples encounter many of the same dilemmas as couples do in their first marriages in building what Berger and Kellner (1964) have referred to as a "marital nomos," a shared view of the world, although the process of constructing marriage may take a somewhat divergent path.

Basically, then, our disagreement with Cherlin rests partly on a difference in sociological emphasis. We believe that it is more useful to explore the adaptive mechanisms that remarried couples invent for dealing with their everyday problems than to stress the hazards they are likely to face in returning to married life. Our reason for making so much of this difference in emphasis is that we fear that many individuals—remarried or not—are likely to conclude that remarried couples face an especially high risk of marital failure and to act on the basis of this erroneous conclusion.

We view the differential risk of marital dissolution as minor, especially in view of the complexities of managing parenthood in reconstituted families. Thus, the central empirical problem becomes not explaining the disparity in marital stability, but understanding the adaptive mechanisms that remarried couples employ in solving the dilemmas of everyday life.

Appendix: Study of Divorce and Remarriage

INSTITUTE FOR SURVEY RESEARCH
TEMPLE UNIVERSITY
-*Of The Commonwealth System Of Higher Education*-
1601 NORTH BROAD STREET
PHILADELPHIA, PENNSYLVANIA 19122

SUMMER 1979   STUDY #599-400-77

STUDY OF DIVORCE AND REMARRIAGE

DR. FRANK F. FURSTENBERG, JR.
UNIVERSITY OF PENNSYLVANIA

DR. GRAHAM B. SPANIER
PENNSYLVANIA STATE UNIVERSITY

CASE #: ☐☐☐ – ☐

Time interview began: _____ A.M. _____ P.M.

Time interview ended: _____ A.M. _____ P.M.

INTERVIEWER'S NAME:_____ ID#:_____ DATE:_____

INTERVIEWER:_____ ID#:_____ CASE #:_____ DATE:_____

1.) I want to begin by asking you some questions about your present marital situation. Are you currently married, separated, divorced or widowed (or have you never been married)?

Married	1
Separated	2
Divorced	3
Widowed	4
Never been married	5

(SKIP TO Q. 3 AND CIRCLE CODE 1) appears next to "Never been married"

(CHECK APPROPRIATE BOX ON RECALL AID #1A)

2. Altogether, how many times have you been married?

_____
(NUMBER OF MARRIAGES)

(RECORD ON RECALL AID #1B)

	FIRST		SECOND		THIRD		FOURTH	
(ASK QQ. 2A TO 2C FOR EACH MARRIAGE IN Q. 2, STARTING WITH THE FIRST, THEN SECOND, THIRD, ETC.)								
2A. When were you married (the first/second/ etc., time)? That is, in what month and year?	(MONTH) ‾‾‾‾‾‾‾ (YEAR)		(MONTH) ‾‾‾‾‾‾‾ (YEAR)		(MONTH) ‾‾‾‾‾‾‾ (YEAR)		(MONTH) ‾‾‾‾‾‾‾ (YEAR)	
2B. How did that marriage end (or is this your current marriage)? (IF CURRENT MARRIAGE, SKIP TO 2D)	Current Marriage 1 Divorce 2 Separation 3 Death 4		Current Marriage 1 Divorce 2 Separation 3 Death 4		Current Marriage 1 Divorce 2 Separation 3 Death 4		Current Marriage 1 Divorce 2 Separation 3 Death 4	
2C. In what month and year did that (first/ second/ etc.) marriage end?	Separa-tion	Divorce/ Death	Separa-tion	Divorce/ Death	Separa-tion	Divorce/ Death	Separa-tion	Divorce/ Death
	(MONTH) ‾‾‾‾‾‾ (YEAR)	(MONTH) ‾‾‾‾‾‾ (YEAR)	(MONTH) ‾‾‾‾‾‾ (YEAR)	(MONTH) ‾‾‾‾‾‾ (YEAR)	(MONTH) ‾‾‾‾‾‾ (YEAR)	(MONTH) ‾‾‾‾‾‾ (YEAR)	(MONTH) ‾‾‾‾‾‾ (YEAR)	(MONTH) ‾‾‾‾‾‾ (YEAR)
	(IF ANOTHER MARRIAGE, RETURN TO Q. 2A)							

2D. (IF PRIMARY R AND ONLY ONE MARRIAGE, ASK): Later I'll be referring to (SPOUSE ON LABEL). Was this marriage to (him/her)?

(IF CURRENT MARRIAGE TO SPOUSE ON LABEL, RECORD ON RECALL AID #1B)	Yes	1
(CLARIFY R'S RELATIONSHIP TO SPOUSE ON LABEL)	No	2

(IF PRIMARY R AND MORE THAN ONE MARRIAGE, ASK): Later I'll be referring to (SPOUSE ON LABEL). Which marriage was to (him/her)?

‾‾‾‾‾‾‾‾‾‾‾‾ ⟶ (IF CURRENT MARRIAGE IS TO SPOUSE ON
(# OF MARRIAGE)   LABEL, RECORD ON RECALL AID #1B)

(IF SECONDARY R: IF EVER MARRIED PRIOR TO THIS RELATIONSHIP, RECORD ON RECALL AID #1B AND ASK): Later I'll have some questions about your previous spouse. What shall I call (him/her)?

(RECORD NAME ON CALL REPORT FORM LABEL. THIS PERSON IS THE SPOUSE ON LABEL. NOW SKIP TO Q. 4)

(IF CURRENTLY MARRIED IN Q. 1, SKIP TO Q. 4)

3. Are you currently living with someone of the opposite sex?

Yes	1
No	2

(RECORD RESPONSE ON RECALL AID, #1A)

4. What is your date of birth?

_____   _____   _____
     (MONTH)   (DAY)   (YEAR)

5. What is the highest grade of school you have completed?

(CIRCLE HIGHEST GRADE COMPLETED)	Elementary School	1	2	3	4	5	6
	High School	7	8	9	10	11	12
	College or Trade School	13	14	15	16		
	Graduate or Professional School	17	18	19	20+		

6. What is your current occupation? That is, what is your job title?

_____
                        (OCCUPATIONAL TITLE)

(IF HOUSEWIFE, STUDENT, OR NONE, SKIP TO Q. 9)

7. Tell me a little bit more about what you actually do at your job? What are your main duties?

_____

_____
                              (DUTIES)

8. What kind of company or business do you work for?

_____
                        (COMPANY OR BUSINESS)

8A. Do you work full time or part time? That is, do you work at least 35 hours per week or less?

Full time (35 hours)	1
Part time (less than 35 hours)	2

8B. Are you self-employed or do you work for someone else?

Self-employed	1
Someone else	2
Other (SPECIFY): _____	3

9. What is your religious preference, if any?

	Protestant	1
(SKIP	Roman Catholic	2
TO	Jewish	3
Q. 11)	Other (SPECIFY): _____	4
(SKIP TO INSTRUCTIONS ABOVE Q. 13)	Atheist, Agnostic, None	5

10. What denomination is that?

_____
(PROTESTANT DENOMINATION)

11. Would you say you are:

very religious,	1
somewhat religious,	2
slightly religious, or	3
not religious at all?	4

12. How frequently do you attend religious services or activities? Do you attend:

at least twice a week,	1
about once a week,	2
at least once a month,	3
a few times during the year,	4
rarely, or	5
do you never attend?	6

(IF PRIMARY R NOT CURRENTLY MARRIED OR LIVING WITH A PARTNER, SKIP TO Q. 26)

(ALL SECONDARY Rs, SKIP TO Q. 26)

13. I have some questions about your (husband/wife/partner). What shall I call (him/her)?

_____
(RECORD WHAT R SAYS)

13A. What is (SPOUSE'S/PARTNER'S) date of birth?

_____   _____   _____
(MONTH)   (DAY)   (YEAR)

14. What is the highest grade of school (he/she) has completed?

(CIRCLE HIGHEST GRADE COMPLETED)	Elementary School	1	2	3	4	5	6
	High School	7	8	9	10	11	12
	College or Trade School	13	14	15	16		
	Graduate or Professional School	17	18	19	20+		

15. What is (his/her) current occupation? That is, what is (his/her) job title?

_____
(OCCUPATIONAL TITLE)

(IF HOUSEWIFE, STUDENT, OR NONE, SKIP TO Q. 18)

16. Tell me a little bit more about what (he/she) actually does in that job? What are (his/her) duties?

_____

_____
(DUTIES)

17. What kind of company or business does (he/she) work for?

_____
(COMPANY OR BUSINESS)

17A. Does (he/she) work full time or part time? That is, does (he/she) work at least 35 hours per week or less?

Full time (35 hours)	1
Part time (less than 35 hours)	2

17B. Is (he/she) self-employed or does (he/she) work for someone else?

Self-employed	1
Someone else	2
Other (SPECIFY):	3

18. What is (his/her) religious preference, if any?

	Protestant	1
(SKIP	Roman Catholic	2
TO	Jewish	3
Q. 20)	Other (SPECIFY):	4
(SKIP TO Q. 22)	Atheist, Agnostic, None	5

19. What denomination is that?

_____
(PROTESTANT DENOMINATION)

20. Would you say (he/she) is:

very religious,	1
somewhat religious,	2
slightly religious, or	3
not religious at all?	4

21. How frequently does (he/she) attend religious services or activities? Does (he/she) attend:

at least twice a week,	1
about once a week,	2
at least once a month,	3
a few times during the year,	4
rarely, or	5
does (he/she) never attend?	6

22. How many times was (he/she) married before your current (marriage/relationship)?

_____
(NUMBER OF PREVIOUS MARRIAGES)

(IF NONE, SKIP TO Q. 26)

		FIRST	SECOND	THIRD
	(ASK QQ. 23 TO 25 FOR EACH PREVIOUS MARRIAGE OF THE CURRENT SPOUSE/PARTNER, STARTING WITH THE FIRST, THEN SECOND, ETC.)			
23.	Did (his/her) (first/second, etc.) marriage end by death, divorce, or separation?	Death 1 Divorce 2 Separation 3	Death 1 Divorce 2 Separation 3	Death 1 Divorce 2 Separation 3
24.	How long did that marriage last?	‾‾(MONTHS)‾‾ OR ‾‾(YEARS)‾‾	‾‾(MONTHS)‾‾ OR ‾‾(YEARS)‾‾	‾‾(MONTHS)‾‾ OR ‾‾(YEARS)‾‾
25.	How many children did (he/she) have in that marriage?	‾‾(NUMBER OF CHILDREN)‾‾	‾‾(NUMBER OF CHILDREN)‾‾	‾‾(NUMBER OF CHILDREN)‾‾

(IF ANOTHER PREVIOUS MARRIAGE, RETURN TO Q. 23; IF LAST PREVIOUS MARRIAGE, GO TO Q. 26)

26. Not counting yourself, what are the first names of all the people 18 and older who are living in your household at the present time? Don't include the names of any children (or stepchildren).

(LIST FIRST NAMES OF ALL HOUSEHOLD MEMBERS 18 AND OLDER IN COLUMN A BELOW. FOR EACH LISTED HOUSEHOLD MEMBER, ASK Q. 26A.)

R IS ONLY HOUSEHOLD MEMBER 18 AND OLDER ☐ → (SKIP TO Q. 27A)

26A. What is (FIRST NAME)'s relationship to you? (RECORD IN COLUMN B BELOW)

#	COLUMN A FIRST NAME	COLUMN B RELATIONSHIP TO RESPONDENT
1		
2		
3		
4		
5		
6		

26B. In addition to the people we just talked about, are there any other people 18 and older living in your household at the present time?

	(RETURN TO Q. 26)	Yes	1
		No	2

(ASK Q. 27A, THEN ASK B, C AND D ABOUT EACH CHILD.)

27A. Including all children regardless of their ages, and starting with the oldest child first, tell me the names of all of the children who are presently living in your household. Include both your own children and any stepchildren living with you.

NO CHILDREN LIVING IN HOUSEHOLD ☐ ⟶ (RECORD ON RECALL AID #3A AND SKIP TO Q. 28A)

A. What is the (oldest/next to oldest/etc.) child's first name?	B. What is (his/her) date of birth?	C. (IF NOT OBVIOUS): Is (NAME OF CHILD) a male or female?		D. Who are (NAME OF CHILD)'s natural parents:			
		MALE	FEMALE	You and (SPOUSE ON LABEL)?	You and (CURRENT SPOUSE/PARTNER)?	Your (CURRENT SPOUSE/PARTNER) and (his/her) previous mate?	OTHER (SPECIFY):
1. _____ (FIRST NAME)	⟶ ___/___ (MONTH) (YEAR)	1	2	1	2	3	4 _____
2. _____ (FIRST NAME)	___/___ (MONTH) (YEAR)	1	2	1	2	3	4 _____
3. _____ (FIRST NAME)	___/___ (MONTH) (YEAR)	1	2	1	2	3	4 _____
4. _____ (FIRST NAME)	___/___ (MONTH) (YEAR)	1	2	1	2	3	4 _____
5. _____ (FIRST NAME)	___/___ (MONTH) (YEAR)	1	2	1	2	3	4 _____
6. _____ (FIRST NAME)	___/___ (MONTH) (YEAR)	1	2	1	2	3	4 _____

(IF ANOTHER CHILD, RETURN TO Q. 27B; IF LAST CHILD, CONTINUE WITH Q. 27E.)

27E. Have you now given me all of the children living in the household?

	Yes	1
	No	2

(RETURN TO Q. 27A)

27F. (ON RECALL AID #3, CHECK BOX B IF NO CHILDREN UNDER 18.
ON RECALL AID #4, RECORD NAMES OF CHILDREN WHO ARE UNDER 18 YEARS OF AGE AND WHO HAVE CODE 1 CIRCLED IN Q. 27D.
ON RECALL AID #5, RECORD NAMES OF CHILDREN WHO ARE UNDER 18 YEARS OF AGE AND WHO HAVE CODE 3 CIRCLED IN Q. 27D.)

(ASK Q. 28A, THEN ASK B, C, D, AND E ABOUT EACH CHILD.)

(28A) Now tell me about your children (and your spouse's/partner's children) who are not living in your household. Including all children regardless of their ages, and starting with the oldest child first, tell me the names of all of the children who are not living in your household.

NO CHILDREN LIVING OUTSIDE HOUSEHOLD ☐ → (RECORD ON RECALL AID #3C AND GO TO PAGE 12)

A. What is the (oldest/next to oldest/etc.) child's first name?	B. What is (his/her) date of birth?	C. (IF NOT OBVIOUS): Is (NAME OF CHILD) a male or female?		D. Who are (NAME OF CHILD)'s natural parents:				E. With whom is (NAME OF CHILD) living now?
		MALE	FEMALE	You and (SPOUSE ON LABEL)?	You and (CURRENT SPOUSE/ PARTNER)?	Your (CURRENT SPOUSE/PARTNER) and (his/her) previous mate?	OTHER (SPECIFY):	
1. _____ (FIRST NAME)	_____ / _____ (MONTH) / (YEAR)	1	2	5	6	7	8 _____	_____ (RELATIONSHIP TO CHILD)
2. _____ (FIRST NAME)	_____ / _____ (MONTH) / (YEAR)	1	2	5	6	7	8 _____	_____ (RELATIONSHIP TO CHILD)
3. _____ (FIRST NAME)	_____ / _____ (MONTH) / (YEAR)	1	2	5	6	7	8 _____	_____ (RELATIONSHIP TO CHILD)
4. _____ (FIRST NAME)	_____ / _____ (MONTH) / (YEAR)	1	2	5	6	7	8 _____	_____ (RELATIONSHIP TO CHILD)
5. _____ (FIRST NAME)	_____ / _____ (MONTH) / (YEAR)	1	2	5	6	7	8 _____	_____ (RELATIONSHIP TO CHILD)
6. _____ (FIRST NAME)	_____ / _____ (MONTH) / (YEAR)	1	2	5	6	7	8 _____	_____ (RELATIONSHIP TO CHILD)

(IF ANOTHER CHILD, RETURN TO Q. 28B; IF LAST CHILD, CONTINUE WITH Q. 28F.)

28F. Have we missed any children who are <u>not</u> living in the household?

(RETURN TO Q. 28A)	Yes	1
	No	2

28G. ON RECALL AID #3, CHECK BOX D IF NO CHILDREN UNDER 18.

ON RECALL AID #6, RECORD NAMES OF CHILDREN WHO ARE UNDER 18 YEARS OF AGE AND WHO HAVE CODE 5 CIRCLED IN Q. 28D.

ON RECALL AID #7, RECORD NAMES OF CHILDREN WHO ARE UNDER 18 YEARS OF AGE AND WHO HAVE CODE 7 CIRCLED IN Q. 28D.

INTERVIEWER: BEFORE PROCEEDING, CHECK AS MANY SECTIONS AS APPLY. AT LEAST ONE MUST BE CHECKED. THEN ASK ALL APPROPRIATE QUESTIONS.

☐ IF NO CHILDREN CHECKED IN RECALL AID #3 A & C, SKIP TO Q. 91 ON PAGE 38.

☐ IF NO CHILDREN CHECKED IN RECALL AID #3 A & D OR #3 B & C, SKIP TO Q. 86 ON PAGE 36.

☐ IF PRIMARY R IS CURRENTLY MARRIED TO SPOUSE ON LABEL (RECALL AID #1B) AND HAS CHILDREN, SKIP TO Q. 86 ON PAGE 36.

☐ IF RECALL AID #4 CHECKED, ASK QQ. 29 TO 47, STARTING ON PAGE 13.

☐ IF RECALL AID #5 CHECKED, ASK QQ. 66 TO 75, STARTING ON PAGE 27.

☐ IF RECALL AID #6 CHECKED, ASK QQ. 48 TO 65, STARTING ON PAGE 21.

☐ IF RECALL AID #7 CHECKED, ASK QQ. 76 TO 85, STARTING ON PAGE 32.

☐ IF NONE OF THE ABOVE (IN QQ. 27D AND 28D, THE ONLY CODES CIRCLED ARE 2, 4, 6, OR 8), SKIP TO Q. 86 ON PAGE 36.

Now I want to ask you a few questions about the child(ren) from your marriage to (SPOUSE ON LABEL)--the ones who are living with you and are under 18.

29. About how often do (NAMES FROM RECALL AID, #4) get a chance to see their (father/mother):

	almost every day,	1
	a few times a week,	2
	a few times a month,	3
	once a month or so,	4
	occasionally during the year,	5
	hardly ever, or	6
(SKIP TO Q. 31)	never?	7
(RECORD ON RECALL AID #2 & SKIP TO Q. 35)	Deceased/whereabouts unknown	0
	Other (SPECIFY): _____	8

30. Do their visits usually follow a regular schedule?

	Yes	1
	No	2

31. During the past two years, have there been any changes in the custody arrangement which was worked out at the time of your divorce (separation)?

	Yes	1
(SKIP TO Q. 32)	No	2

31A. What changes have occurred?

_____

_____

_____

32. How satisfied are you with the current custody arrangement? Are you:

very satisfied,	1
somewhat satisfied,	2
somewhat dissatisfied, or	3
very dissatisfied?	4

33. How satisfied would you say (SPOUSE ON LABEL) is with the current custody arrangement? Is (he/she):

	very satisfied,	1
	somewhat satisfied,	2
	somewhat dissatisfied, or	3
	very dissatisfied?	4
(DO NOT READ)	Don't know	8

34. Concerning your feelings about how to raise (NAMES FROM RECALL AID, #4), do you and (he/she):

	always agree,	1
	usually agree,	2
	sometimes agree, or	3
	do you never agree?	4
(DO NOT READ)	Other (SPECIFY): _____	5

35. In dividing up the various responsibilities of raising (NAMES FROM RECALL AID, #4), can you tell me who generally does what? (HAND R CARD 1)
For example, looking at Card 1: (CIRCLE ALL THAT APPLY)

	RESPONDENT	FORMER SPOUSE	R'S RELATIVES	FORMER SPOUSE'S RELATIVES	FORMER SPOUSE'S CURRENT PARTNER	R'S CURRENT SPOUSE/ PARTNER	THE CHILD(REN)	SOMEONE ELSE (SPECIFY):	DOES NOT APPLY
a. Who usually contributes to their financial support?	1	2	3	4	5	6	7	8 _____	0
b. Who usually supervises the children after school?	1	2	3	4	5	6	7	8 _____	0
c. Who usually sees that they are doing their homework?	1	2	3	4	5	6	7	8 _____	0
d. Who usually makes plans for their birthdays?	1	2	3	4	5	6	7	8 _____	0
e. Who usually selects their summer camp or summertime activities?	1	2	3	4	5	6	7	8 _____	0
f. Who usually arranges for them to see their relatives?	1	2	3	4	5	6	7	8 _____	0
g. Who usually makes decisions about their religious training?	1	2	3	4	5	6	7	8 _____	0
h. Who usually attends school conferences?	1	2	3	4	5	6	7	8 _____	0
i. Who usually gets involved if there is a serious discipline problem?	1	2	3	4	5	6	7	8 _____	0

36. In raising the children, do you think you end up taking:

too much responsibility,	1
about the right amount, or	2
too little responsibility?	3

(IF FORMER SPOUSE IS DECEASED OR WHEREABOUTS UNKNOWN, RECALL AID #2, SKIP TO Q. 41)

36A. What about your former spouse? Does (he/she) take too much, about the right amount, or too little responsibility for raising the children?

Too much	1
About right	2
Too little	3

37. In making decisions about the children, do you think (he/she) has:

a great deal of influence,	1
some, or	2
very little influence?	3

38. During the past two years, has (his/her) influence:

increased,	1
stayed about the same, or	2
decreased?	3

39. During the past two years, has (his/her) closeness to the children:

increased,	1
stayed the same, or	2
decreased?	3

40. Would you say (his/her) relationship with the children is now:		
	very close,	1
	fairly close, or	2
	not so close?	3

41. How about your relationship with them? Is it:		
	very close,	1
	fairly close, or	2
	not so close?	3

42. Here is a list of relatives. (HAND R CARD 2) Looking at Card 2, how often do (NAMES FROM RECALL AID, #4) get a chance to see each of the following people:

	DOES NOT APPLY	ABOUT EVERY DAY	ONCE OR TWICE A WEEK	ONCE OR TWICE A MONTH	OCCASIONALLY DURING THE YEAR	HARDLY EVER	NEVER
a. either of your parents	0	6	5	4	3	2	1
b. any of your brothers and sisters	0	6	5	4	3	2	1
c. any of your other relatives	0	6	5	4	3	2	1
d. either of (SPOUSE ON LABEL)'s parents	0	6	5	4	3	2	1
e. any of (SPOUSE ON LABEL)'s brothers and sisters	0	6	5	4	3	2	1
(ASK IF MARRIED OR LIVING WITH PARTNER):							
f. either of (SPOUSE/PARTNER)'s parents	0	6	5	4	3	2	1
g. any of (SPOUSE/PARTNER)'s brothers and sisters	0	6	5	4	3	2	1

(IF NOT MARRIED OR LIVING WITH A PARTNER, SKIP TO NEXT SECTION OF QUESTIONS CHECKED ON PAGE 12; IF NO OTHER SECTIONS CHECKED ON PAGE 12, SKIP TO Q. 86)

43. In making decisions concerning the children, does (spouse/partner) have:

a great deal of influence,	1
some, or	2
very little influence?	3

44. In raising the children, does your (spouse/partner) end up taking:

too much responsibility,	1
about the right amount, or	2
too little responsibility?	3

45. Would you say that (his/her) relationship with the children is:

very close,	1
fairly close, or	2
not so close?	3

46. What do the children call (him/her) when they are speaking to (him/her)?

_____

_____

(IF SPOUSE ON LABEL IS DECEASED OR (HIS/HER) WHEREABOUTS ARE UNKNOWN [RECALL AID #2], SKIP TO NEXT SECTION OF QUESTIONS CHECKED ON PAGE 12; IF NO OTHER SECTIONS CHECKED ON PAGE 12, SKIP TO Q. 86 ON PAGE 36)

47. Concerning the children, how often do disagreements come up between (spouse/partner) and <u>(SPOUSE ON LABEL)</u>? Is it:

	frequently,	1
	sometimes,	2
	rarely, or	3
(SKIP TO NEXT SECTION OF QUESTIONS CHECKED ON PAGE 12; IF NO OTHER SECTIONS CHECKED, SKIP TO Q. 86 ON PAGE 36)	never?	4
(DO NOT READ)	Inapplicable (SPECIFY):	0

47A. When disagreements arise, what are they usually about?

_____

_____

_____

_____

(ALL SKIP TO NEXT SECTION OF QUESTIONS CHECKED ON PAGE 12; IF NO OTHER SECTIONS CHECKED, SKIP TO Q. 86 ON PAGE 36)

Now I want to ask you a few questions about the child(ren) from your marriage to (SPOUSE ON LABEL)--the ones who are not living with you and are under 18.

48.   About how often do you get a chance to see (NAMES FROM RECALL AID, #6):

	almost every day,	1
	a few times a week,	2
	a few times a month,	3
	once a month or so,	4
	occasionally during the year,	5
	hardly ever, or	6
(SKIP TO Q. 50)	never?	7
	Other (SPECIFY):	8

49.   Do these visits usually follow a regular schedule?

Yes	1
No	2

(IF RESPONDENT ANSWERED QQ. 29 TO 47, SKIP TO Q. 53)

50.   During the past two years, have there been any changes in the custody arrangement which was worked out at the time of your divorce (separation)?

	Yes	1
(SKIP TO Q. 51)	No	2

50A.   What changes have occurred?

_____

_____

51. How satisfied are you with the current custody agreement? Are you:

very satisfied,	1
somewhat satisfied,	2
somewhat dissatisfied, or	3
very dissatisfied?	4

(IF SPOUSE ON LABEL DECEASED OR WHEREABOUT UNKNOWN [RECALL AID #2], SKIP TO Q. 54)

52. How satisfied would you say your <u>(SPOUSE ON LABEL)</u> is with the current custody arrangement? Is (he/she):

	very satisfied,	1
	somewhat satisfied,	2
	somewhat dissatisfied, or	3
	very dissatisfied?	4
(DO NOT READ)	Don't know	8
(RECORD ON RECALL AID #2 & SKIP TO Q. 54)	Deceased/Whereabouts unknown	0

53. Concerning your feelings about how to raise <u>(NAMES FROM RECALL AID #6)</u>, do you and (he/she):

	always agree,	1
	usually agree,	2
	sometimes agree, or	3
	do you never agree?	4
	Other (SPECIFY): _____	5

54. In dividing up the various responsibilities of raising (NAMES FROM RECALL AID, #6), can you tell me who generally does what?   (HAND R CARD 1)
For example, looking at Card 1:   (CIRCLE ALL THAT APPLY)

	RESPONDENT	FORMER SPOUSE	R'S RELATIVES	FORMER SPOUSE'S RELATIVES	FORMER SPOUSE'S CURRENT PARTNER	R'S CURRENT SPOUSE/ PARTNER	THE CHILD(REN)	SOMEONE ELSE (SPECIFY):	DOES NOT APPLY
a. Who usually contributes to their financial support?	1	2	3	4	5	6	7	8 _____	0
b. Who usually supervises the children after school?	1	2	3	4	5	6	7	8 _____	0
c. Who usually sees that they are doing their homework?	1	2	3	4	5	6	7	8 _____	0
d. Who usually makes plans for their birthdays?	1	2	3	4	5	6	7	8 _____	0
e. Who usually selects their summer camp or summertime activities?	1	2	3	4	5	6	7	8 _____	0
f. Who usually arranges for them to see their relatives?	1	2	3	4	5	6	7	8 _____	0
g. Who usually makes decisions about their religious training?	1	2	3	4	5	6	7	8 _____	0
h. Who usually attends school conferences?	1	2	3	4	5	6	7	8 _____	0
i. Who usually gets involved if there is a serious discipline problem?	1	2	3	4	5	6	7	8 _____	0

(IF FORMER SPOUSE IS DECEASED OR WHEREABOUTS UNKNOWN, RECALL AID #2, SKIP TO Q. 55A)

55. In raising the children, do you feel that your former spouse ends up taking:

too much responsibility,	1
about the right amount, or	2
too little responsibility?	3

55A. (What about you?) Do you end up taking too much, about the right amount, or too little responsibility for the children?

Too much	1
Right amount	2
Too little	3

56. In making decisions about the children, do you think you have:

a great deal of influence,	1
some, or	2
very little influence?	3

57. During the past two years, has your influence:

increased,	1
stayed the same, or	2
decreased?	3

58. During the past two years, has your closeness to the children:

increased,	1
stayed the same, or	2
decreased?	3

59. Is your relationship with them:

very close,	1
fairly close, or	2
not so close?	3

60. Here is a list of relatives. (HAND R CARD 2) Looking at Card 2, how often do (NAMES FROM RECALL AID, #6) get a chance to see each of the following people:

	DOES NOT APPLY	ABOUT EVERY DAY	ONCE OR TWICE A WEEK	ONCE OR TWICE A MONTH	OCCA-SIONALLY DURING THE YEAR	HARDLY EVER	NEVER
a. either of your parents	0	6	5	4	3	2	1
b. any of your brothers and sisters	0	6	5	4	3	2	1
c. any of your other relatives	0	6	5	4	3	2	1
d. either of (SPOUSE ON LABEL)'s parents	0	6	5	4	3	2	1
e. any of (SPOUSE ON LABEL)'s brothers and sisters	0	6	5	4	3	2	1
(ASK IF MARRIED OR LIVING WITH PARTNER):							
f. either of (SPOUSE/PARTNER)'s parents	0	6	5	4	3	2	1
g. any of (SPOUSE/PARTNER)'s brothers and sisters	0	6	5	4	3	2	1

(IF NOT MARRIED OR LIVING WITH A PARTNER, SKIP TO NEXT SECTION OF
QUESTIONS CHECKED ON PAGE 12; IF NO OTHER SECTIONS CHECKED, SKIP TO Q. 86,
PAGE 36)

61. In making decisions concerning the children does (spouse/partner) have:

	a great deal of influence,	1
	some, or	2
	very little influence?	3
(SKIP TO NEXT SECTION OF (DO NOT READ) QUESTIONS CHECKED ON PAGE 12; IF NO OTHER SEC-TIONS CHECKED ON PAGE 12, SKIP TO Q. 86 ON PAGE 36)	No contact	4

62. In raising the children does (he/she) end up taking:

	too much responsibility,	1
	about the right amount, or	2
	too little responsibility?	3

63. Would you say that (his/her) relationship with the children is:

	very close,	1
	fairly close, or	2
	not so close?	3

64. What do the children call (him/her) when they are speaking to (him/her)?

_____

_____

(IF SPOUSE ON LABEL IS DECEASED OR (HIS/HER) WHEREABOUTS ARE UNKNOWN, RECALL AID #2, SKIP TO NEXT SECTION OF QUESTIONS CHECKED ON PAGE 12; IF NO OTHER SECTIONS CHECKED ON PAGE 12, SKIP TO Q. 86 ON PAGE 36)

65. Concerning the children, how often do disagreements come up between (spouse/partner) and (SPOUSE ON LABEL)? Is it:

	frequently,	1
	sometimes,	2
	rarely, or	3
(SKIP TO NEXT SECTION OF QUESTIONS CHECKED ON PAGE 12; IF NO OTHER SEC- TIONS CHECKED, SKIP TO Q. 86 ON PAGE 36) (DO NOT READ)	never?	4
	Inapplicable (SPECIFY): _____	0

65A. When disagreements arise, what are they usually about?

_____

_____

(ALL SKIP TO NEXT SECTION OF QUESTIONS CHECKED ON PAGE 12; IF NO OTHER SECTIONS CHECKED, SKIP TO Q. 86 ON PAGE 36)

66. Now I want to ask you a few questions about the child(ren) from (SPOUSE/PARTNER'S) previous marriage(s)--the ones who are living with you now and are under 18.

About how often do (NAMES FROM RECALL AID #5) get a chance to see their (father/mother)?

	almost every day,	1
	a few times a week,	2
	a few times a month,	3
	once a month or so,	4
	occasionally during the year,	5
	hardly ever, or	6
(SKIP TO Q. 68)	never?	7
	Other (SPECIFY):_____	8
	Deceased/Whereabouts unknown	0

(IF CODE 7 OR 0, CHECK RECALL AID #5A)

67. Do the visits usually follow a regular schedule or not?

Yes	1
No	2

68. In dividing up the various responsibilities of raising (NAMES FROM RECALL AID, #5), can you tell me who generally does what? (HAND R CARD 3) For example, looking at Card 3: (CIRCLE ALL THAT APPLY)

	RESPONDENT	R'S PARTNER	PARTNER'S FORMER SPOUSES	R'S RELATIVES	PARTNER'S RELATIVES	PARTNER'S FORMER SPOUSES' RELATIVES	THE CHILDREN	SOMEONE ELSE (SPECIFY):	DOES NOT APPLY
a. Who usually contributes to their financial support?	1	2	3	4	5	6	7	8 _____	0
b. Who usually supervises the children after school?	1	2	3	4	5	6	7	8 _____	0
c. Who usually sees that they are doing their homework?	1	2	3	4	5	6	7	8 _____	0
d. Who usually makes plans for their birthdays?	1	2	3	4	5	6	7	8 _____	0
e. Who usually selects their summer camp or summertime activities?	1	2	3	4	5	6	7	8 _____	0
f. Who usually arranges for them to see their relatives?	1	2	3	4	5	6	7	8 _____	0
g. Who usually makes decisions about their religious training?	1	2	3	4	5	6	7	8 _____	0
h. Who usually attends school conferences?	1	2	3	4	5	6	7	8 _____	0
i. Who usually gets involved if there is a serious discipline problem?	1	2	3	4	5	6	7	8 _____	0

-28-

69. In raising (NAMES FROM RECALL AID #5), would you say that you end up taking:

too much responsibility,	1
about the right amount, or	2
too little responsibility?	3

70. In making decisions about the children, do you think that you have:

a great deal of influence,	1
some, or	2
very little influence?	3

71. Is your relationship with them:

very close,	1
fairly close, or	2
not so close?	3

72. What do the children call you when they are talking to you?

_____

_____

73. Here is a list of relatives. (HAND R CARD 2) Looking at Card 2, how often do (NAMES FROM RECALL AID, #5) get a chance to see each of the following people:

	DOES NOT APPLY	ABOUT EVERY DAY	ONCE OR TWICE A WEEK	ONCE OR TWICE A MONTH	OCCA-SIONALLY DURING THE YEAR	HARDLY EVER	NEVER
a. either of your parents	0	6	5	4	3	2	1
b. any of your brothers and sisters	0	6	5	4	3	2	1
c. any of your other relatives	0	6	5	4	3	2	1
d. either of (SPOUSE/PARTNER)'s parents	0	6	5	4	3	2	1
e. any of (SPOUSE/PARTNER)'s brothers and sisters	0	6	5	4	3	2	1
f. the children's grandparents on their (mother's/father's) side	0	6	5	4	3	2	1
g. the children's uncles or aunts on their (mother's/father's) side	0	6	5	4	3	2	1

(IF CHILDREN HAVE NO CONTACT WITH PARENT OUTSIDE HOUSEHOLD, RECALL AID #5A, SKIP TO NEXT SECTION OF QUESTIONS CHECKED ON PAGE 12; IF NO OTHER SECTIONS CHECKED ON PAGE 12, SKIP TO Q. 86 ON PAGE 36)

74. How often do you and the children's (mother/father) discuss matters concerning the children? Is it:

	frequently,	1
	sometimes,	2
	rarely, or	3
(SKIP TO NEXT SECTION OF QUESTIONS CHECKED ON PAGE 12; IF NO OTHER SECTIONS CHECKED ON PAGE 12, SKIP TO Q. 86 ON PAGE 36)	never?	4

75. How often do disagreements come up between the two of you? Is it:

	frequently,	1
	sometimes,	2
	rarely, or	3
(SKIP TO NEXT SECTION OF QUESTIONS CHECKED ON PAGE 12; IF NO OTHER SECTIONS CHECKED ON PAGE 12, SKIP TO Q. 86 ON PAGE 36)	never?	4

75A. When disagreements arise, what are they usually about?

_____

_____

(ALL SKIP TO NEXT SECTION OF QUESTIONS CHECKED ON PAGE 12; IF NO OTHER SECTION CHECKED ON PAGE 12, SKIP TO Q. 86 ON PAGE 36)

Now I want to ask you a few questions about your (spouse/partner's) children--the ones who are <u>not</u> living with you and are under 18.

76. About how often do you get a chance to see <u>(NAMES FROM RECALL AID #7)</u>?
    Is it:

	almost every day,	1
	a few times a week,	2
	a few times a month,	3
	once a month or so,	4
	occasionally during the year,	5
	hardly ever, or	6
(CHECK "NO CONTACT" ON RECALL AID #7A AND SKIP TO Q. 78)	never?	7
	Other (SPECIFY): _____	8

77. Do the visits usually follow a regular schedule or not?

	Yes	1
	No	2

78. In dividing up the various responsibilities of raising (NAMES FROM RECALL AID, #7), can you tell me who generally does what? (HAND R CARD 3)
For example, looking at Card 3: (CIRCLE ALL THAT APPLY)

	RESPONDENT	R'S PARTNER	PARTNER'S FORMER SPOUSES	R'S RELATIVES	PARTNER'S RELATIVES	PARTNER'S FORMER SPOUSES' RELATIVES	THE CHILDREN	SOMEONE ELSE (SPECIFY):	DOES NOT APPLY
a. Who usually contributes to their financial support?	1	2	3	4	5	6	7	8 _____	0
b. Who usually supervises the children after school?	1	2	3	4	5	6	7	8 _____	0
c. Who usually sees that they are doing their homework?	1	2	3	4	5	6	7	8 _____	0
d. Who usually makes plans for their birthdays?	1	2	3	4	5	6	7	8 _____	0
e. Who usually selects their summer camp or summertime activities?	1	2	3	4	5	6	7	8 _____	0
f. Who usually arranges for them to see their relatives?	1	2	3	4	5	6	7	8 _____	0
g. Who usually makes decisions about their religious training?	1	2	3	4	5	6	7	8 _____	0
h. Who usually attends school conferences?	1	2	3	4	5	6	7	8 _____	0
i. Who usually gets involved if there is a serious discipline problem?	1	2	3	4	5	6	7	8 _____	0

79. In raising the children, do you feel that you end up taking:

too much responsibility,	1
about the right amount, or	2
too little responsibility?	3

80. In decisions affecting the children, do you have:

a great deal of influence,	1
some, or	2
very little influence?	3

(IF NO CONTACT, RECALL AID #7A, SKIP TO Q. 86 ON PAGE 36)

81. How close is your relationship to the children? Is it:

very close,	1
fairly close, or	2
not so close?	3

82. What do they call you when they are talking to you?

_____

_____

83. Here is a list of relatives. (HAND R CARD 2) Looking at Card 2, how often do (NAMES FROM RECALL AID, #7) get a chance to see each of the following people:

	DOES NOT APPLY	ABOUT EVERY DAY	ONCE OR TWICE A WEEK	ONCE OR TWICE A MONTH	OCCA- SIONALLY DURING THE YEAR	HARDLY EVER	NEVER
a. either of your parents	0	6	5	4	3	2	1
b. any of your brothers and sisters	0	6	5	4	3	2	1
c. any of your other relatives	0	6	5	4	3	2	1
(ASK IF MARRIED OR LIVING WITH PARTNER):							
d. either of (SPOUSE/PARTNER)'s parents	0	6	5	4	3	2	1
e. any of (SPOUSE/PARTNER)'s brothers and sisters	0	6	5	4	3	2	1

84. How often do you and the children's (mother/father) discuss matters concerning the children? Is it:

	frequently,	1
	sometimes,	2
	rarely, or	3
	never?	4
(DO NOT READ)	Deceased/Whereabouts unknown	0

(IF CODES "4" OR "0", SKIP TO Q. 86)

85. How often do disagreements come up between the two of you? Is it:

	frequently,	1
	sometimes,	2
	rarely, or	3
(SKIP TO Q. 86)	never?	4

85A. When disagreements arise, what are they usually about?

_____

_____

86. Have your feelings about being a parent changed very much in the last couple of years or remained pretty much the same?

	Changed	1
(SKIP TO Q. 87)	Remained the same	2

86A. How and why have they changed? (PROBE FOR CAUSES OF CHANGE)

_____

_____

87. Many parents feel worn out from time to time with the burdens of raising a family. How often do you feel tired, worn out, or exhausted from raising your family? Is it:

all the time,	1
most of the time,	2
sometimes,	3
rarely, or	4
never?	5

88. How often, if ever, have you had times when you lost control of your feelings and felt you might hurt your child? Would you say:

often,	1
sometimes,	2
hardly ever, or	3
never?	4

89. As a parent, how would you rate yourself? Would you say you were:

excellent,	1
good,	2
fair,	3
poor, or	4
terrible?	5

(IF R NOT REMARRIED OR LIVING WITH A PARTNER AFTER PREVIOUS MARRIAGE, SKIP TO Q. 91)

90. Since you remarried (started living together), do you find it more or less difficult to manage the various tasks of raising your child(ren)?

	More difficult	1
	Less difficult	2
(SKIP TO Q. 91)	About the same	3

90A. Why has it become (more/less) difficult?

_____

_____

_____

91. Here are some beliefs that people sometimes have about families with stepchildren. Do you agree or disagree with these beliefs:

	AGREE	DISAGREE	DEPENDS (SPECIFY):
a. It is generally harder to love a stepchild than to love one's own child.	1	2	3 _____
b. Generally, remarried persons have more difficulty disciplining their spouse's children than their own children.	1	2	3 _____
c. Remarried parents usually favor their own children over their spouse's children.	1	2	3 _____
d. There really isn't much difference between the way families with stepchildren operate and the way other families operate.	1	2	3 _____
e. There are often problems in getting grandparents to accept stepchildren.	1	2	3 _____
f. It is not good for a child to have more than one home.	1	2	3 _____
g. Remarried couples often have problems raising children because they don't share the same standards.	1	2	3 _____
h. Stepparents do better if they think of themselves more as a friend to their stepchildren than as a parent.	1	2	3 _____
i. Raising children part-time is much more difficult than raising them full-time.	1	2	3 _____
j. People still regard stepmothers negatively.	1	2	3 _____
k. It is harder to be a stepparent than to be a natural parent.	1	2	3 _____
l. Children frequently play their natural parents and their stepparents off against each other.	1	2	3 _____
m. It's better if children don't call their stepparents Mom or Dad.	1	2	3 _____
n. All things considered, children have fewer problems if they grow up with their two natural parents than if they grow up with one natural parent and a stepparent.	1	2	3 _____
o. Children have a hard time establishing relationships with new relatives after their parents remarry.	1	2	3 _____
p. A stepparent can't really take the place of a natural parent in the child's emotional life.	1	2	3 _____

92. Are you planning to have any (more) children in the future?

	Yes	1
(SKIP TO Q. 95)	No	2
	Undecided (SPECIFY): _____	3
(SKIP TO Q. 96)	Not applicable/sterility, past childbearing age	4

93. How many (more) children in all do you think you would <u>like</u> to have?

_____
(NUMBER)

94. How many (more) children do you think you will <u>actually</u> end up having?

_____
(NUMBER)

95. Suppose a pregnancy occurred in the next few months. (HAND R CARD 4) Looking at Card 4, which of the following statements would best describe the way you would feel?

I am hoping there will be a pregnancy and would be very happy.	1
I am not planning on a pregnancy now but would be happy anyhow.	2
I would rather not have a pregnancy but would not be too upset.	3
I don't want a pregnancy and would be somewhat upset.	4
I don't want a pregnancy and would be very upset.	5
I am pregnant/My partner is pregnant.	6

(IF SPOUSE ON LABEL DECEASED, RECALL AID #2, SKIP TO Q. 102)

(IF R MARRIED TO SPOUSE ON LABEL, SKIP TO Q. 116)

(IF SECONDARY R WAS NEVER SEPARATED OR DIVORCED, SKIP TO Q. 116)

96. Now I'd like to talk about your relationship with your (SPOUSE ON LABEL/ PREVIOUS SPOUSE). In what state does (he/she) live?

USA: _____ (STATE)		1
NOT USA: _____ (COUNTRY)		2
(SKIP TO Q. 100)	Spouse's whereabouts unknown	3

(HAND R CARD 5)

97. Looking at Card 5, during the past few weeks, how often have you:

		DOES NOT APPLY	ALMOST EVERY DAY	A FEW TIMES A WEEK	ONCE A WEEK	ONLY ONCE OR TWICE	NOT AT ALL
(IF ANY CODE 2-5, ASK Q. 98)	a. gone out socially with your former spouse?	0	5	4	3	2	1
	b. spoken to your former spouse in person?	0	5	4	3	2	1
	c. spoken to your former spouse by phone?	0	5	4	3	2	1
	d. heard from your former spouse by letter?	0	5	4	3	2	1
(SKIP	e. written to your former spouse?	0	5	4	3	2	1
TO	f. heard about your former spouse through family?	0	5	4	3	2	1
Q. 99)	g. heard about your former spouse through friends?	0	5	4	3	2	1
	h. seen your former spouse, but not talked to (him/her)?	0	5	4	3	2	1

98. When you talk to your former spouse, do you usually discuss:

		YES	NO
	a. your relationship?	1	2
	b. daily happenings?	1	2
	c. personal problems?	1	2
	d. practical problems such as home repairs?	1	2
(IF NO CHIL-DREN, SKIP TO g)	e. your child(ren)?	1	2
	f. child support?	1	2
	g. other things? What? (SPECIFY): _____	1	2

99. Thinking about the amount of contact you actually have with your former spouse, would you like to have:

more contact,	1'
about the same amount of contact, or	2
less contact?	3

(HAND R CARD 6)

100. Which one of the choices on this card **best** describes your feelings toward your former spouse now?

I still love (him/her).	1
I still like (him/her), but I don't love (him/her).	2
I don't feel much of anything for (him/her).	3
I hate (him/her).	4
I both love and hate (him/her).	5
Other (SPECIFY): _____	6

101. Is your former spouse now married or living with someone?

	Married	1
	Living with someone	2
(SKIP TO Q. 102)	Neither	3
	Don't know	8

101A. Before (he/she) (married/started living with someone), did you know of (his/her) plans?

	Yes	1
	No	2

101B. Before that happened, did you know the person (he/she) (married/started living with)?

	Yes	1
	No	2

(HAND R CARD 7)

101C. Tell me all the words on this card which describe your reaction to (his/her) relationship.

Supportive	1
Relieved	2
Pleased	3
Rejected	4
Uninvolved	5
Jealous	6
Other (SPECIFY): _____	7

(HAND R CARD 8)

102. Please look at Card 8, which contains pairs of different statements about your former marriage, and tell me the letter for the statement in each pair that best reflects your view.

Statement	A	B	Don't Know
1st pair	1	2	8
2nd pair	1	2	8
3rd pair	1	2	8
4th pair	1	2	8
5th pair	1	2	8
6th pair	1	2	8

(IF MARRIED, SKIP TO Q. 116).   (IF LIVING WITH PARTNER, SKIP TO Q. 113)

Now I'm going to ask you some questions about your social life.

103. How often do you go out with someone of the opposite sex? Do you go out:

daily,	1
a few times a week,	2
about once a week,	3
a few times a month,	4
about once a month,	5
less than once a month, or	6
never?	7

104. Are you satisfied with the frequency with which you go out on dates or would you like to go out more or less often?

more often	1
satisfied	2
less often	3

(IF NO CHILDREN, RECALL AID #3A & C , SKIP TO Q. 107)

105. In what ways, if any, do you think your child(ren) influence your chances of going out on dates? Do you think your child(ren):

increase your chances,	1
have no effect, or	2
decrease your chances?	3

106. In what ways, if any, do you think your child(ren) influence your chances for remarriage? Do you think your child(ren):

increase your chances,	1
have no effect, or	2
decrease your chances?	3

107. During the last year, have you had sexual relations:

	frequently,	1
	occasionally,	2
	rarely, or	3
(SKIP TO Q. 110)	not at all?	4

108. On the average, how many times a month do you have sexual intercourse?

_____
(NUMBER)

109. Are your sexual relations:

very satisfactory,	1
somewhat satisfactory,	2
a little unsatisfactory, or	3
very unsatisfactory?	4

110. Are you satisfied with the frequency with which you are having sexual intercourse or would you like to have sex more or less often?

more often	1
satisfied	2
less often	3

111. During your marriage with (SPOUSE ON LABEL), what were your views about extramarital sex? Did you:

	strongly disapprove,	1
	disapprove,	2
	approve, or	3
	strongly approve?	4
(DO NOT READ)	Other (SPECIFY): _____	5

112. What are your views now? Do you:

	strongly disapprove,	1
	disapprove,	2
	approve, or	3
	strongly approve?	4
(DO NOT READ)	Other (SPECIFY):	5

113A. People have many alternatives in deciding how to live today (HAND R CARD 9). Looking at the alternatives on Card 9, which do you think is the best for you?

(RECORD RESPONSE, THEN ASK Q. 113B): And which is the worst?

	Q.113A BEST	Q.113B WORST
a. not get involved in a permanent relationship with someone else.	1	1
b. live with someone and never remarry.	2	2
c. live with someone before remarrying.	3	3
d. remarry without living with someone beforehand.	4	4

114. Why do you think that (RESPONSE FROM Q. 113A) is the best choice for you?

_____

_____

_____

115. Why do you think that (RESPONSE FROM Q. 113B) is the worst choice for you?

_____

_____

_____

116. Here are some beliefs that people sometimes hold about remarriage. Please tell me whether you agree or disagree that:

	AGREE	DISAGREE	DEPENDS (SPECIFY): _____
a. People treat remarried couples differently than couples in their first marriages.	1	2	3 _____
b. Remarried couples have an easier time dividing up household chores than couples in their first marriages.	1	2	3 _____
c. Remarried couples have more problems getting along with their in-laws than couples in their first marriages.	1	2	3 _____
d. People often make the same mistakes when getting married the second time as they did the first time.	1	2	3 _____
e. Remarried couples have a different conception of love than couples in their first marriages.	1	2	3 _____
f. People who marry a second time have different expectations of marriage than they did in their first marriages.	1	2	3 _____
g. Sex is less important in second marriages than in first marriages.	1	2	3 _____
h. Even after they remarry, people continue to be emotionally attached to their former mates.	1	2	3 _____
i. Remarried people usually feel that it is less important to be sexually faithful than people in their first marriages.	1	2	3 _____
j. Remarriage changes the way people feel about themselves.	1	2	3 _____
k. Remarriages generally work out better than first marriages.	1	2	3 _____
l. Remarried couples are less likely to stay married if they are not happy together than people in their first marriages.	1	2	3 _____

(IF R <u>NOT</u> MARRIED OR <u>NOT</u> LIVING WITH PARTNER, SKIP TO Q. 156)

(IF R MARRIED TO SPOUSE ON LABEL, SKIP TO Q. 156)

117. Now I'd like to talk with you about the background of your current (marriage/relationship). How long did you and (spouse/partner) know each other before you were (married/started living together)?

_____   OR   _____
   (MONTHS)   (YEARS)

118. How long did you date before you were (married/started living together)?

_____   OR   _____
   (MONTHS)   (YEARS)

(IF LIVING TOGETHER, SKIP TO Q. 120)

119. Did you live together before you were married?

Yes	1
(SKIP TO Q. 120) No	2

119A. For how long?

_____   OR   _____
   (MONTHS)   (YEARS)

120. Did any of the following individuals affect your decision to (remarry/live together)?

	YES	NO	Q.120A (IF YES: How was your decision affected)?
a. Your relatives	1	2	
b. Your (spouse's/partner's) relatives	1	2	
c. Your friends	1	2	
d. Your former spouse	1	2	
(IF R HAS CHILDREN:) e. Your children	1	2	
(IF SPOUSE/PARTNER HAS CHILDREN:) f. Your (spouse/partner)'s children	1	2	

121. Did you and your (SPOUSE/PARTNER) ever discuss the possibility that
the (marriage/relationship) might not work out before you decided to
(marry/live together)?

Yes	1
No	2

122. People describe the process of meeting new family members in different
ways. Would you say that meeting (SPOUSE'S/PARTNER's) relatives have
been:

(SKIP TO Q. 123)	mostly comfortable and pleasant, or	1
(ASK Q. 122A)	somewhat uncomfortable or unpleasant?	2
(SKIP TO Q. 123) (DO NOT READ)	Other (SPECIFY):_____	3

122A. What made it uncomfortable or unpleasant?

_____

_____

123. How about (SPOUSE/PARTNER)'s experience with meeting your relatives?
Was it:

(SKIP TO Q. 124)	mostly comfortable and pleasant, or	1
(ASK Q. 123A)	somewhat uncomfortable or unpleasant?	2
(SKIP TO Q. 124) (DO NOT READ)	Other (SPECIFY):_____	3

123A. What made it uncomfortable or unpleasant?

_____

_____

(IF SECONDARY R NOT PREVIOUSLY MARRIED, SKIP TO Q. 133)

(IF R HAS NO CHILDREN FROM PREVIOUS MARRIAGES, SKIP TO Q. 125)

124. How about your children's experience with meeting (SPOUSE/PARTNER)'s relatives? Was it:

		mostly comfortable and pleasant, or	1
	(SKIP TO Q. 125)		
	(ASK Q. 124A)	somewhat uncomfortable or unpleasant?	2
(SKIP TO Q. 125)	(DO NOT READ)	Other (SPECIFY): _____	3

124A. What made it uncomfortable or unpleasant?

_____

_____

125. In deciding to marry (SPOUSE ON LABEL), what were (his/her) qualities that were important to you?

_____

_____

126. In deciding to enter your current relationship, what qualities were important this time?

_____

_____

127. In what ways was your decision to (marry SPOUSE/live with PARTNER) different from your decision to marry (SPOUSE ON LABEL)?

_____

_____

128. Before you (remarried/started living together), did your former (husband/wife) know of your plans?

	Yes	1
	No	2
	Don't know	8
(SKIP TO Q. 133)	Spouse dead/whereabouts unknown	0

129. Did your former (husband/wife) know (SPOUSE/PARTNER) before you (remarried/started living together)?

		Yes	1
	(SKIP TO Q. 131)	No	2

130. How did they know one another?

_____

_____

(HAND R CARD 7)

131. Which of the terms on this card <u>best</u> describes (his/her) reaction to your (remarriage/relationship)?

	Supportive	1
	Relieved	2
	Pleased	3
	Rejected	4
	Uninvolved	5
	Jealous	6
	Other (SPECIFY): _____	7

132.   Has your (remarriage/relationship) affected your feelings for your
        former (husband/wife)?

	Yes	1
(SKIP TO Q. 133)	No	2

132A.   How have your feelings been affected?

_____

_____

_____

133.	I am going to read you some statements about areas of disagreement that some people have in relationships. (HAND R CARD 10) Looking at Card 10, please tell me which of the choices best describes how much you and (SPOUSE/PARTNER) agree or disagree on:						

	ALWAYS AGREE	ALMOST ALWAYS AGREE	OCCA-SIONALLY DISAGREE	FRE-QUENTLY DISAGREE	ALMOST ALWAYS DISAGREE	ALWAYS DISAGREE	NA
a. Handling household finances.	6	5	4	3	2	1	0
b. Matters of recreation.	6	5	4	3	2	1	0
c. Religious matters.	6	5	4	3	2	1	0
d. Demonstrations of affection.	6	5	4	3	2	1	0
e. Friends.	6	5	4	3	2	1	0
f. Sex relations.	6	5	4	3	2	1	0
g. Conventionality--that is, correct or proper behavior.	6	5	4	3	2	1	0
h. Philosophy of life.	6	5	4	3	2	1	0
i. Ways of dealing with parents or relations.	6	5	4	3	2	1	0
j. Aims, goals, and things believed important.	6	5	4	3	2	1	0
k. Amount of time spent together.	6	5	4	3	2	1	0
l. Making major decisions.	6	5	4	3	2	1	0
m. Household tasks.	6	5	4	3	2	1	0
n. Leisure time interests and activities.	6	5	4	3	2	1	0
o. Career decisions.	6	5	4	3	2	1	0
(IF CHILDREN LIVING IN HOUSEHOLD):							
p. Childcare arrangements.	6	5	4	3	2	1	0
q. Disciplining the children.	6	5	4	3	2	1	0

(HAND R CARD 11)

134. Looking at the choices on Card 11, please tell me how often these situations occur:

	ALL OF THE TIME	MOST OF THE TIME	MORE OFTEN THAN NOT	OCCA- SIONALLY	RARELY	NEVER
a. How often do you discuss or consider (divorce or separa- tion/terminating your relationship)?	1	2	3	4	5	6
b. How often do you or (SPOUSE/ PARTNER) leave the house after a fight?	1	2	3	4	5	6
c. In general, how often do you think that things between you and (SPOUSE/PARTNER) are going well?	1	2	3	4	5	6
d. Do you confide in (him/her)?	1	2	3	4	5	6
e. Do you ever regret that you (married/started living together)?	1	2	3	4	5	6
f. How often do you and (SPOUSE/ PARTNER) quarrel?	1	2	3	4	5	6
g. How often do you and (SPOUSE/ PARTNER) get on each other's nerves?	1	2	3	4	5	6

135. Do you kiss (SPOUSE/PARTNER):

never,	0
rarely,	1
occasionally,	2
almost every day, or	3
every day?	4

136. How many outside interests do you engage in together:

none,	0
very few,	1
some,	2
most, or	3
all of them?	4

(HAND R CARD 12)

137. Please refer now to Card 12. How often would you say the following events occur between you and (SPOUSE/PARTNER)? How often do you:

	NEVER	LESS THAN ONCE A MONTH	ONCE OR TWICE A MONTH	ONCE OR TWICE A WEEK	ONCE A DAY	MORE THAN ONCE A DAY
a. have a stimulating exchange of ideas?	0	1	2	3	4	5
b. laugh together?	0	1	2	3	4	5
c. calmly discuss something?	0	1	2	3	4	5
d. work together on a project?	0	1	2	3	4	5

138. During the past few weeks, has being too tired for sex caused differences of opinion or been a problem in your relationship?

Yes	1
No	2

138A. During the past few weeks, has not showing love caused differences of opinion or been a problem in your relationship.

Yes	1
No	2

(HAND R CARD 13)

139. On Card 13 there are dots representing different degrees of happiness in your relationship. The middle point "happy" represents the degree of happiness of most relationships. Please tell me which dot best describes the degree of happiness, all things considered, of your relationship.

0	1	2	3	4	5	6
.	.	.	.	.	.	.
Extremely Unhappy	Fairly Unhappy	A little Unhappy	Happy	Very Happy	Extremely Happy	Perfect

(HAND R CARD 14)

140. On Card 14 there are six statements that describe how many people feel about the future of their relationships. Which <u>best</u> describes the future of yours?

I want desperately for my relationship to succeed, and would go to almost any length to see that it does.	6
I want very much for my relationship to succeed, and will do all I can to see that it does.	5
I want very much for my relationship to succeed, and will do my fair share to see that it does.	4
It would be nice if my relationship succeeded, but I can't do much more than I am doing now to help it succeed.	3
It would be nice if it succeeded, but I refuse to do more than I am doing now to keep the relationship going.	2
My relationship can never succeed, and there is no more that I can do to keep it going.	1

141. Now I'd like to know how you and <u>(SPOUSE/PARTNER)</u> divide up the household jobs. For example, who:

	R	BOTH	SPOUSE OR PARTNER	NEITHER
a. repairs things around the house?	1	2	3	4
b. services the car?	1	2	3	4
c. keeps track of the money and bills?	1	2	3	4
d. does the grocery shopping?	1	2	3	4
e. cleans the house?	1	2	3	4
f. does the evening dishes?	1	2	3	4

142. Now, what about who makes the decisions. For example, who decides:

	R	BOTH	SPOUSE OR PARTNER	NEITHER
a. whether the male should take a certain job?	1	2	3	4
b. what car to buy?	1	2	3	4
c. where to go on vacations?	1	2	3	4
d. what house or apartment to live in?	1	2	3	4
e. whether the female should work or not?	1	2	3	4
f. how much money you can afford to spend per week on food?	1	2	3	4

(IF IN FIRST MARRIAGE, SKIP TO Q. 144)

143. Is this different or the same as the way decisions were made in your former marriage?

	Different	1
(SKIP TO Q. 144)	Same	2

143A. How is it different?

_____

_____

_____

144. Who do you think is boss in your relationship?

Man	1
Woman	2
Both	3

145. Some people feel that disagreement and conflict in a relationship is normal, while others try to avoid it at all costs. When conflict develops in your relationship, is it:

something you readily accept as normal,	1
something you dislike but live with, or is it	2
something you try to avoid at all costs?	3

(IF IN FIRST MARRIAGE, SKIP TO Q. 147)

146. Is this different or the same as the way you felt in your former marriage?

	Different	1
(SKIP TO Q. 147)	Same	2

146A. How is it different?

_____

_____

_____

Now just a few questions about your sexual relationship.

147. On the average, how many times a month do you and your (husband/wife/partner) have sexual intercourse?

_____
(NUMBER PER MONTH)

148. Do you and (he/she) have sexual intercourse:

more often than you would like,	1
about as often as you like, or	2
less often than you would like?	3

149. Is sexual intercourse:		
	very satisfactory,	1
	somewhat satisfactory,	2
	a little unsatisfactory, or	3
	very unsatisfactory?	4

150. How many months after you started dating did you first have sexual intercourse?

_____
(NUMBER OF MONTHS)

(IF IN FIRST MARRIAGE, SKIP TO Q. 153)

151. During your former marriage, what were your views about having extramarital sex? Did you:

	strongly disapprove,	1
	disapprove,	2
	approve, or	3
	strongly approve?	4
(DO NOT READ)	Other (SPECIFY): _____ _____	5

152. What about your former spouse's views? Did (he/she):

	strongly disapprove,	1
	disapprove,	2
	approve, or	3
	strongly approve?	4
(DO NOT READ)	Other (SPECIFY): _____ _____	5
	Don't know	8

153. What are (SPOUSE/PARTNER)'s views about extramarital sex? Does (he/she):

strongly disapprove,	1
disapprove,	2
approve, or	3
strongly approve?	4
(DO NOT READ) Other (SPECIFY): _____ _____	5
Don't know	8

154. And what are your views now? Do you:

strongly disapprove,	1
disapprove,	2
approve, or	3 .
strongly approve?	4
(DO NOT READ) Other (SPECIFY): _____ _____	5
Don't know	8

155A. Have you had sexual intercourse with anyone other than (SPOUSE/PARTNER) since you have been (married/living together)?

Yes	1
No	2

155B. How about (SPOUSE/PARTNER)? Do you think that (he/she) has had sexual intercourse with anyone else since you have been (married/living together)?

Yes	1
No	2

Now I would like to ask you some questions about your family and friends.

(IF NOT MARRIED OR NOT LIVING WITH A PARTNER, HAND R CARD 15A.

IF A PREVIOUS MARRIAGE AND NOW MARRIED OR LIVING WITH A PARTNER, HAND R CARD 15B.

IF NOW IN FIRST MARRIAGE OR LIVING WITH A PARTNER, HAND R CARD 15C)

(156.) Which of the people listed on Card 15 live within an hour's drive of you:

(IF DECEASED OR NONEXISTENT, CIRCLE CODE "0")

	LIVE WITHIN HOUR'S DRIVE	DOES NOT APPLY
a. R's parents?	1	0
b. R's brothers and sisters?	2	0
c. R's other relatives?	3	0
d. R's former spouse?	4	0
e. R's former spouse's parents?	5	0
f. R's former spouse's brothers and sisters?	6	0
g. R's current (spouse's/partner's) parents?	7	0
h. R's current (spouse's/partner's) brothers and sisters?	8	0

(ALLOW R TO KEEP CARD 15 TO ANSWER QQ. 159-165)

(IF R NEVER MARRIED OR NOW IN FIRST MARRIAGE, SKIP TO Q. 159)

157. Some people who have been divorced still think of their former spouse's family as their own relatives and some do not. Do you still consider these people as <u>your</u> relatives: (IF DECEASED OR NONEXISTENT, CIRCLE CODE "0")

	YES	NO	DOES NOT APPLY
a. your former (husband's/wife's) mother or father?	1	2	0
b. any of your former (husband's/wife's) sisters and brothers?	1	2	0
c. any of your former (husband's/wife's) other relatives?	1	2	0
d. your former (husband/wife)?	1	2	0

(IF R HAS NO CHILDREN FROM (HIS/HER) PREVIOUS MARRIAGE LIVING IN HOUSEHOLD, RECALL AID #4, SKIP TO Q. 159)

158. How about your children from your former marriage (NAMES FROM RECALL AID #4). Do they still consider these people as their relatives:

(IF DECEASED OR NONEXISTENT, CIRCLE CODE "0")

	YES	NO	DOES NOT APPLY
a. your former (husband's/wife's) mother or father?	1	2	0
b. any of your former (husband's/wife's) sisters and brothers?	1	2	0
c. any of your former (husband's/wife's) other relatives?	1	2	0
d. your former (husband/wife)?	1	2	0

159. Now looking back at Card 15, about how often do you get a chance to see the people on the list? Do you get to see them almost every day, once or twice a week, once or twice a month, occasionally during the year, hardly ever, or never? (REPEAT CATEGORIES AS NECESSARY.)

(IF RELATIVES DECEASED OR NONEXISTENT, CIRCLE CODE "0")

	ALMOST EVERY DAY	ONCE OR TWICE A WEEK	ONCE OR TWICE A MONTH	OCCA-SIONALLY DURING THE YEAR	HARDLY EVER	NEVER	DOES NOT APPLY
a. R's parents	6	5	4	3	2	1	0
b. R's brothers and sisters	6	5	4	3	2	1	0
c. R's other relatives	6	5	4	3	2	1	0
d. R's former spouse	6	5	4	3	2	1	0
e. R's former spouse's parents	6	5	4	3	2	1	0
f. R's former spouse's brothers and sisters	6	5	4	3	2	1	0
g. R's current (spouse's/ partner's) parents	6	5	4	3	2	1	0
h. R's current (spouse's/ partner's) brothers and sisters	6	5	4	3	2	1	0

	Q. 160	Q. 161	Q. 162	Q. 163	Q. 164	Q. 165
160. Looking again at Card 15, in the past few weeks, from which of these people have you received any help such as babysitting, errands, housework, or home repairs?						
161. In the past few weeks, for which of these people have you provided any help such as babysitting, errands, housework, or home repairs?						
162. In the past few weeks, from which of these people have you received any financial help?						
163. In the past few weeks, to which have you given any financial help?						
164. In the past few weeks, from which of these people have you received any moral support such as advice or encouragement?						
165. In the past few weeks, to which have you provided any moral support such as advice or encouragement?						

	Q. 160	Q. 161	Q. 162	Q. 163	Q. 164	Q. 165
a. R's parents	1	1	1	1	1	1
b. R's brothers and sisters	1	1	1	1	1	1
c. R's other relatives	1	1	1	1	1	1
d. R's former spouse	1	1	1	1	1	1
e. R's former spouse's parents	1	1	1	1	1	1
f. R's former spouse's brothers and sisters	1	1	1	1	1	1
g. R's current (spouse's/ partner's) parents	1	1	1	1	1	1
h. R's current (spouse's/ partner's) brothers and sisters	1	1	1	1	1	1

166. How many close friends do you have living in this area?

_____
(NUMBER)

(IF "NONE," SKIP TO INSTRUCTIONS ABOVE Q. 168)

167. How many of these friends have you made in the past two years?

_____
(NUMBER)

(IF R IS MARRIED, OR LIVING WITH PARTNER, ASK Q. 168; OTHERWISE, SKIP TO Q. 169)

168. Considering all the friends you and (SPOUSE/PARTNER) have, would you say that:

a. you each mostly have your own separate friends,	1
b. you have both some separate friends and some mutual or shared friends, or	2
c. you mostly have mutual or shared friends?	3 .

169.	(Excluding your partner)(and your children), think about the three persons you feel closest to <u>right now</u>. Starting with the one closest to you, please tell me their names. (RECORD BELOW) (ASK QQ. 169A-C ABOUT ONE AT A TIME)			
		FIRST	SECOND	THIRD
		(FIRST NAME)	(FIRST NAME)	(FIRST NAME)
169A.	What is your relationship to _____? (NAME)			
	a member of R's family,	1	1	1
	a member of R's current (spouse's/partner's) family,	2	2	2
	a member of R's former spouse's family or	3	3	3
	a friend?	4	4	4
	Other (SPECIFY):	5	5	5
169B.	Is _____: (NAME)			
	married,	1	1	1
	separated or divorced,	2	2	2
	widowed, or was (he/she)	3	3	3
	never married?	4	4	4
169C.	On the average, how often do you have contact with _____ now? Is it: (NAME)			
	daily,	1	1	1
	a few times a week,	2	2	2
	about once a week,	3	3	3
	about once a month,	4	4	4
	less than once a month, or	5	5	5
	never?	6	6	6

-64-

170. Now we'd like to know how satisfied you are with your day-to-day life (HAND R CARD 16). Looking at Card 16, please tell me how satisfied you are with:

	EXTREMELY SATISFIED	SOMEWHAT SATISFIED	NOT SATISFIED
a. the work you do?	1	2	3
b. where you live?	1	2	3
c. your way of life?	1	2	3
d. the things you do for enjoyment?	1	2	3
e. your health?	1	2	3

171. Taking all these things together, how would you say things are going for you these days. Would you say things are:

very good,	1
pretty good,	2
so-so,	3
not too good, or	4
not good at all?	5

172. Sometimes people think about suicide (after a divorce or separation). During the past two years, did you ever:

	YES	NO
a. make an attempt to take your own life?	1	2
b. make plans about how you would go about taking your life?	1	2
c. reach the point where you seriously considered taking your own life?	1	2
d. think about doing this even if you would not really do it?	1	2

(HAND R CARD 17)

(173.) Card 17 has a picture of a ladder. Suppose we say that the top of the ladder (POINT TO 10) represents the best possible life for you and the bottom (POINT TO 0) represents the worst possible life for you. Where on the ladder--at what step--do you personally see yourself at the present time?

_____
(ENTER NUMBER) [STEP]

(174.) I am again going to read some statements to you (HAND R CARD 18). From Card 18, please tell me how strongly you agree or disagree with each statement.

	STRONGLY AGREE	AGREE SOMEWHAT	DISAGREE SOMEWHAT	STRONGLY DISAGREE
a. I feel I'm a person of worth, at least on an equal basis with others.	1	2	3	4
b. I feel I have a number of good qualities.	1	2	3	4
c. All in all, I am inclined to feel that I'm a failure.	1	2	3	4
d. I am able to do things as well as most other people.	1	2	3	4
e. I feel I do not have much to be proud of.	1	2	3	4
f. I take a positive attitude toward myself.	1	2	3	4
g. On the whole, I am satisfied with myself.	1	2	3	4
h. I wish I could have more respect for myself.	1	2	3	4
i. I certainly feel useless at times.	1	2	3	4
j. At times I think I am no good at all.	1	2	3	4

(HAND R CARD 19)

175. Please look at Card 19. Tell me how often during the past week you felt:

	NEVER	ONCE	SEVERAL TIMES	OFTEN
a. particularly excited or interested in something?	1	2	3	4
b. so restless you couldn't sit long in a chair?	1	2	3	4
c. very angry at somebody or something?	1	2	3	4
d. that things were going your way?	1	2	3	4
e. upset because someone criticized you?	1	2	3	4
f. on top of the world?	1	2	3	4
g. very lonely, not close to other people?	1	2	3	4
h. pleased about having accomplished something?	1	2	3	4
i. bored?	1	2	3	4
j. down or discouraged because nothing seemed to be going right for you?	1	2	3	4
k. proud because someone complimented you on something you had done?	1	2	3	4

176. Do you have any health or physical problems that bother you now?

	Yes	1
(SKIP TO Q. 177)	No	2

176A. What are they?

_____

_____

_____

177. How many times have you seen a doctor within the past year?

_____
(NUMBER OF TIMES)

178. I am going to read you a list of common conditions that people experience. (HAND R CARD 20). Please look at this card and for each condition I mention, tell me whether this has increased, remained the same, decreased, or whether you never had this condition at all in the last two years:

		INCREASED	REMAINED THE SAME	DECREASED	NEVER HAD CONDITION
a.	sleeplessness?	1	2	3	0
b.	nervousness?	1	2	3	0
c.	being tired?	1	2	3	0
d.	headaches?	1	2	3	0
e.	indigestion?	1	2	3	0
f.	allergies?	1	2	3	0
g.	colds, flu, or fever?	1	2	3	0
h.	irregularity?	1	2	3	0
i.	moody spells?	1	2	3	0
j.	depression?	1	2	3	0

(ALLOW R TO KEEP CARD 20 TO ANSWER Q. 179)

179. Still looking at Card 20, please tell me if the following activities have increased, remained the same, decreased, or whether you never did this activity at all in the last two years:

		INCREASED	REMAINED THE SAME	DECREASED	NEVER DID THIS
a.	participating in sports and athletics?	1	2	3	0
b.	gambling?	1	2	3	0
c.	drinking with friends socially?	1	2	3	0
d.	drinking when you are alone?	1	2	3	0
e.	smoking?	1	2	3	0
f.	taking drugs with a physician's orders?	1	2	3	0
g.	taking drugs without a physician's orders?	1	2	3	0

(180.) In the past two years, have you worked at any job for pay?

		Yes	1
(SKIP TO Q. 182)		No	2

180A.   Looking at Card 21 (HAND R CARD 21), which of these have happened to you in the past two years:

		HAVE HAPPENED
	a. started work for the first time?	01
	b. gotten to like your work more?	02
	c. gotten to like your work less?	03
	d. changed to a more responsible job?	04
	e. changed to a less responsible job?	05
	f. been promoted?	06
	g. been demoted?	07
	h. been laid off or fired?	08
	i. spent considerably more time at work?	09
	j. spent considerably less time at work?	10
(SKIP TO Q. 182)	k. None of these has happened.	00

181.   In what ways have these changes been related to your (divorce/separation and)(remarriage/new relationship)?

	OR	NO WAY	1

(182.) How stable has your income been in the past two years? Has it been:

very stable,	1
somewhat stable,	2
somewhat unstable, or	3
very unstable?	4

(183.) At present, do you feel:

a lot of financial strain,	1
some financial strain,	2
very little financial strain, or	3
no financial strain at all?	4

(184.) Looking at Card 22 (HAND R CARD 22), please choose the category that corresponds to your family's total yearly income for 1978 before taxes. Just tell me the letter.

a.	less than $5,000	1
b.	$5,000 to $9,999	2
c.	$10,000 to $14,999	3
d.	$15,000 to $19,999	4
e.	$20,000 to $24,999	5
f.	$25,000 to $29,999	6
g.	$30,000 to $39,999	7
h.	$40,000 to $49,999	8
i.	$50,000 and above	9

(HAND R CARD 23)

185. Here is a list of various sources of income. All of these will not apply to you. Please tell me the letters of sources from which you received income in the past year.

a. R's employment	01
b. Employment of partner	02
c. Unemployment compensation	03
d. Veteran's benefits	04
e. Social Security	05
f. Welfare or public assistance	06
g. Child support from your former spouse	07
h. Other assistance from your former spouse	08
i. Assistance from your parents	09
j. Assistance from other relatives	10
k. Investments (stocks/bonds), trust	11
l. Other sources (SPECIFY): _____	12

186. Approximately how much do you spend each month on:

	$ EACH MONTH
a. food?	$_____
b. rent or mortgage?	$_____
c. utilities?	$_____
d. clothing?	$_____
e. recreation?	$_____
f. transportation?	$_____

(IF R NOT PREVIOUSLY MARRIED, SKIP TO Q. 188)

187. Do you have to help support your former spouse?

		SPECIFY AMOUNT
YES ☐	$_____	PER _____
NO ☐		

187A. Do you have to pay any child support?

		SPECIFY AMOUNT
YES ☐	$_____	PER _____
NO ☐		

(IF NOT MARRIED OR LIVING TOGETHER, OR IF R MARRIED TO SPOUSE ON LABEL, SKIP TO Q. 189)

188. Since you (married/started living together), would you say your financial status is:

better off than before,	1
about the same as before, or	2
worse off than before?	3

189. Do you own or rent the place where you are currently living or are you living in someone else's home at the present time?

Own	1
Rent	2
Living in someone else's home	3

190. How long have you been living in your current residence?

_____ OR _____
(MONTHS)   (YEARS)

191. How long do you expect to be living (there/here)?

_____ OR _____
(MONTHS)   (YEARS)

(IF THE RESPONDENT PLANS TO LEAVE CURRENT RESIDENCE WITHIN 12 MONTHS, ASK Q. 192; OTHERWISE, SKIP TO Q. 193)

192. Why do you expect to be moving?

_____

_____

193. Although we have asked you a lot of questions, sometimes interviews such as this don't really cover all of the important topics.

Is there anything else which you would like to tell us? (PROBE: Is there any additional information which you think might be helpful to us in trying to understand separation, divorce, and remarriage)

_____

_____

_____

_____

_____

_____

_____

_____

_____

_____

_____

_____

(GO TO Q. 195)

(ASK QQ. 195-198 AND THEN COMPLETE THE FOLLOWING OBSERVATIONS IN PRIVACY IMMEDIATELY AFTER YOU LEAVE R)

194A. Where did the interview take place?

R's home	1
Public place (lounge, restaurant, etc.)	2
Other (SPECIFY): _____	3

194B. Who was present?

No one else present	1
Others present--out of hearing range (SPECIFY WHO):	2
Others present--within hearing range (SPECIFY WHO):	3

194C. What is R's race or ethnic group?

White	1
Black	2
Asian	3
Latin American	4
Other (SPECIFY): _____	5

194D. Was the respondent:

(1)	cooperative,	1
	partially cooperative, or	2
	uncooperative?	3

(2)	suspicious,	1
	somewhat suspicious, or	2
	not suspicious?	3

(3)	hostile,	1
	somewhat hostile, or	2
	not hostile?	3

(4)	communicative,	1
	partially communicative, or	2
	not communicative?	3

(5)	somewhat ugly, homely,	1
	average, or	2
	nice looking?	3

(6)	slovenly, untidy, not clean,	1
	average, or	2
	clean, well-groomed, neatly dressed?	3

194E. Did R show any signs of:

		YES	NO
a.	drunkenness?	1	2
b.	drug intoxication?	1	2
c.	nervousness or emotional upset?	1	2

194F. During the interview, were there:

no interruptions,	1
only minor interruptions, or	2
some major interruptions? (DESCRIBE): _____ _____ _____	3

194G. Were there any significant problems in the interview?

Yes (EXPLAIN): _____ _____ _____	1
No	2

194H. How truthful do you believe the respondent was?

	Always truthful	1
(SPECIFY QUESTION NUMBERS OR QUESTION CONTENT)	Occasionally untruthful, or distorting the truth	2
	Frequently untruthful, or distorting the truth	3

194I. How much difficulty did R have in comprehending the questions?

None	1
Slight	2
Fair amount	3
A lot	4

195. Would you be interested in having us mail you a summary of the findings of this study which should be ready in about six months?

	Yes	1
	No	2

196. If we should want to contact you in the future, what is your phone number? (MY SUPERVISOR MAY BE CALLING TO VERIFY THE INTERVIEW)

CURRENT HOME PHONE:_____ CURRENT WORK PHONE:_____

197. If another follow-up were conducted in the next couple of years, would you be willing to participate?

(RECORD	Yes	1
ANY COMMENTS)	Maybe	2
(SKIP TO Q. 198)	No	3

197A. Would you tell me the names and addresses of two persons who would always know your address if you should decide to move.

NAME:_____

ADDRESS:_____

```
        CITY            STATE            ZIP
```

PHONE:_____ (RELATIONSHIP TO R)_____

NAME:_____

ADDRESS:_____

```
        CITY            STATE            ZIP
```

PHONE:_____ (RELATIONSHIP TO R)_____

198. Dr. Furstenberg and Dr. Spanier are planning to write a book on divorce and remarriage based in part on the results of this research. Part of the book will feature case studies which go beyond this interview.

Would you be available for another interview in the next month or two for the purpose of providing the additional material they need? Such case studies would, of course, be presented anonymously. You would be called for an appointment.

	Yes	1
(ASK Q. 198A)	Maybe	2
	No	3

198A. Under what conditions would you be willing to participate?

_____

_____

(ALL INTERVIEWERS: RECORD TIME INTERVIEW ENDED HERE AND ON COVER)
                                                  TIME ENDED:_____

(COMPLETE Q. 194A-1 AS SOON AS YOU LEAVE R)

References

ADAMS, B. N. (1971) "Isolation, function, and beyond: American kinship in the 1960's," pp. 163–185 in C. B. Broderick (ed.) A Decade of Family Research and Action: Journal of Marriage and the Family. Minneapolis, MN: National Council of Family Relations.

—————— (1968) Kinship in an Urban Setting. Chicago: Markham.

ANSPACH, D. F. (1976) "Kinship and divorce." Journal of Marriage and the Family 38: 323–330.

BACHRACH, L. L. (1975) "Marital status and mental disorder: an analytical review.' DHEW Publication (ADM) 75–217. Washington, DC: U.S. Government Printing Office.

BALTES, P. B. and O. G. BRIM [eds.] (1979) Life–Span Development and Behavior vol 2a. New York: Academic Press.

BANE, M. J. (1979) "Marital disruption and the lives of children," pp. 276–286 in G. Levinger and O.C. Moles (eds.) Divorce and Separation: Context, Causes and Consequences. New York: Basic Books.

BECKER, G. S., (1977) E. M. LANDES and R. T. MICHAEL "An economic analysis of marital instability." Journal of Political Economy 85: 1141–1187.

BERGER, P. and H. KELLNER (1964) "Marriage and the construction of reality," in R. L. Coser (ed.) The Family: Its Structures and Functions. New York: St. Martin's Press.

BERNARD, J. (1973) The Future of Marriage. New York: Bantam Books.

—————— (1956) Remarriage: A Study of Marriage. New York: Dryden Press.

BLOOM, B. L., S. J. ASHER, and S. W. WHITE (1978) "Marital disruption as a stressor: a review and analysis." Psychological Bulletin 85: 867–894.

BLOOM, B. L., S. W. WHITE and S. J. ASHER (1979) "Marital disruption as a stressful life event," in G. Levinger and O. C. Moles (eds.) Divorce and Separation: Contexts, Causes, and Consequences. New York: Basic Books.

BOHANNON, P. (1970) Divorce and After. Garden City, NY: Doubleday.

BRADBURN, N. M. (1969) The Structure of Psychological Well Being. Chicago: Aldine Publishing.

BRODY, E. (1978) "The aging of the family." The Annals of the American Academy of Political and Social Science.

BROWN, P. (1974) "A study of women coping with divorce," in D.G. McGuigan (ed.) New Research of Women and Sex Roles. University of Michigan: Center for Continuing Education.

BUMPASS, L. L. (1983) "Demographic aspects of children's second-family experience," Working paper, Center for Demography and Ecology, University of Wisconsin, Madison.

—————— (1982) "Children and marital disruption: a replication and update." Working paper, Center for Demography and Ecology, University of Wisconsin, Madison.

—————— (1979) "The changing linkage of nuptiality and fertility in the United States." Working paper 79-6, Center for Demography and Ecology, University of Wisconsin, Madison.

CAMPBELL, A., P. E. CONVERSE, and W. L. RODGERS (1976) The Quality of American Life. New York: Russell Sage Foundation.

CANTRIL, H. (1965) The Pattern of Human Concerns. New Brunswick: Rutgers University Press.

CHAMIE, J. and S. NSULY (1981) "Sex differences in remarriages and spouse selection," Demography 18: 335–348.

CHERLIN, A. (1981) Marriage, Divorce, Remarriage: Changing Patterns in the Postwar United States. Cambridge: Harvard University Press.

—————— (1980) "Religion and remarriage: reply to Halliday." American Journal of Sociology 86: 636–640.

—————— (1978) "Remarriage as an incomplete institution." American Journal of Sociology 84: 634–650.

—————— (1977) "The effects of children on marital dissolution." Demography 14: 265–272.

—————— and F. F. FURSTENBERG, Jr. (1980) "Grandparent-parent-grandchild relations after divorce: proposal submitted to the National Institute on Aging."

CHERLIN, A. and J. MCCARTHY (1983) "Remarried couples households." Presented at the annual meeting of the Population Association of America.

CHIRIBOGA, D. A., J. ROBERTS, and J. A. STEIN (1978) "Psychological well being during marital separation." Journal of Divorce 2: 21–36.

CLAYTON, R. R. and J. BOKEMEIER (1980) "Premarital sex in the seventies." Journal of Marriage and the Family 42: 759–775.

DEAN, G. and D. T. GURAK (1978) "Marital homogamy the second time around." Journal of Marriage and the Family 40: 559–570.

DEGLER, C. N. (1980) At Odds: Women and the Family in America from the Revolution to the Present. New York: Oxford University Press.

DEMOS, J. and S. S. BOOCOCK (1978) Turning Points: Historical and Sociological Essays on the Family. Chicago: University of Chicago Press.

ELDER, G. H., Jr. (1974) "Approaches to social change and the family," p. S1–S38 in J. Demos and S. S. Boocock (eds.) Turning Points: Historical and Sociological Essays on the Family. Chicago: University of Chicago Press.

ESPENSHADE, T. J. and R. E. BRAUN (1982) "Life course analysis and multistate demography: an application to marriage, divorce, and remarriage." Journal of Marriage and the Family 44:1025–1036.

FARBER, B. (1973) Family and Kinship in Modern Society. Glenview, IL: Scott, Foresman and Company.

FURSTENBERG, F. F., Jr. (1983) "Marital disruption and childcare." Working paper, Family Impact Seminar, National Center for Family Studies, Catholic University, Washington, DC.

—————— (1982a) "Conjugal succession: reentering marriage after divorce," in P. B. Baltes and O. G. Brim (eds.) Life Span Development and Behavior, Vol. 4. New York: Academic Press.

—————— (1982b) "Childcare after divorce and remarriage." MacArthur Foundation, Conference on Child Care, Chicago.

—————— (1981) "Remarriage and intergenerational relations," in R. Fogel et al. (eds.) Stability and Change in the Family. New York: Academic Press.

—————— (1979) "Recycling the family: perspectives for researching a neglected family form." Marriage and Family Review 2: 12–22.

—————— (1976) Unplanned Parenthood: The Social Consequences of Teenage Childbearing. New York: The Free Press.

—————— and C. W. NORD (1982) "Parenting apart: patterns of childrearing after divorce." Presented at the annual meeting of the American Sociological Association, San Francisco.

FURSTENBERG, F. F., Jr. and J. SELTZER (1983) "Divorce and child development." Presented at the annual meeting of the Orthopsychiatric Association, Boston.

FURSTENBERG, F. F., Jr. and K. G. TALVITIE (1980) "Children's names and paternal claims: bonds between unmarried fathers and their children." Journal of Family Issues 1: 31–58.

FURSTENBERG, F. F., Jr. and N. ZILL (1979) "A national longitudinal study of marital disruption." Proposal to the National Institute of Mental Health, prepared in response to NIMH Marital Disruption Prevention Program.

FURSTENBERG, F. F., Jr., R. LINCOLN, and J. MENKEN (1981) Teenage Sexuality, Pregnancy, and Childrearing. Philadelphia: University of Pennsylvania Press.

FURSTENBERG, F. F., Jr., C. W. NORD, J. L. PETERSON, and N. ZILL (et al., 1983a) The life course of children of divorce: marital disruption and parental contact." American Sociological Review 48: 656–668.

FURSTENBERG, F. F., Jr., J. SELTZER, P. ALLISON, and C. W. NORD (et al., 1983b) "Encountering divorce: childrens' responses to family dissolution and reconstitution." Presented at the annual meeting of the American Sociological Association, Detroit.

GLENN, N. O. (1981) "The well being of persons remarried after divorce." Journal of Family Issues 2: 61–75.

——— C. WEAVER (1977) "The marital happiness of remarried divorced persons." Journal of Marriage and the Family 39: 331–337.

GLICK, P. C. (1984) "Prospective changes in marriage, divorce, and living arrangements." Journal of Family Issues 1.

——— (1980) "Remarriage: some recent changes and variation." Journal of Family Issues 1: 455–479.

——— (1979) "Children of divorced parents in demographic perspective." Journal of Social Issues 35: 170–182.

——— A. I. NORTON (1977) "Marrying, divorcing, and living together in the U.S. today." Population Bulletin 32: 5.

GLICK, P. C. and G. B. SPANIER (1980) "Married and unmarried cohabitation in the United States." Journal of Marriage and the Family 42: 19-30.

GOODE, W. J. (1956) Women in Divorce. New York: The Free Press.

GRANOVETTER, M. S. (1973) "The strength of weak ties." American Journal of Sociology 76: 1360-1380.

GRIFFITH, J. D. (1980) "Economy, family, and remarriage: theory of remarriage and application to preindustrial England." Journal of Family Issues 1: 479–497.

GUTMAN, H. G. (1977) The Black Family in Slavery and Freedom. New York: Vintage Books.

HALEM, L. C. (1980) Divorce Reform: Changing Legal and Social Perspectives. New York: The Free Press.

HALLIDAY, T. C. (1980) "Remarriage: the more complete institution?" American Journal of Sociology 86: 630–635.

HAREVEN, T. K. (1978) "Family time and historical time," pp. 57–70 in A. S. Rossi et al. (eds.) The Family. New York: W. W. Norton.

HERZOG, E. and C. E. SUDIA (1971) Boys in Fatherless Families. Washington, DC: U.S. Government Printing Office.

HETHERINGTON, E. M., M. COX, and R. COX (1982) "Effects of divorce on parents and children," M. Lamb (ed.) Nontraditional Families. Hillsdale, NJ: Lawrence Erlbaum.

——— (1978) "The Aftermath of Divorce," J. H. Stevens, Jr. and M. Matthews (eds.) Mother-Child, Father-Child Relations. Washington, DC: National Association for the Education of Young Children.

HILL, R. B. (1977) Informal Adoption Among Black Families. Washington, DC: National Urban League.

HIRSCHHORN, L. (1977) "Social policy and the life cycle: a developmental perspective." Social Service Review (September): 434–450.

HUNT, M. M. (1966) The World of the Formerly Married. New York: McGraw-Hill.

JACOBSON, P. (1959) American Marriage and Divorce. New York: Holt, Rinehart and Winston.

JEFFERS, C. (1967) Living Poor: A Participant Observer Study of Priorities and Choices. Ann Arbor, MI: Ann Arbor Publishers.

KESHET, J. K. (1980) "From separation to stepfamily: a subsystem analysis." Journal of Family Issues 1: 517–532.

KETT, J. F. (1977) Rites of Passage: Adolescence in America, 1790 to the Present. New York: Basic Books.

KITSON, G. C. and H. J. RASCHKE, (1981) "Divorce research: what we know; what we need to know." Journal of Divorce 4: 1–37.

KOO, H. P. and C. M. SUCHINDRAN, (1980) "Effects of children on women's remarriage prospects." Journal of Family Issues 1: 497–515.

KULKA, R. A. and H. WEINGARTEN (1979) "The long-term effects of parental divorce in childhood on adult adjustment." Journal of Social Issues 35: 50–78.

LASCH, C. (1977) Haven in a Heartless World: The Family Besieged. New York: Basic Books.

LEVINGER, G. and O. C. MOLES [eds.] (1979) Divorce and Separation: Context, Cause, and Consequences. New York: Basic Books.

LEVITIN, T. E. (1979) "Children of divorce." Journal of Social Issues 35: 1–25.

LEWIS, R. A. and G. B. SPANIER (1979) "Theorizing about the quality and stability of marriage," pp. 268–294 in W. Burr, et al. (eds.) New York: The Free Press.

LONGFELLOW, C. (1979) "Divorce in context: its impact on children" in G. Levinger and O. C. Moles (eds.) Divorce and Separation: Context, Causes, and Consequences. New York: Basic Books.

MACKLIN, E. D. (1978) "Nontraditional family forms: a decade of research." Journal of Marriage and the Family 42: 905–922.

MASNICK, G. and M. J. BANE (1980) The Nation's Families: 1960–1990. Cambridge, MA: Joint Center for Urban Studies of MIT and Harvard University.

McCARTHY, J. F. (1978) "A comparison of the probability of dissolution of first and second marriages." Demography 15: 345–359.

MEAD, M. (1971) "Anomalies in American postdivorce relationship," in P. Bohannon (ed) Divorce and After. Garden City, NY: Doubleday.

MILLS, C. W. (1959) The Sociological Imagination. New York: Oxford University Press.

MODELL, J. (1980) "Normative aspects of American marriage timing since World War II." Journal of Family History 5: 210–234.

——— F. F. FURSTENBERG, Jr., and T. HERSHBERG (1976) "Social change and transitions to adulthood in historical perspective." Journal of Family History 1: 7–32.

MODELL, J., F. F. FURSTENBERG, Jr., and D. STRONG (1978) "The timing of marriage in the transition to adulthood: continuity and change, 1860–1975." American Journal of Sociology, 84: S120–S150.

NAGER, L., D. CHIRIBOGA, and L. CUTLER (1977) "Stress and relief during the process of divorce: a psychosocial study." Presented at the annual meeting of the Western Psychological Association, Seattle.

ORTNER, D. K. and K. LEWIS (1979) "Evidence of single-father competence in childrearing." Family Law Quarterly 13: 27–47.

PARSONS, T. (1943) "The kinship system of the contemporary United States." American Anthropologist 45: 22–38.

PETERS, J. F. (1976) "A comparison of mate selection and marriage in the first and second marriages in a selected sample of the remarried divorced." Journal of Comparative Family Studies 7: 483–491.

PLATERIS, A. (1979) Divorces by Marriage Cohort. DHEW Publication (PHS) 79-1912. Washington, DC: U.S. Government Printing Office.

PRESTON, S. H. (1975) "Estimating the proportion of American marriages that end in divorce." Sociological Methods and Research 3: 435–460.

—— and J. MCDONALD (1979) "The incidence of divorce within cohorts of American marriages contracted since the Civil War." Demography 16: 1–25.

PRICE-BONHAM, S. and J. O. BALSWICK (1980) "The non-institutions: divorce; desertion, and remarriage." Journal of Marriage and the Family 42: 959–972.

RAPOPORT, R. and R. RAPOPORT (1976) Dual Career Families: New Integrations of Work and Family. New York: Harper & Row.

REISS, I. and F. F. FURSTENBERG, Jr. (1981) "Sociology and human sexuality," in H. I. Lief (ed.) Sexual Problems in Medical Practice. Chicago: American Medical Association.

RENNE, K. S. (1971) "Health and marital experience in an urban population." Journal of Marriage and the Family. 33: 338–350.

RILEY, M. W. (1979) "Age and aging: from theory generation to theory testing." Presented at the annual meeting of the American Sociological Association, Boston. (Forthcoming in volume edited by H. M. Blalock, Jr.)

ROSENBERG, G. S. and D. F. ANSPACH (1973) Working Class Kinship. Lexington, MA: Lexington Books.

ROSENBERG, M. (1965) Society and the Adolescent Self-Image. Princeton: Princeton University Press.

ROSS, H. and I. V. SAWHILL (1975) Time of Transition: The Growth of Families Headed by Women. Washington, DC: The Urban Institute.

RUBIN, L. B. (1979) Women of a Certain Age. New York: Harper & Row.

SANDERS, R. and G. B. SPANIER (1979) "Divorce, child custody, and child support." U.S. Bureau of the Census, Current Population Reports, Series P-23, No. 84. Washington, DC: U.S. Government Printing Office.

SAWHILL, I. V. (1978) "Economic perspectives on the family," A. S. Rossi et al. (eds.) The Family. New York: W. W. Norton.

SCHNEIDER, D. M. (1980) American Kinship: A Cultural Account. Englewood Cliffs, NJ: Prentice-Hall.

—— and C. B. COTTRELL (1975) The American Kin Universe: A Genealogical Study: The University of Chicago Studies in Anthropology Series in Social, Cultural and Linguistic Anthropology, 3. Chicago: Department of Anthropology, University of Chicago.

SCHONROCK, G. (forthcoming) Changes in Courtship, Conceptions of Marriage and Love. Ph.D. dissertation, University of Pennsylvania.

SHANAS, E. (1973) "Family-kin networks and aging in cross-cultural perspective." Journal of Marriage and the Family 35: 505–511.

SHORTER, E. (1975) The Making of the Modern Family. New York: Basic Books.

SPANIER, G. B. (1976) "Measuring dyadic adjustment: new scales for assessing the quality of marriage and similar dyads." Journal of Marriage and the Family 38: 15–28.

—— and E. A. ANDERSON (1979) "The impact of the legal system on adjustment to marital separation." Journal of Marriage and the Family 41: 605–613.

SPANIER, G. B. and R. F. CASTO (1979) "Adjustment to separation and divorce: a qualitative analysis," in G. Levinger and O. C. Moles (eds.) Divorce and Separation: Context, Causes and Consequences. New York: Basic Books.

SPANIER, G. B. and F. F. FURSTENBERG, Jr. (1982) "Remarriage after divorce: a longitudinal analysis of well-being." Journal of Marriage and the Family 44: 709–720.

SPANIER, G. B. and P. C. GLICK (1981) "Marital instability in the United States: some correlates and recent changes." Family Relations 30: 329–338.

——— (1980a) "Paths to remarriage." Journal of Divorce 3: 283–298.

——— (1980b) "The life cycle of American families: an expanded analysis." Journal of Family History 5: 97–111.

SPANIER, G. B. and R. MARGOLIS (1983) "Marital separation and extramarital sexual behavior." Journal of Sex Research 19: 12–48.

SPANIER, G. B., R. A. LEWIS, and C. L. COLE (1975) "Marital adjustment over the family life cycle: the issue of curvilinearity." Journal of Marriage and the Family 37: 263–275.

SPICER, J. W. and G. D. HAMPE (1975) "Kinship interaction after divorce." Journal of Marriage and the Family 37: 113–119.

STACK, C. (1974) All Our Kin. Chicago: Aldine.

STAPLES, R. (1978) The Black Family: Essays and Studies. Belmont, CA: Wadsworth.

STEIN, P. J. [ed.] (1981) Single Life: Unmarried Adults in Social Context. New York: St. Martin's.

SUSSMAN, M. B. (1976) "The family life of old people," in R. H. Birstock and E. Shanas (eds.) Handbook of Aging and the Social Sciences. New York: Van Nostrand Reinhold Company.

THOMPSON, L. (1981) The Aftermath of Separation and Divorce. Unpublished doctoral dissertation, Pennsylvania State University.

TROLL, L. E., S. J. MILLER, and R. C. ATCHLEY (1979) Families in Later Life. Belmont, Calif.: Wadsworth Publishing Company, Inc.

TUFTE, V. and B. MYERHOFF [eds.] (1979) Changing Images of the Family. New Haven: Yale University Press.

U.S. Bureau of the Census (1979) Current Population Reports, Series P-23, No. 84. "Divorce, child custody and child support." Washington, DC: U.S. Government Printing Office.

——— (1977) Current Population Reports, Series P-20, No. 312. "Marriage, divorce, widowhood, and remarriage by family characteristics: June 1975." Washington, DC: U.S. Government Printing Office.

——— (1976) Current Population Reports, Series P-20, No. 297. "Number, timing and duration of marriages and divorces in the United States: June 1975." Washington, DC: U.S. Government Printing Office.

VAUGHAN, D. (1979) "Uncoupling: the process of moving from one lifestyle to another." Alternative Life-Styles 2: 415–442.

VISHER, E. B. and J. S. VISHER (1979) Stepfamilies: A Guide to Working Stepparents and Stepchildren. New York: Brunner/Mazel.

Vital and Health Statistics (1980) "Remarriage of women 15–44 years of age whose first marriage ended in divorce: United States, 1976." No. 58 (February 14). Hyattsville, Md.: National Center of Health Statistics.

——— (1973) "100 years of marriage and divorce statistics: United States, 1867–1967." Series 21: 24 (December). Washington, DC: U.S. Government Printing Office.

——— (1970) "Children of divorced couples: United States, selected years." Series 21: 18 (February). Washington, DC: U.S. Government Printing Office.

WALKER, K., J. ROGERS, and L. MESSINGER (1977) "Remarriage after divorce: a review." Social Casework 58: 276–285.

WALLERSTEIN, J. S. and J. B. KELLY (1980) Surviving the Breakup. New York: Basic Books.

WEED, J. A. (1980) "National estimates of marriage dissolution and survivorship: United States." Vital and Health Statistics: Series 3, Analytic Statistics; No. 19.

DHHS Publication No. (PHS) 81–1403. Hyattsville, MD: National Center for Health Statistics; Office of Health Research, Statistics and Technology; Public Health Service, U.S. Department of Health and Human Services.

WEINGARTEN, H. (1980) "Remarriage and well-being: national survey evidence of social and psychological effect." Journal of Family Issues 1: 533–559.

WEISS, R. S. (1975) Marital Separation. New York: Basic Books.

WHITE, L. K. (1979) "Sex differentials in the effects of remarriage on global happiness." Journal of Marriage and the Family 41: 869–876.

WRONG, D. (1961) "The oversocialized conception of man in modern sociology." American Sociological Review 26: 183–193.

ZELNIK, M. and J. F. KANTNER (1980) "Sexual activity, contraceptive use and pregnancy among metropolitan area teenagers: 1971–1979." Family Planning Perspectives 12: 230–237.

ZILL, N. (1984) Happy, Healthy and Insecure. New York: Doubleday.

Index

About the Authors

FRANK F. FURSTENBERG, Jr., is Professor of Sociology and Research Associate in the Population Studies Center at the University of Pennsylvania. His interest in the American family began at Columbia University where he received his Ph.D. While there he carried out historical research on family life in the nineteenth century, conducted a study of the intergenerational transmission of values, and initiated a longitudinal investigation of teenage childbearing that eventuated in the publication of *Unplanned Parenthood: The Social Consequences of Teenage Childbearing* (Free Press, 1976). This study explores mechanisms by which poverty is perpetuated through the social, economic, family, and personal consequences of being "off schedule" in the social timetable for growing up. Currently the adolescent parents from the original sample described in *Unplanned Parenthood* are being reinterviewed along with their children who are now, 15 years later, teenagers themselves. Recent essays on adolescent parenthood appear in *Perspectives on Teenage Sexuality, Pregnancy, and Childbearing* (University of Pennsylvania Press, 1980) which he coedited with Richard Lincoln and Jane Menken.

Furstenberg has been exploring the transformation of the American family—and especially in the most recent decades in response to the sharp rise in rates of marital disruption. This volume is the result of the research based on a survey conducted in Central Pennsylvania. Using a national data set, he is continuing to examine the consequences of marital dissolution on the functioning of the American kinship system. A study of grandparents, conducted with Andrew Cherlin, is presently being concluded.

GRAHAM B. SPANIER is Vice Provost for Undergraduate Studies and Professor of Sociology and Psychiatry at the State University of New York at Stony Brook. Prior to his appointment there he served as Associate Dean of the College of Human Development and Professor of Human Development and Sociology at the Pennsylvania State University. He received his Ph.D. in sociology from Northwestern University where he was a Woodrow Wilson Fellow.

Spanier is the author, editor, or coauthor of eight books and has published more than 80 articles in professional journals. He is the founding editor of the Journal of Family Issues, has served as Associate Editor of the Journal of Marriage and the Family, and was a member of the editorial board of the Journal of Marriage and Family Counseling. He has regularly reviewed for more than 20 other social science journals.

He has held many elective offices in professional associations, recently serving as Vice President of the National Council on Family Relations and Chair of the Family Selection of the American Sociological Association. He is a clinical member and fellow of the American Association for Marriage and Family Therapy, and an elected member of the International Academy of Sex Research.

His primary research and teaching interests focus on the quality and stability of marital relations across the life course, divorce and remarriage, family demography, and family policy. He is currently writing about the changing demography of the American family.